FROM GREAT POWER TO WELFARE STATE

FROM GREAT POWER
TO WELFARE STATE

300 YEARS OF SWEDISH SOCIAL DEVELOPMENT

KURT SAMUELSSON

LONDON
GEORGE ALLEN AND UNWIN LTD
RUSKIN HOUSE   MUSEUM STREET

Title of the original Swedish edition
FRÅN STORMAKT TILL VÄLFÄRDSSTAT

PRINTED IN GREAT BRITAIN
in 11 on 12 pt. Times type
BY UNWIN BROTHERS LIMITED
WOKING AND LONDON

CONTENTS

FOREWORD

THIS book has been written at the request of *Sveriges Riksbank* (National Bank of Sweden), which in connection with its three hundredth anniversary in 1968 asked for a broad survey of Swedish social development during the centuries of the bank's operation. Within that framework I was given a free hand. I have chosen to limit myself to the economic, social and power-political aspects of the period, and have tried to give an account of the development within these spheres and their interaction.

Even this limitation has entailed challenging problems of selection. Which parts of this complex development should be singled out; how could such a wealth of material be compressed into manageable proportions; and how could a broad survey be sufficiently detailed to avoid a preponderance of the sort of abstraction so often found in 'synopses'? How could the need for simplification, the presentation of broad trends, be reconciled with the demands on space made by the equivocal and the controversial?

In one respect I knew that my ambitions would have to be circumscribed from the start. No matter how much a survey of this sort draws on previous scholarship, it may never hope to satisfy the specialists in any given phase or period. I can only hope, however, that they may be conciliated by the fact that readers who desire more complete information are directed, both in the text and in the references at the end, to more specialized sources. It is my earnest hope that this book may inspire many readers to explore these sources and thus to some degree repay my debt to the many historians and social scientists from whose works I, with ever increasing admiration, have drawn knowledge, ideas and inspiration.

KURT SAMUELSSON

1

THE POWER AND THE GLORY

I

OUR story opens on a note of personal tragedy. On July 22, 1668, Johan Wittmacher Palmstruch was sentenced to death by the Svea Court of Appeal. The bank he had founded under royal charter eleven years earlier had been swept away with gale force by a sudden lack of public confidence. It was replaced by a new institution, *Sveriges Riksbank* (National Bank of Sweden). Its articles of association were signed on September 28th, but were antedated September 22, 1668.

Palmstruch's career was in a way illustrative of the Sweden in which he worked and died. He was a foreigner, born in Riga though of Dutch extraction. He had for some time worked in the Netherlands where he was thrown into prison; we are not certain of the charges, possibly economic espionage. It was via Riga that he came to Sweden, where he received royal charter in 1656 to establish a bank in Stockholm on the model of the famous Amsterdam bank. Palmstruch was but one of many foreigners who during the seventeenth century had entered the service of the Swedish state. Their numbers included officers, businessmen, public administrators, scientists and industrialists. Most of them, however, met with a better fate than the unfortunate Palmstruch.

These immigrants were evidence of the economic and political interest that Sweden had aroused in Europe. Sweden was a country subject to considerable international influence, politically, economically and culturally.

This was not an entirely new phenomenon. One might regard foreign influences as having been of even greater importance more than a century earlier, before Martin Luther, Gustavus Vasa and the Reformation. Influences then, in that Catholic era, were of a more uniform quality: chiefly religious and cultural, but in consequence

11

also social and political. This uniformity was lost through the emergence of the national state, the divorce of the Church from Rome, and the wars of religion on the Continent.

Now, however, in this more divided seventeenth-century world, Sweden's foreign relations had assumed a more reciprocal character. 'Ultima Thule' was no longer a passive recipient up in the far north, but a first-rate military and political power whose actions to a large degree decided the fate of Europe. This was emphatically demonstrated in that same year, 1668: Louis XIV was forced to abandon his plans for the conquest of the Spanish Netherlands and accept peace, when Sweden, together with England and the Netherlands, formed the Triple Alliance.

These four states which, after the Thirty Years' War, had assumed the old Hapsburg hegemony of Spain and Austria, met in alliance and contrast: France and Sweden politically and militarily dominant, England and the Netherlands economically and commercially dominant. The relative strengths of the four countries varied from decade to decade and from year to year; but it is no exaggeration to say that they held the trump cards in seventeenth-century power politics.

In all four states important internal developments explain the exterior strength. In France there emerged after decades of construction by Richelieu and Mazarin, the most powerful central government of that day, Louis XIV's absolute monarchy. Within a few years similar central governments were formed in the Netherlands under William of Orange and in Sweden under Charles IX. In Sweden, the centralized administrative machinery on which the absolute monarchy was largely to be based, had been built up over a period of four or five decades. In England the centralized rule of the Cromwellian Protectorate was followed by a struggle between the Crown and Parliament in the reigns of Charles II and James II. With the expulsion of James II, the accession to the throne of William and Mary of Orange and the Declaration of Rights, the struggle ended with the victory of Parliament.

The world had expanded. Hegemony over Europe was not the only prize at stake. In 1664, four years before the Triple Alliance was signed, the British conquered the Dutch in that area of North America which was to become New York State. Capitulation was forced on the Governor of New Amsterdam, Peter Stuyvesant (who nine years earlier had increased his domain by taking New Sweden, in present-day Delaware, from Sweden). New Amsterdam was renamed New York after the Duke of York (later James II, deposed

12

in 1689), who had been granted the new American conquests by his brother, Charles II.

Before the end of the seventeenth century the world was expanding eastwards as well. Under Peter the Great, who within fourteen years made himself the absolute ruler over all Russians, Asiatic Russia strove to beome an integral part of Europe, heir not only to Sweden's trans-Baltic possessions but also to the Swedish system of centralized administration, and to a share in the Western European culture and technology.

The complex political struggle had by this time begun to assume a form which was to persist for some long time. This was the virtually continuous attempt, first by the Netherlands and then also by England, to maintain a balance of power against the most powerful military and expansionist states: Sweden, France, again Sweden, again France—and much, much later, Germany. It was for the sake of this balance of power that the Triple Alliance was formed. This was also the purpose of the coalition mobilized by William of Orange, in which the Spanish and Austrian Hapsburg dynasties, Denmark and a number of German states, among them Brandenburg, joined to counterbalance the alliance of Sweden, England and France. A year later William of Orange had prevailed on the English Parliament to compel Charles II to break the alliance with France, and again, as during the Triple Alliance, place England on the side of 'power balance'.

In this unstable Europe, Swedish power was undeniably a colossus on feet of clay. The violent territorial expansion initiated by Gustavus Adolphus and continued by Charles X could not be adequately sustained by Sweden's small population. There was a lack of financial resources. Money for the wars and for the administration of new territories became an overwhelming problem. These possessions created further difficulties, as they were poorly located according to military logistics: besides being scattered, their often long, open frontiers bordered on countries itching for revenge, with the result that Swedish troops ultimately exhausted themselves by constantly having to keep on the move. There may be some truth in the popular contention that Charles X and his grandson, Charles XII, were forced onwards by the restless Palatinate blood flowing through their veins. However it would be truer to say that these two warriors had no other alternative. Their vital task was to strike fast with a small force in one place and then rapidly remove elsewhere, thus giving the enemy the impression that Sweden commanded an inexhaustible arsenal. This stratagem paid off time and again, but it was inevitably doomed to failure. The whole situation created a feeling of uncertainty. The regency which, on the strength of the Triple Alliance in 1668, had joined forces with the Netherlands against France, was torn internally by divided counsels. It was not only a question of which country to fight, but also from which country the badly needed subsidies were to come.

Charles X had found his own 'solution' to the problems created by the combination of great-power status with straitened finances, namely to commit Sweden to almost uninterrupted warfare, which was thought to finance itself and give more strength and better revenues from new, conquered provinces in the future. His son, Charles XI, was to try another method: the overhauling of the treasury as part of a major reorganization of the administrative system. Charles XII for his part chose to turn the clock back to the days of his grandfather. Presumably nothing could have averted the final disaster, no matter what was done. After 1718 it was left to a 'parliamentary' government under Arvid Horn to unravel the great bankruptcy—as did Cardinal Fleury under Louis XV in France at about the same time.

Naturally it was more than a thirst for power, more than religious fanaticism which lay behind Sweden's expansionist policy and her stubborn defence of her position as a great power, although these were contributory factors. Of greater importance was the fact that the country's real interests were largely to be found on the other side of the Baltic Sea. This sea was vital to her for commerce and shipping, and because the great granaries lay in the Baltic provinces—even if they did not fill any domestic need at that stage. Only a very limited quantity of grain was imported before the end of the seventeenth century; but the international trade and shipping and the resultant customs revenues were all the more important. After the signing of the Armistice with Poland at Altmark in 1629, the year before Gustavus Adolphus entered the Thirty Years' War, Sweden controlled all the leading Baltic ports except those in Denmark. Of the 1,686 ships which in 1631 passed from the Baltic through Öresund strait, 1,273 came from ports where Sweden collected duty.

Actually the Baltic had long been a cockpit of power politics. Earlier, and especially during the fifteenth century, the Hanseatic League had attempted to dominate the Baltic. In this quest the League met competition from Denmark which was bent on unifying the whole of Scandinavia—hence the help rendered by Lübeck to Gustavus Vasa and the Swedish struggle for independence. The Dutch interest in Baltic power politics caused the Netherlands to

14

support first the Swedes in their struggle against Denmark, and later the general Danish policy towards Sweden. Ultimately, the formation of alliances depended on the particular interests which were uppermost in trade and economic policy.

In the course of a century or more, Europe had undergone a definite change in character. Religious, political and economic power had shifted from the Mediterranean to the Atlantic and Baltic coasts. The entrepôts of Italy had not lost all their earlier significance: they remained important financial capitals for a long time, and even after they had virtually ceased to play that role, they continued to export able citizens and knowledge to the new power centres. Nevertheless, the voyages of discovery had shifted the focus of trade and industry to western Europe. To say this may be to put the case too strongly, for the undermining of Mediterranean dominance would have occurred even without the explorers. Italy's decline had been ushered in much earlier, when the Turks cut off the important Levantine trade, and her prominence was further diminished by the rise of the Hanseatic League and, from the thirteenth century onwards, by the rise of the Netherlands and England. For various reasons Spanish supremacy was relatively short-lived.

A long period of developing expansive power lay behind the discoveries and the new colonization. The countries involved in these enterprises had, over the two or three preceding centuries, undergone a slow but certain economic and political advance. Thus, for example, the economic rise of the Netherlands, usually dated as from the beginning of the sixteenth century, had its roots in several centuries of development. That country had occupied a leading position in the textile trade and industry since the thirteenth century, if not before. Her position was strengthened by the decline of the German Hanseatic cities. Their decline, a significant factor in the evolution of the powers whose progress we are following, was assisted by the northern state's extrication from earlier economic and political dependence on them. Gustavus Vasa called on the League for aid when he first sought to free Sweden from Danish rule, but gradually he came to realize that his goal of a sovereign state would be empty of meaning unless Hanseatic influence also was crushed. The Thirty Years' War is another case in which increased power became a *casus belli*: ostensibly Gustavus II Adolphus and Axel Oxenstierna entered the war on religious grounds but as the willing support of Cardinal Richelieu's Catholic France demonstrated, the conflict developed into a struggle for markets and financial positions. When Charles X, in 1658, subdued the Danish-held provinces in southern

15

Sweden, he wrested the 'key to the Baltic' from Danish hands at the same time.

It is clear that Swedish expansion was not 'planned' beforehand. The wars and conquests, and the involvement in European politico-military affairs that went with them were the result of a gradual development. Facing the most crucial decision of all—entry into what became the Thirty Years' War—Gustavus Adolphus and his Chancellor hesitated. Oxenstierna advised the King against joining the army in Germany; he believed that Gustavus Adolphus should concentrate on gaining the supremacy over Scandinavia and the Baltic area. The primary sphere of interest lay further north: the protection of Finland and the newly won territories in the Baltic provinces; and in the ending of Polish Vasa descendants' claims on the Swedish throne. But the balance against Denmark, the need to protect new territories by further conquests and, undeniably, a strong desire to aid Protestant brethren in Germany, forced the newly great power to commit itself further. The modern term escalation could certainly be applied both to Gustavus II Adolphus' foundation of, and Charles X Gustavus' expansion of the Swedish empire. One action triggered off another in a never-ending upward spiral. This escalation partially explains the poor foundation on which the Swedish power rested; the economic, financial and political difficulties which accompanied its greatness; and finally the far-reaching changes in Sweden's national life which this political position was bound to produce. The opportunity to consolidate was never given.

II

It is difficult to give any detailed account of the Swedish economy during this period. We do not know enough about important sections of it—and must remain ignorant for the lack of statistics. First we lack information in regard to population and its distribution. Swedish census statistics, which are the oldest in the world, did not start in consecutively numbered series until 1749—although relatively sound information can be gained for the period dating back to 1720, with the aid of certain supplementary 'historical' accounts. It is not until the nineteenth century, however, that we have information concerning such significant facts as the proportions of rural and urban elements in the population—an especially important factor in considering the attempts of official policy during the seventeenth century to accelerate urban development.

According to certain very rough estimates which can be made for 1668, the population of Sweden proper—that is, including the provinces taken from Denmark ten years earlier—would appear to have fallen short of one million. It is also probable that Stockholm, which grew very fast throughout this period, increased its numbers from about 10,000 at the beginning of Gustavus II Adolphus' reign to between 40,000 and 45,000 at the time the *Riksbank* was founded. A peak of approximately 50,000–55,000 inhabitants is believed to have been reached in 1674, and it is unlikely that Stockholm ever passed the 60,000 mark before the decline which set in during the reign of Charles XII and brought the population figures back to the 45,000 mark by the end of his reign.

These figures, though low by twentieth-century standards, ranked Stockholm as an internationally important city. It was not until the end of the eighteenth century that more than a score of European cities had over 100,000 inhabitants, and then only 300 towns had over 10,000 inhabitants. Stockholm would certainly seem to have been one of the ten or fifteen largest cities in Europe in 1668 (at about which time it had only just been surpassed by Copenhagen). As for the two giants, London and Paris, they already appear to have passed the half-million mark by 1668. Here again, of course, we are able to make rough estimates only.

No other Swedish town could aspire to Stockholm in size. According to certain calculations Göteborg had about 4,000–5,000 inhabitants during the 1670s, and it is possible that Norrköping because of a considerable growth of industry there during the seventeenth century may perhaps have been somewhat larger than Göteborg; but the difference between them cannot have been great, and other 'cities' such as Uppsala, Gävle and Jönköping either had not, or had only just, reached the 3,000 mark.

According to a very rough estimate no more than 6 or 7 per cent of the total population can have been urban. Included in this classification, moreover, are a great many communities which as recipients of royal privileges were titled as towns and officially recognized as such; most of the approximately eighty towns, however, were overgrown villages rather than towns in any real economic sense.

If allowance is made for a number of built-up areas which, though not incorporated as towns were in some cases larger than towns, at least 90 per cent of Sweden's population at that time was rural. About 80 to 85 per cent were engaged in agriculture. The composition of this agricultural population (i.e. the percentage of farmers—

independent, or tenants under either the crown or the nobility—and the percentage of agricultural labourers employed by farmers), is unknown. It is certain that the number of landless agricultural labourers, who either hired out their services to others or spent a large part of the year in enforced idleness, greatly increased during the eighteenth century. However, far less is known of the conditions prevailing during the seventeenth century.

We are sure that the authorities then encouraged the breaking of new ground and the building of new homesteads—although one of their chief motives for this was to increase the national tax revenues. That there was no lack of land for settling on is evidenced by the Finnish immigration, which began towards the end of the sixteenth and continued until the middle of the seventeenth century. Since the prime requisite for getting people to be willing to bring virgin land under the plough was an increase in population, Finnish immigration was at first eagerly welcomed and encouraged. (Later it was opposed because the Finnish method of burn-beating destroyed the forests which Swedish farmers used as a primary reserve for cattle pasture, and which were of crucial importance for iron smelting; also, to make matters worse, the Finns offered keen competition in the hunt for game.) The population did not increase, and we can assume that this helped to prevent the growth during the seventeenth century of a landless class which would have been forced to seek employment from the land-owning farmers. The surplus manpower which nevertheless existed could be absorbed by the mining trades and on the manorial estates which then were forming. In addition the recurring need for men to fight the country's wars acted as an effective check on the development of a rural proletariat.

Strictly speaking, only a small proportion of the agriculturalists consisted of independent farmers, or tax farmers as they were called. Most of the land belonged to the crown and the nobility; towards the end of the seventeenth century these two forms of ownership embraced between 70 to 80 per cent of all homesteads in Sweden. Thus only a quarter or a third of the peasants were independent. Economically this had little significance except in regard to the forming of manorial estates. To an overwhelming extent agriculture was conducted as a family enterprise, regardless of whether the land was the family's own or belonged to the crown or to the nobility. The rapid increase in noble landholdings, chiefly at the expense of the crown, had little effect on the organization and conduct of agriculture. On the whole, agriculture retained its traditional character. There were two features peculiar to this traditional agriculture and these were to persist for more than a century: the open field system which had developed from the prevailing manner of dividing land among all the sons in a family, and the close connection between agriculture and forestry.

The origins of divided ownership are not certain. Clearly the inheritance system intensified the fragmentation of the land, as its purpose was to provide each of the heirs with equally good land, so that if there were three sons a farm would not be partitioned simply into thirds, but instead each field would be broken into three parts. It often happened that the units of land thus cut up would become so small as to render individual cultivation impossible. A farmer had to sow when his neighbours sowed, and reap when his neighbours reaped. Indeed a common pattern of cultivation seems to have been ordered by the villages with fixed times for planting and harvesting. In regard to the actual farming the peasants thus formed a collective whose members worked assigned lots in proportion to the acreage they owned or rented, and no one functioned as 'sole farmer'. Just how important this arrangement was for the efficiency of farming is difficult to say. The system had been defended on the grounds that it was rational in view of contemporary technology. According to this argument, long, narrow strips were better suited to the harrow and plough than shorter and wider strips. A likely consequence in any case was a pronounced conservatism in farming methods. Strip farming reinforced a natural caution caused partly by a dependence on the quality of the soil and climate, and partly by tradition. The sons learned from their fathers. When the adoption of new methods or approaches required unanimity, or at least a majority, it is reasonable to assume that innovations encountered a stubborn resistance. New methods such as the eighteenth-century enclosure reforms and the introduction of the potato were not first tried on peasant farms, but on the new manorial estates and on church land.

Conservatism in farming methods, regardless of its causes, appears to have been solidly established. One of its most pronounced features was a great emphasis on grain, little attention being given to root crops. The result was a continuous impoverishment of the soil—a tendency aggravated in many places by the practice of planting the same kind of cereal crop in the same field year after year, giving the earth no opportunity to lie fallow. In many areas, however, the two-field system had been introduced, whereby spring and autumn planting were alternated on the soil. The three-field system, which divided the land among autumn crops, spring crops and fallow, made headway more slowly, although it had been common on the Continent for at least two centuries. Barley, the predominant crop during the sixteenth century, was beginning to meet serious competition from rye. Oats and wheat played a subordinate role, and were to do so for a long time to come; hence the comparative rarity of white bread, which was regarded as a rare luxury in Sweden until well into the twentieth century.

The predominance of cereal cropping must be considered in relation to the farmers' use of the forests (other than as sources of fuel and game). Grain was the chief crop because it was the best food available for human beings. The animals were largely left to fend for themselves on forest pasture which was owned in common. This practice had at least two important consequences. Firstly, the loss of soil nutrients, caused by the partiality for cereal cropping, was exacerbated by the fact that the soil seldom if ever was fertilized: the biological balance was thus violated. Secondly, it became difficult to get sufficient fodder for livestock during the winter. Cattle was therefore by necessity butchered on a large scale in the autumn; during certain periods hides seem to have been an important export item. The surviving stock were undernourished, which meant that farmers could expect very little return from them, i.e. in the form of dairy products. Although the condition of these animals usually improved in the following spring, summer and autumn, they never fully recovered from the hardships of winter. Not even in the most productive periods could the yields of meat or milk come anywhere near the levels attainable by modern methods. The situation can be compared with that in some under-developed countries today. Such practices obviously affected the human diet. Even if we disregard their effect on longevity (where so many factors are involved that it would be wrong to limit the explanation to Malthusianism), we need not look far to understand why the Swedes of that day were of such short stature. This is a source of amazement to many the first time they are faced with authentic seventeenth century clothes. Charles XII was regarded in his time as an unusually impressive figure on account of his five feet six inches, which today would classify him as short.

We have noted above some of the reasons for the maintenance of traditional agricultural methods. However, it would certainly be a mistake to consider ignorance, rigid conservatism and possible incompetence as the only factors restricting agricultural techniques and encouraging the reliance on woodlands. It must be noted that the farmlands were surrounded not only by forests, but often also by bogs, marshes, and other land unsuitable for cultivation. During the sixteenth and seventeenth centuries this picture gradually changed as the geological process of land elevation continued, with the result that agriculture came to be conducted more and more extensively and the old methods of livestock raising gradually declined in importance; instead of setting the livestock out to pasture, often several miles from the homestead, farmers increasingly cultivated fodder crops.

The importance of the woodland for the farming population cannot be exaggerated. The forest not only provided pasture for animals, and fuel and timber for human dwellings, but also acted as a game reserve for much of the year. Hunting was an important economic pursuit and any attempt to limit their hunting rights was met with stern opposition from the peasants. Game was not valued for the meat alone. The hides and furs played an important part, augmenting the family wardrobe and featuring as articles of sale on the domestic as well as the export markets. Free access to the woods was as important to the farmer as the farming operation itself. This is especially true if the list of 'forest occupations' is made to include fishing (excluding marine fishing). It is probable that fishing was of even greater economic value for farmers than hunting and trapping.

Farming and 'forest occupations' thus occupied a dominant position in the total national economy. Perhaps, however, we should also mention the home crafts (*sloyd*) in all their different forms. The vast majority of farms were very nearly self-sufficient. The members of a family were often jacks-of-all-trades: farmers, livestock raisers, hunters, fishers, bakers, brewers, smiths, shoemakers, and so on.

The products of domestic arts and crafts were not necessarily restricted to use in the self-contained household. Some crafted products were made for sale, and a measure of regional specialization was common during the seventeenth century. Per Nyström gives the following examples, among others: the manufacture of rough woollen cloth in the Borås area, woodenware in Västergötland, linen in Hälsingland and Småland; nail-making in Bergslagen, and copper-smithing in Hälsingland. Although production of these goods took place in farming households, specialization had in some cases undoubtedly reached the point where *sloyd* had become a chief occupation, that is a handicraft in the truer sense.

In addition to homecraft, which received more or less consistent encouragement from the authorities, the making of articles by hand was also practised by itinerant artisans. Many of these had presumably worked previously in towns, employed by other craftsmen, but for some reason or another found rural freelancing more to their liking. Furthermore, there were different types of artisans employed on the larger noble estates, which were self-sufficient to a much greater extent than the normal farming households. These estates also provided a home for the decorative arts as the nobility took a great interest in beautifully appointed interiors. During the seventeenth century the fancier aspects of joinery and furniture-making in particular flourished; but apart from that, artisans were also engaged to satisfy more mundane needs, such as blacksmithing, construction work, tailoring, shoemaking, baking and brewing. The royal estates employed an even greater number of men. With the more elaborate royal households which were first introduced by Erik XIV and John III, and later brought to an extravagant level by Queen Christina, there developed a great demand for handmade goods of a more exclusive nature.

While individual items produced for the nobility were valued, both intrinsically and more especially as status symbols, and their manufacture gave employment to a number of artisans, their contribution to the national economy was only minor. Of greater significance, though again of relatively limited scope, were the independent handicrafts. During the seventeenth century these were largely confined to the towns, but we do not know how many people were employed in them, or how big their output was. This lack of knowledge is especially glaring in regard to the purely rural crafts, both in their combination with domestic *sloyd* and in the more specialized forms they assumed. Thanks to a documented source (making due allowance for inaccuracies), we are better informed about the urban crafts. On the basis of the statistics available, Ernst Söderlund has estimated the total number of craftsmen and their hired workers at about 8,000, equivalent to between 2 or 3 per cent of the total adult male population at the end of the seventeenth century. Söderlund assumes that close to 3,000 persons were engaged in handcraft in Stockholm and about the same number in other towns, adding up to a total of 6,000; but since the estimates for the latter probably have exaggerated the total employed in rural towns, the total estimate is more likely to be close to 5,000. Söderlund believes that at least 2,000 persons were engaged in rural handicrafts. These figures cannot be regarded as wholly accurate, but they do afford a basis for general observations. Thus we may conclude that even if the value of handicrafts represented a very small percentage of the 'national income', they must have been rather important to those particular branches of industry

22

in which the majority of crafts were conducted, namely shoemaking, tailoring, smithing and cabinet-making.

Their distribution over the country was most uneven. There is nothing remarkable about this; the distribution of population was uneven, especially in regard to communities which in an economic sense merited the title of 'towns'. Stockholm stood in a class by itself as may be seen from the figures cited above. It headed the list not only in sheer numbers of artisans, but also in the number of different trades followed, the size of their output, and the number of people employed in a workship. According to Söderlund, and his estimates seem to be rather high, the employee-artisan ratio averaged at one-half in the rural towns and between 1·6 and 1·7 in Stockholm. In other words, the capital employed between three to three and a half times as many persons per workshop.

The shoemakers and tailors were predominant both in Stockholm and in the provincial towns. Together they probably accounted for nearly one-third of all the workshops in the capital and about the same proportion elsewhere, although the tailors were relatively more important in Stockholm. Next came the smiths and carpenters. In the capital, fifth and sixth rankings were held by the bakers and the brewers although both these trades were very modestly represented in the provincial towns. The disproportionately large number of butchers in Stockholm was also striking. Proceeding from there to the 'fancier' crafts (fancy in the sense of entailing a larger artistic component), we find that Stockholm virtually monopolized the supply of goldsmiths, bookbinders, painters, sculptors, stonecutters, chair-makers, gold braiders, wigmakers, lace makers and watchmakers. The same thing is true of a number of other specialities, more 'practical' than artistic, practised by the tanners, the makers of buttons and needles, and the cordwainers, who were primarily concerned with the tanning of hides and skins for furniture upholstery and travelling bags. Coppersmiths and hatters, on the other hand, appear to have been much more widely represented in the provincial towns than in Stockholm. In part, this is simply a statistical consequence of the fact that other trades were so richly represented in the capital; but it was also due to the fact that the products of coppersmiths and hatters enjoyed a relatively greater demand in rural areas.

Conditions varied in different provincial towns. As a result, the averages given above for Sweden excluding Stockholm cannot be considered typical of any one of its towns. Norrköping, for example, definitely set the provincial pace in regard to the number of crafts and their differentiation. The industrialization of Norrköping, launched by Louis de Geer, which secondarily affected the shipping trade, was inevitably reflected in the size and diversity of the town's handicrafts. Handicrafts were important in Göteborg too, though they tended to be specialized due to the concentration there on shipping and the absence of other industry. In Karlskrona the handicrafts took on a similarly specialized pattern towards the end of the seventeenth century when the town started to develop into Sweden's naval headquarters. If we estimate that somewhat more than one-third of the urban artisans worked in Stockholm and another one-third in the towns mentioned above, we should get a fair idea of how the handicrafts were distributed locally.

If urban handicrafts were supported by the authorities, official support was even more readily forthcoming in regard to the so-called manufactories, a blanket term here indicating the processes by which products were made on an industrial scale, and the actual establishments where they were made. The iron manufactories formed a separate branch, which is natural in view of the position held by Swedish iron and its significance for weaponry. A second important group of manufactories were involved in producing foodstuffs, textiles and other commodities of more vital everyday economic importance.

There were good reasons for lending official support to the manufactories, even though the ultimate results were at great variance with those originally sought. Blessed with resources of high-grade iron ore, and impelled by the need to maintain a good standard of production, Sweden had every incentive to foster a higher degree of processing. In addition, the preferences of foreign customers for special sizes, thicknesses and other particular design specifications tended to encourage specialization and professional skill at the manufacturing stage. A further incentive for improvement came from the spectre of ruinous competition for the staple product, bar iron, where Sweden was in danger of pricing herself out of the market because of high freight costs. A higher degree of processing could increase the selling value of bar iron per unit of weight shipped, and thereby reduce the ratio of freight costs to total revenue. The general predilection of that day, by no means unjustified, for increasing the value of exports by incorporating a greater component of domestic processing, did not make the manufacturing schemes any the less tempting.

The only sort of hardware manufacture in which production became better organized during the seventeenth century was the armament industry. A royal decree of 1620 forced the closure of peasant forges which until then had formed the arms industry together with a number of manufactories located in castles. The proprietors were forced to choose between moving to certain designated towns—Söderhamn, Norrtälje, Örebro, Norrköping and Jönköping—or staying where they were. This change encountered stubborn resistance. As late as the 1640s county governors were engaged in upending rural forges and confiscating bellows. Nevertheless, a permanent body of specialized, skilled gunsmiths and armourers, limited to a few districts, was successfully mustered. When Louis De Geer took over management of the factories in 1627, he could rely almost completely on domestic labour in contrast with conditions in the iron industry itself. At Eskilstuna, where manufacturing had roots going back to the time when Charles IX was the Duke of Södermanland, the Rademacher enterprises were established in the 1650s. Although of limited importance during this period, the Rademacher enterprises did lay the foundations of Eskilstuna's subsequent fame as a metalworking centre. The anchor-forge at Söderfors was started in 1676. Because of the shipbuilding boom at that time—especially in England—this line of manufacture proved to be among the most profitable. Exactly at the turn of the century, the Stjärnsund manufactory entered the picture, its production being based on the patents of the noted inventor Christoffer Polhem. Actually this enterprise counted for little in the total scheme of things, but there is no mistaking the part it played in fulfilling one of the most cherished economic dreams of the age.

However, important as were the creation of new iron-working industries, other new types of manufacture were still more eagerly pursued, and in these different spheres the seventeenth century left its most significant imprint. Before we proceed, a few concepts must first be clarified. Per Nyström, in his book on the Swedish manufacturing industry before the nineteenth century, has called attention to the fluid boundary lines between handicrafts and manufactories on the one hand, and manufactories and home *sloyd* on the other. The chief distinction between manufactories and handicrafts was that products of the former were placed directly on the open market, while crafted products were sold by the artisans to their customers and very often fabricated to order. The chief distinction between manufactories and home *sloyd*, the products of which were sold openly too, was that manufactories gradually came to rely more and more on industrial processes. This is not to suggest that the manufactories already existing could generally be regarded as industrial enterprises, or even that they were characterized to a greater extent by large-scale operation than the leading handicrafts. The tendency, nevertheless, undoubtedly lay in this direction. Indeed, as the word 'manufactories' came to be used in the seventeenth century, it seems to have covered all types of production which could compete with and preferably obviate imports of finished goods. The manufacturing industry was accordingly made to include textile, leather and metal production, the processing of imported cane sugar, of paper, glass and glazed earthenware, and the production of small wares and sundry other articles which the craftsmen did not deal with. Activities which were conducted by such artisans as clothes-makers, locksmiths, cabinet-makers, housebuilders and shoe-makers, fell outside the definition of manufactories owing to the cited differences in selling methods.

With regard to the emergence of manufactories on a more industrial scale—many of them vested in undertakings which started under letters patent and vanished comparatively early from the scene—these were almost exclusively located in the larger towns, particularly Stockholm, Göteborg, Malmö, Norrköping, Jönköping, Kalmar and Gävle. The reason for this was, firstly, the pro-urban spirit of the Government, which meant that privileges would not be granted for any other type of location; and secondly, the fact that towns provided the most appropriate environment, especially since the crown was often the only customer. Of undoubted importance, too, was the special type of business organization which became common, whereby a merchant or a trading house held the proprietary interest and provided the working capital, while responsibility for actual production was vested in a staff of employed engineers, almost all of whom were imported from abroad. Considering that the foremost manufactories were textiles, a close tie with home *sloyd* might have been expected. From all indications, however, a working relationship was never established. That is not as strange as it may sound: the skills required for industrial processing were not of the kind that could be recruited from the ranks of *sloyd* practitioners. Besides, the two sectors had separate markets and channels of distribution.

The larger-scale industrial activities were chiefly limited to the most important export items: tar, timber, copper and iron. This terminology does not signify the emergence of factory production in the modern sense, except perhaps in the fields of copper and iron. It does mean, however, that tendencies towards large-scale operation, and a subsequent increase in organization and capital requirements, became more prevalent in the production of these goods, as they already had in foreign trade and shipping.

Copper, iron and tar, were the origins of foreign interest in Sweden, and provide the background against which her expansion and long reign as a great power must be seen. Admittedly these three products did not count for very much in quantitative terms: their contribution to the national income was small. But over long periods they preponderated heavily in the country's exports, ranging from 80 to 90 per cent of the total. Above all, their role was crucial for the government's financial position and its weight in power politics. Therefore, they came to have a powerful impact on social conditions. When Engelbrekt, the Stures and Gustavus Vasa enlisted the men of Dalarna and Västmanland provinces as assault troops in their struggles against Denmark, they did not, as is the popular conception, rely so much on liberty-loving farmers and cattle raisers, as on the mine owners in these provinces and their Hanseatic connections across the Baltic. Sweden exercised a virtual monopoly over tar, iron and copper (particularly copper), until the beginning of the eighteenth century. The exports of these products enabled her to finance both her long wars and, to some extent, the administration of conquered territories.

It is one of the ironies of history that Swedish ascendancy in copper, which also contributed indirectly to the expansion of the Netherlands as the marketing country, should have come from Spain's adoption of a copper standard at the end of the sixteenth century. Sweden was thereby enabled to export more copper and to command a much higher price for it, which in turn helped to finance many seventeenth-century military campaigns. Indeed it can be said that Spain, when it adopted a copper standard, provided the technical and financial means for the northward shift of economic and political power which accelerated during the seventeenth century.

Incidentally, this trade in copper had not a little bearing on the genesis of the *Riksbank*. Johan Palmstruch's brilliant, but in the long run unfortunate, idea was to issue notes as receipts for the deposits of the bulky copper coins. This copper standard had been introduced by Gustavus Adolphus in 1624 in order to create a domestic demand for copper, as a means of regulating supply and prices on the world market. The bank notes (the first Sweden had seen) very soon acquired a premium rate *vis-à-vis* copper, precisely because they were so much easier to handle. Palmstruch then lost both common sense and decency. He yielded to the temptation to issue more notes than the prevailing rates of exchange for copper could accommodate; he even issued bank loans in the form of paper notes which did not correspond to any existing copper deposits. Inevitably a run was caused on the bank by depositors anxious to redeem their paper for metal. The resulting panic precipitated the bank crash we mentioned earlier, which compelled the founding of the *Riksbank*. The first real paper monetary system of Europe had failed with a crash and more than fifty years were to pass before Sweden was ready to try such a system again. In any event, blame for the tragedy—or perhaps the honour for having ventured to modernize the monetary system at so early a date—ultimately fell upon Swedish copper policy and on the peculiarities, to be described later on, which it engendered in an already confused monetary system.

Successful in the copper trade, Sweden was also well placed during this age in regard to the other two chief exports, iron and tar. These three together serve to explain how the country was able to achieve its position as a first-rank military and political power.

Iron took a much greater part than copper in the value of Swedish exports; during the period here under review, the ratio was about two to one. For various reasons, however, its position on the European market could not be compared with that of copper. In the first place, iron was a less important commodity generally. Secondly, most of the countries in need of iron produced their own and were therefore not dependent on imports. The principal importing country was the Netherlands, followed by England, whose own production had been on the decline chiefly owing to a shortage of charcoal. Yet even in England, iron accounted for no more than a very small percentage of total imports. Nevertheless, despite the relatively minor role of iron in the economies of importing countries, Sweden, as virtually the only exporting country and endowed moreover with ores of unusually high purity (which given the technology then existing made all the difference as far as the usefulness of iron was concerned) enjoyed what may be called an extremely strong marginal position. This role of iron was steadily gaining significance, and thus ironworking was increasingly becoming a major factor in the Swedish economy.

As for tar, its importance must be seen in relation to the boom in shipbuilding, especially in England, the Netherlands and France, which were expanding their navies and merchant marines. As long as tar and pitch could be extracted from wood only, the Swedish-Finnish tar industry possessed a great advantage. As woodlands had been depleted all over Europe, Sweden and Finland possessed virtually the only remaining forest reserves. This favoured position was ruthlessly exploited to create high prices. To be sure, the combined export value of pitch and tar did not usually exceed 6 per cent of the total, and certainly never more than 7 per cent. However, in combination with the monopoly of copper, and a near-monopoly of iron exports, the monopoly of tar products constituted a commercial supremacy without which the politico-military expansion would have been unattainable.

The economic significance of tar derived not only from the demand for it in shipbuilding. It was also an easy article to produce, requiring little capital investment. Thus it became a thriving rural industry wherever trees grew in abundance and transport conditions were favourable for sale. The relative costs of processing and transport on the one hand, and the market value of the product on the other, created a highly advantageous balance in favour of the producer.

Conditions were the reverse for the lumber industry, whose inferior position had been excerbated by an embargo on exports of oak, the supplies of which were needed for the building of Sweden's own navy. Consequently the two staples of this industry, logs and boards, had a combined export value far below that of tar and pitch. Well over 50 per cent of the lumber exports appear to have been shipped within the Baltic area; further westward, the competition from Norway was too keen. The most important exporting areas were the Småland and Värmland regions, while Norrland (Northern Sweden) still played a subordinate role.

Let us return to a consideration of the important ironworking industry. Iron was worked in Sweden long before the birth of Christ, and had become an export item by the fifth century. Until the twelfth century, however, the ore was not extracted from mines but from lakes and bogs in the south of Sweden, particularly in the province of Småland. As far as we know, ironworking was exclusively undertaken by the peasants; the extraction of ore required little organizational and technical skill. Possibly this pattern of operation did not alter much when rock deposits were first exploited. For a long time, ironworking remained a sideline of agriculture and forestry. During the thirteenth and fourteenth centuries the mining of ore became increasingly concentrated in areas of what had formerly been wasteland situated in the provinces north-west of Lake Mälaren and known collectively as Bergslagen. Gradually the ore exploitation became a more specialized activity. Some families became the owners of several ore deposits, and began to operate more or less co-operatively on a large scale with permanently employed or seasonally hired labour. In the sixteenth century the crown commenced its acquisition of a large proprietary interest, although it was originally more concerned with copper mining. During the seventeenth century, with its reliance on private business combined with public control, the industry was again restored almost completely to private hands. However this was accompanied by a regulatory system which, in combination with certain technical changes, was to leave its imprint on Swedish ironworking for almost two centuries.

The breakthrough of pig iron processing dates from the sixteenth century. This change entailed the use of hotter furnaces which were better able to produce the crude intermediate between ore and malleable iron than the former constructions of timber and earth (*mulltimmerhyttor*). It appears that initially the results of pig-making were quite unforeseen, and even caused no little anxiety, until the advantages were seen in first converting all the ore into pig iron, and then having the pig refined into malleable iron in special furnaces. The advantages of this process were at first limited by the use of the same furnaces to make both the pig and the malleable product. It was not until the last decades of the sixteenth century that separate furnaces were adopted for each and the blast-furnace operation took hold in earnest. In this new form, ironworking came to be concentrated in two areas, both outside the Bergslagen region defined above. One was in north-eastern Uppland, where mills were started in the sixteenth century based on the mines at Dannemora; towards the end of the century the industry there was organized on a more ambitious scale by Welam de Wijk, an immigrant from the southern Netherlands. The other area was in Värmland, a province which was to account for nearly a quarter of Sweden's iron output before the end of the century.

At that time two innovations from abroad had reached Sweden, and there has been much discussion as to which of them was more important, the Walloon forge or the German forge. The essential difference between them was of quality. Walloon iron proved to be superior in the production of steel, and although it accounted for barely more than 10 per cent of the total iron exports (a small proportion, compared with German-forged iron), the recognition of its fine working qualities greatly affected the industry. For over two centuries the emphasis on quality became the industry's best asset on the international market. Another difference between the two types of forge lay in the kind of blast furnace employed. The German forges relied on the old timber-earth constructions, enlarged and with added provision for a vastly improved blasting method. Walloon forges used masoned furnaces, usually of stone—the so-called 'French' furnaces. However, the similarities between these forges were more important than their differences. Beginning in the 1630s, the leather bellows in both were replaced by bellows of wood which had been introduced by the German, Hans Steffen. Wooden bellows provided a stronger and more even heat, thereby increasing the capacity. Of special importance was the adoption of alternate blowing of two bellows in the same furnace, which made it possible to build much larger blast furnaces. The advantages of this new technique gained special significance when an improved bulwarking technique developed at the same time allowed the exploitation of power from waterways which were too violent for the earlier mills. Both of the new types of blast furnace, the 'French' in particular, were much larger and more costly than the old furnaces, which was one reason for the transition to larger-scale enterprises. Also, thanks to the continuous operation which the improved pig-making process permitted, it became possible to run the subsequent processes of refining and forging on a large scale.

Naturally enough, this development altered the techniques of corporate management and organization. A gradual and at times accelerated advance towards large-scale operation developed, though without entirely eliminating the traditional small ironmakers. These changes would presumably have occurred in any case, given the technical knowledge, but there can be no doubt that this development was stimulated by the government regulations applied to ironworking in the seventeenth century. It turned out to be a fortunate example of economic planning. That the controls succeeded so well in this case is due to the fact that they coincided both with technical-economic trends and with the interests of entrepreneurs. The small ironmakers were assured of protection for their mining and pig-making activities, and could therefore be reasonably reconciled to the curtailment of their forging rights. The ironworks owners were given a monopoly of the refining processes plus guranteed access to cheap raw materials and semi-manufactures.

Four main lines of thought lay behind the promotion of this policy. (1) Preference was to be given to large-scale enterprise and financially strong types of business organizations at the processing stages. (2) The maintenance of stable prices for raw materials was believed necessary to ensure continued price stability on the world market, since it was feared competitors with inferior natural advantages might otherwise impose poorer terms of trade. (3) Guarantees were sought to maintain standards of quality. For this purpose it was easier to control the mill-owners than the small ironmakers; the system involved the compulsory use of 'iron stamps', a designation of origin certifying that the iron produced by any one mill had the right quality. (4) To prevent the depletion of forests on the scale that had taken place elsewhere in Europe, the authorities wanted to locate the industry in areas away from the sources of raw materials. Thus, it seemed natural to permit pig-making to remain close to these sources; pig iron was easier to ship than ore and, as noted earlier, the production of pig and its refinement into malleable iron (called bar iron because of the shape it assumed after hammering), could best be carried out in separate furnaces anyway.

It would be wrong to make exaggerated claims for the uniqueness of this policy. Certainly Sweden was in an exceptionally favourable position to expand her iron industry: she had the forests for making charcoal (now taking care not to burn down her advantage), and she had ores of low phosphorus content. Even so, it had become an established tendency in almost all iron-producing countries to scatter production so as to separate the later processing stages from the actual mining and the first processing stage.

Neither would it be correct to say that this policy was pursued with fervent and relentless dedication. On the contrary, the four dicta were applied with considerable flexibility—which surely explains so great a success. The division of labour was never carried to the extreme of prohibiting the operation of all bar-iron forges in Bergslagen. It was the formation of new enterprises that the authorities wanted to prevent. Similarly, at the other end of production, the iron mills were not prevented from integrating their own mines and pig-making activity with the production of bar iron. Indeed, the possession of mines was regarded as a special asset when letters patent were sought for opening an iron mill.

At all events, the successful application of these ideas resulted in the classic rise of the Swedish ironworking industry, with its ramifications in the technical, economic, social and cultural spheres. Even though the eighteenth century was well under way before this structure acquired its final character, the foundations were undoubtedly laid during the seventeenth century.

The aims of the government policy on ironworking were most gratifyingly realized. Exports began to rise during the 1620s. At the beginning of that decade an estimated 7,000 tons of iron were shipped from Sweden annually. Twenty years later this figure had, through a relatively continuous increase, reached approximately 17,000 tons, and by mid-century, 18,000 tons. A figure of nearly 25,000 tons coincided with the founding year of the *Riksbank*. By the end of the century, exports apparently were stabilized at about 27,000 tons annually, allowing for annual fluctuations.

Up to the middle of the seventeenth century, the boom in Swedish ironworking was sustained chiefly by Dutch demand, reflecting the expansion of the Netherlands in foreign trade and shipping. Much of the iron and wood coming from Sweden was channelled directly into the construction of ships. At the same time, however, iron was required for other uses. The Dutch towns were growing fast. Factories had to be built to accommodate the country's thriving crafts and industries. Dutch interest in Swedish iron was further stimulated by the Thirty Years' War. A double-pronged effect was at work here: the war impeded the procurement of supplies of iron from Germany, just when the Netherlands needed more iron to manufacture armaments. Accordingly the increased Dutch demand neatly matched the Swedish desire to boost exports. An essential consideration for Sweden, concerned with financing her own war effort, was to find buyers who were willing to put up capital in advance and who would also be responsible for the technical side of the expansion in ironworking. It was fortunate for Sweden that the Dutch iron industry lacked the means for making substantial progress, both qualitatively and quantitatively: these deficiencies may account for the emigration to Sweden of De Geer's Walloons, who were destined to play such an important role in the genesis of the Swedish quality steels.

The war boom had spent its force by mid-century, and the Dutch-sponsored investments had tapered off. Prices, which until then had risen, began to be stabilized. In the light of this it becomes easier to appreciate the Swedish dread of increased manufacturing costs which dictated the above-mentioned official attempts to regulate prices of ore and pig iron. At this juncture, however, England became a new market giving promise of a second period of expansion. We have already noted the stagnation which ensued in English iron production, partly explained by the depletion of forests and the resulting grave shortage of charcoal. But as Karl-Gustav Hildebrand has demonstrated, this explanation does not tell the whole truth. Actually the English had managed to overcome their plight: the iron mills, formerly clustered in the south, were relocated in the Midlands and the northern counties, and charcoal was extracted from forests with rapid regrowth. Of equal importance, perhaps even more so from the Swedish point of view, was that England, beginning under the rule of Cromwell in the mid-seventeenth century, expanded vigorously in virtually all sectors: commerce and shipping, domestic industry, the development of towns, and the founding of colonies. England was at the dawn of an empire, whose face then was largely turned towards North America, particularly the 'thirteen colonies'. These territories admittedly covered only a small part of that continent, but they became most powerful in population, organization and armed might. The recurring wars at sea, such as the conflict with the Netherlands from 1651 to 1658 over the Navigation Act, created a great need for new investments in men-of-war and merchant vessels. Losses in battle, together with those occurring from more normal causes (shipwrecks were fairly common), maintained a steady market for shipbuilding which ensured a demand for iron. These developments contained the seeds of what was to take place in the eighteenth century when Swedish pre-industrial ironworking was to reach its economic, social and political zenith. However, it also reached a top level in the sense of stagnation—an elevated standstill. The role of iron as one of the pillars of Swedish great-power status was brought to an end ultimately.

It may be appropriate to say a few words here about some of the men who helped build up the new Sweden of the seventeenth century. An initial reference has already been made to the Dutchman, Welam de Wijk, who reorganized the iron industry of Uppland. He started his Swedish career in the service of Duke Charles, later Charles IX, in order to promote the development of ironworking in his master's duchy. That relationship foundered on differences of opinion, after which de Wijk became an agent of the crown under John III. It was in this capacity that he rendered his primary contribution in helping to lay the foundations of the iron industry. Among the iron mills he administered for the crown or leased from it were Österby, Forsmark, Ortala, Leufsta, Gimo and Västland, all in the Uppland province, and Finspång in Östergötland. Willem de Besche (1573–1629), a fellow countryman from the southern Netherlands, succeeded him as ironmaster under Duke Charles. To a certain degree de Besche also became the 'heir' of his predecessor, presumably in consequence of the Duke's accession to the throne. Thus he came to lease Finspång as from 1616 and Österby, Gimo and Leufsta as from 1626. Money was the prerequisite for these activities, and this need for money explains future developments. Yet another Dutchman, Louis De Geer (1587–1652), entered the iron business as financier. As from 1627, De Geer openly appeared as a partner of de Besche, and later as successor to the latter's leases. To repay its debts to him the crown allowed De Geer to acquire the sole proprietary interest in the most important of the above-mentioned mills at the beginning of the 1640s. At Finspång he finished what de Besche had started by converting a large part of the mill into an arms manufactory. At Österby, Gimo and Leufsta, production was concentrated on Walloon iron; this 'Öregrund iron' (from the Swedish place name Öregrund) was, thanks to its high quality, best suited to the fabrication of steel, and it has become forever connected with the name of Louis De Geer.

While this trio of Dutchmen may have made the greatest impression on posterity, they were far from being the only men of significance in the developing industry. A very large number of Swedish nobles who had domains in the iron provinces were enabled by the new policy to become ironmasters (*brukspatron*). Often enough, the owner would lease the mill to a 'staple-town' merchant, who in due course might also acquire the proprietary interest. Such transfers generally took place according to the same principle which held for the old crown works, which were first leased out and later sold. In both cases the leasing would be motivated by the owner's inability to run the business; the nobility, of course, had other duties to fulfil, in particular as officers and administrators. Then, too, they needed the money. As for the lessee, the advantages of this arrangement were obvious. He did not have to put up all the capital which an immediate purchase would have required. After paying the rent, he could invest instead in an expansion of the plant. In due course, when a good rate of return had improved his financial position, a favourable opportunity would come for outright purchase. Profits which made this possible, as well as the general success of official ironworking policy, were naturally related to the flourishing conditions which prevailed in this industry.

Exports fulfilled another function beyond that of financing military campaigns. They were also meant to balance the imports of commodities. Imports were not viewed with friendly eyes by the authorities. Indeed their quest for national self-sufficiency manifested itself in many different spheres. It lay behind the zeal with which domestic manufactories and crafts were encouraged, and the preference for importing talented persons to exercise their skills within the borders of the realm rather than import foreign products. The considerations of economic policy which guided these endeavours will be dealt with in another context. Some further observations on the pattern of external trade must be made at this point.

Just as two or three commodities completely dominated the export trade, so a few particular imports, namely textiles, small wares, salt and beverages prevailed. Grains did not achieve any considerable importance until nearly the end of the seventeenth century; they were to comprise one of the leading import commodities throughout the eighteenth century. Textiles accounted for, roughly, between 30 and 35 per cent of the total, with a slight decline setting in as the seventeenth century drew to a close. Small wares constituted about 20 per cent and salt about 10 per cent. The key commodity for the great majority of the population was salt, though its use for the preservation of food would appear to have been exaggerated by some economic historians. Eli F. Heckscher, for instance, speaks of 'green-salted' butter—certainly a misunderstanding on his part. If butter changes colour from salting, it tends to turn orange rather than green. In older usage, 'green' butter simply referred to the fresh, unsalted product. Drying and perhaps freezing also played a major role, and it is reasonable to assume that hunting and fishing contributed more fresh fare to the table than is generally estimated. Nevertheless, even if the importance of salt has been overrated—it was never imported on the scale required to fulfil the purposes ascribed to it—there can be no doubt that it was essential for the storage economy of an agrarian country. The relative preponderance of finished textiles and small wares stems from the fact that imports, if one disregards salt and some fish, played a subordinate role in contributing to the necessities of life. In other words, imported goods consisted largely of luxuries suited to the tastes of the upper class and the well-to-do middle class. Silk stockings for ladies of refinement were in particular demand, so much so that a lively smuggling traffic developed. This emphasis on luxury items also explains the sporadic government attempts to suppress much of the import trade and to promote domestic manufacture in its place in order to get greater financial freedom of action by an improved balance of trade.

During the seventeenth century the importance of Swedish merchant tonnage greatly increased not only in absolute terms, but presumably also in relation to the total Swedish foreign trade. Of all the ships passing through Öresund strait more than 10 per cent were to carry the Swedish flag. Of a total of Swedish and Dutch vessels, the former comprised about one-fifth. In 1670 the Swedish merchant marine is believed to have fallen just short of 34,000 registered tons. Dutch ships totalled at the same time about 370,000 tons; Great Britain and the Hanseatic cities had about 70,000 tons each; and France about 45,000 registered tons. One indication of the strong position which the Swedish merchant navy held at this time is that the tonnage registered in 1670 was exceeded by only a few hundred tons exactly a hundred years later. Towards the end of Charles XI's reign, the tonnage is known to have greatly exceeded the figures for both 1670 and 1770. That peak was reached during the boom touched off in shipping by the naval wars of the 1690s, when Sweden elected to remain neutral. A figure of about 33,000 registered tons was then reached in Stockholm alone. This great advantage was to be largely vitiated in the later phases of the Great Northern War.

As usual, we know less of internal conditions than of external, at least as far as trade and transport statistics are concerned. Sweden's relations with the outside world were subject to various controls imposed chiefly for fiscal reasons, and official records provide an abundance of satisfactory source materials. Some fiscal controls were imposed on internal trade also, but the records were never kept with the same order and tidiness as were those concerning external trade.

Nevertheless we have some starting points. The authorities sought to concentrate domestic trade, particularly in the foreign-trade staples, in the towns. Their efforts were undoubtedly crowned with a measure of success. The evidence for this is provided by the close relationship between deliveries to and purchases from the large exporting and importing towns, as well as by the importance which handicrafts attained in some of the cities, especially in Stockholm, Göteborg and Norrköping. Many of the new towns developed from long-established marketplaces (köpingar—the prefix 'köp' is Swedish for 'buy'). Even though the granting of a charter did not necessarily mean that these communities became towns in the economic sense, it stands to reason that their new legal status did not detract from whatever commercial importance they may have had. If anything, such status was likely to prove a boon to a town. Alongside the commerce between and within towns and marketplaces, there was also a considerable amount of house-to-house peddling. Peddling was particularly widespread in Västergötland province, as Nils Forssell describes in his Borås stads historia (History of Borås). Perhaps some of the new towns were founded chiefly to legalize and encourage this trade although at this time unlicensed trade became subject to increased persecution. Pedlars seem to have offered an assortment of merchandise, originally consisting of home-made objects of wood and wrought iron, later augmented by textiles. During the course of a pedlar's wanderings these articles would be exchanged for other commodities or new items would be added to the collection. A favourite haunt of the pedlars was the mining district of Bergslagen, which offered a ready market for sale as well as a source of raw materials, especially for the making of wrought-iron articles.

This direct intercourse between Bergslagen and the plains took on added importance with the expansion of the ironworking industry described above. In contrast to the former pattern of operation under small ironmakers, the mills were greatly dependent upon a flow of commodities from the outside to meet the needs of their many

37

employees and the farmers hired to burn charcoal and drive waggons.

Nor was peddling, which at times was virtually indistinguishable from the trade conducted in more regular channels, confined to the regions just mentioned. Nils Forssell has shown that ramifications of the pedlar's trade can be traced to such provinces as Småland, Östergötland, Södermanland and Närke. The pedlars appear to have worked up a particular speciality in cattle, with the foundries once again serving as the ultimate destination. Thus in Örebro, 4,000 head of cattle were cleared through customs in 1665 and 3,500 in 1666. Of the former figure, 1,200 head came from Västergötland and 2,000 from Småland; the contributions of these provinces in 1666 were 800 and 850 head respectively. There was also an important trade in horses: 1,124 head were cleared through customs at Hova and Örebro in 1666. If we add that one horse per owner was exempted from duty, the total head passing through Nova and Örebro comes to 1,800. What we do not know is the proportion of these figures to the total traffic in horses; nor do we know how many of the horses involved were engaged in the actual transportation of goods. None the less, the figures do point to a good-sized market for horses. The foundries had various uses for them apart from the pulling of heavy loads. Perhaps their use as saddle horses or in front of sledges was more important. Given the miserable road conditions of those days, these were the only feasible means of transport over long distances. Oxen were also used as draught animals but were valued more for their meat and for the mining ropes made from their hides.

Owing to the poor communications which prevailed in summer, it has been customary for historians to ascribe crucial importance to winter transportation. The observation may be correct in regard to the transport of iron between the pig-iron furnaces and the foundries, and to lighter, short-distance hauls generally. Several travellers, among them Per Brahe and the French diplomatic secretary, Charles Ogier, record in their diaries how men and women of high station, who never went anywhere without a retinue, much preferred to travel in the winter, when the frozen waterways offered easy passage. However, in regard to long distance commerce the findings made by Forssell suggest that winter transport played a more modest role. Nor is it hard to understand why. Horses have to be fed. In winter, with its shortage of feed, it was anything but easy to find fodder. During the warmer months of the year, however, it was possible to let the draught animals, as well as the cattle being raised for market, feed themselves *en route* by putting them out to the large meadowlands which were held in common or by the crown. To the extent one passed through sparsely settled country this procedure met with no hindrance. Obviously, too, the merchants themselves preferred to travel during the most agreeable seasons, in spite of the technical impediments to travel that might present themselves. Moreover, a part of the wares they were taking with them represented the fruits of the previous winter's home *sloyd*.

Transport by water was of great importance during the warmer parts of the year. Between Finland and Sweden, of course, overwater routes provided the most direct means of communication. However, there was also a good deal of traffic along the coasts, as well as on the large lakes Mälaren, Vänern, Vättern and Hjälmaren, together with the Göta river—the outlet of Lake Vänern. In addition, numerous plans were afoot for the construction of canals. Some of these projects were completed, such as the canal connecting Lake Mälaren with the Baltic through Stockholm, and another between Hjälmaren and Mälaren. If any further proof were needed of the tremendous importance which was attached to water transportation, it lay in the ambitious scope of these engineering projects; they were to be realized through the construction of the Göta Canal during the nineteenth century. In the capital at any rate, small craft from Finland, Norrland and Lake Mälaren were a common sight, and beyond doubt contributed significantly to Stockholm's communications with the rest of the country. The general rule, with certain exceptions for Gävle, was to have all foreign trade originating in the Gulf of Bothnia pass through Stockholm—a policy which strengthened internal shipping and trade with the capital.

The sailing ships depended on weather and wind and could not attain any considerable speeds. On a couple of occasions it took Axel Oxenstierna more than a month to sail from Stockholm to Riga. Even so, it is likely that journeys by water were often faster, more reliable and more comfortable than those undertaken over land. Some idea of the latter may be formed from the posting-inn system for the conveyance and accommodation of travellers. An ordinary traveller had to reckon on stopping somewhere for the night after every twelve miles. This means (and the calculation accords with some of the contemporary narratives), that a journey by horse and carriage averaged a mile and a half per hour on the better roads. The use of a loaded waggon or sledge naturally slowed down the pace even more. Many weeks would certainly be needed by pedlars from the Borås region who were heading for Bergslagen with goods and cattle, with frequent stops along the way for the transaction of business. Parties on horseback could cover between 30 and 35 miles in a day.

Besides, no great percentage of Sweden was covered by anything remotely resembling a road network. All the same, the existing facilities were impressive enough, both in mileage and maintenance. Visitors from abroad were wont to praise Swedish roads as the best in Europe. If Stockholm is taken as the point of origin, a highway followed the Bothnian coast up to Haparanda by way of Uppsala, Gävle, Sundsvall, Umeå and Piteå. Another led to Hälsingborg via Norrköping, Linköping, Ödeshög and Jönköping, traversing a route more or less identical with that of today's European Highway 4. Göteborg and Uddevalla could be reached by way of Eskilstuna, Örebro and Skara or, further north, by way of Västerås and Karlstad. From Linköping and Jönköping, one could take a road to Kalmar on the Baltic coast, and connect from there to Lund by way of Karlskrona and Kristianstad, and from Lund there was a connection leading to 'E4' at Hälsingborg. From Enköping or Västerås one could also proceed northwards to Falun. These routes formed only the core of the network.

Given the simplicity and the modest scale of enterprise which characterized the Swedish seventeenth-century economy as roughly outlined above, it follows that the forms of business organization were rudimentary. The aggregations of capital employed were likewise small, although by contemporary standards the need for capital was great in certain sectors, such as foreign trade, the mining and processing of iron and copper, various other manufactures, and even some of the handicrafts. Accordingly, it became necessary to launch undertakings and financing on the basis of more united efforts. Obviously, the problems posed must not be seen in isolation but in relation to the general economic structure and the size and mobility of that day's capital resources.

First of all, the demands imposed by the expansion of ironworking, foreign trade and shipping, and to a certain extent by the manufacturing system, could not possibly be met exclusively, or even chiefly, by domestic capital. One reason was the overall shortage of capital, but probably more significant was the fact that so little of the available capital could be transferred to new enterprises. Certainly an increased quantity of capital did pass into the hands of noblemen, and some of it was no doubt invested in new enterprises, in particular in the ironworks which they owned. Thus the role of the nobility in the new iron industry acquired great importance in so far as foundries could be conveniently located on the titled landholdings. To a far greater extent, however, the nobles tended to lock their capital: they would buy new land, often acquired in remission of loans granted to the state; or they would indulge an increasingly expensive taste for luxuries, especially as manifested in the many new castles and manor houses often with magnificent interiors and large staffs of servants.

The result was a lack of fluid domestic capital for new enterprises. The traditional alternative, recourse to foreign capital, lay close to hand, and reliance on that seemed the more natural as the new needs were intimately linked with these traditional means of finance. The technique and procedure did not become fully developed until the eighteenth century, but in kind if not in degree, seventeenth-century financing was characterized by the same methodology. Certain of its essential features and their background ought therefore be noted at this stage.

To begin with, control over Swedish foreign trade and shipping had historically been exercised mainly by foreign powers or other external groups. The first financiers were the Hanseatic cities, followed by the Dutch, and finally, to some degree, by the English. The seventeenth-century struggle for a 'national' merchant marine, not to mention other Swedish endeavours on behalf of domestic industry and commerce generally, may be compared to the aspirations of an ex-colony which, having achieved political autonomy, also seeks to throw off the economic yoke. Perhaps the parallel may be even more boldly drawn, though without claiming special consideration for Sweden's case; a similar process was fomenting in other countries too. Just as some of the newly emergent African states have been concerned to retain former colonial officials to help run their economy and public administration, so Sweden during the seventeenth century was concerned to persuade erstwhile financiers and other businessmen from abroad to become Swedish subjects. The idea was to 'Swedify' their capital and capabilities by 'adopting' them. In consequence, a part of the capital borrowed abroad was replaced by Swedish capital, at least to the extent that more of the returns on investment were retained at home, and could be used to expand enterprises already started or to finance new ventures. Louis De Geer provides the most telling example of such a transfer of capital to Sweden. On the other hand, it would be injudicious to ascribe crucial importance to these transfers. Actually it became fairly common practice for the immigrant entrepreneurs to continue to trade with and borrow money from their foreign connections. An even likelier result, though we cannot prove it with statistics, is that there was a net increase in borrowing from abroad. This is true at any rate in respect of the foreign merchant houses which were 'Swedified' during the eighteenth century. The large visible import surplus, especially conspicuous towards the end of Charles XI's reign, does not indicate a decrease in imports of foreign capital.[1]

It was characteristic that both the accumulation of capital and its mobility would be greatest in trade generally, and in foreign trade particularly. The attendant risks were great but, barring misfortunes, the profits were great too. The ability to make a profit was largely dependent on its position in the national economy. There were two ways of operating: the first was to deal in absolute essentials, e.g. by importing salt, or by exporting hardware items, especially weapons or the kind of iron best suited to make weapons. The second was to concentrate on luxuries destined for a wealthy upper class which would be attracted rather than repelled by a fancy price. After all, possession of these articles conferred a status derived from 'conspicuous consumption'. In both cases, the middlemen, that is, the large-scale foreign trade merchants, had plenty of opportunities to 'pad the bill'.

The fact that trade served as a source of capital brought with it at least two typical consequences.

One of these was a system of credit (förlag), which contained the essential elements of the merchant-employer system. The foreign traders advanced producers working capital to cover the expenses of production until receipts from sales began to come in. The producers could then extend credit to their workers and to their suppliers, who in turn could finance their own labour and output. Obviously the system gave the creditors a powerful hold on the debtors at every link of the chain. The creditors were in a strong position to dictate their terms for deliveries and prices. Here was certainly one reason why so much export business was transacted on a commission basis. Goods were not considered sold to the exporter but as held in commission by him until he sold them, which meant that the selling risk was essentially borne by the producers.

Another consequence of this 'commercial capitalism' was the problem of converting mobile capital into fixed capital, that is converting operating capital into investment capital. Since advances from merchants were intended to cover operating expenses, producers could obtain the wherewithal for investment only from the profits they earned. When the profits were inadequate for this purpose, the

1 Not during the seventeenth century either.

42

producers were tempted to ask for larger advances than the immediately ensuing deliveries were worth—in other words, to borrow longer-term capital under short-term conditions. This resulted in increased debts, and often the merchant took over the enterprise. Presumably it was this method which De Geer applied in his dealings with Willem de Besche.

It would be a mistake to think that all the ironworks thus passed into merchant hands, or that producers generally were doomed to slow but sure ruin by this credit system (*förlag*). The generally excellent market for the iron industry enabled many of the mills to consolidate and improve their financial position to the point where they could not only pay their debts regularly, but also plough back profits into expansion. However, during the eighteenth century a number of the most important iron mills became merchant-owned enterprises (with a resulting high degree of integration in many cases), once a wedge had been opened by the *förlag* system of credit.

An attempt was made to form trading companies on an international model where several merchants and certain other interests joined together to finance ventures which were particularly hazardous and expensive. Similar companies, chiefly involved in transoceanic trade, had been founded in England and the Netherlands. In the course of their development they came to perform political and military functions as well as economic by virtue of the state powers conferred on them to engage in conquests and colonization. Seventeenth-century Swedish trading companies were less successful, though similar ideas motivated to some degree the founding of New Sweden in North America. Such significance as these companies did attain was confined on the export side to tar and copper, where both organizations were formed to establish a foreign trading monopoly. On the import side, the most important was the 'Great Salt Company'. There is no reason to dwell further on the activities of these companies which did not exercise any influence worth mention on trade and production as a whole. Their importance lies in their efforts to amass larger capital than could be put up by any one enterprise; the procedure adopted was to float shares which were subscribed by a large number of merchants, members of the aristocracy and high government officials.

The 'joint ventures' in which merchants would underwrite the risks of a single specific undertaking probably accomplished more in the building up of capital. With risks and profits prorated according to each partner's investment, it became possible to transact marginal business of the kind that no one individual would stand the risk for or be interested in. That type of association had long been practised in shipping. It was not at all unusual that merchants owned and loaded vessels in common under a special form of business organization, a shipping company partnership. Instead of acquiring sole title to one or more ships, a merchant elected to share the ownership of a good-sized fleet with other merchants. His reasons were not so much the difficulty of producing capital for his own shipping business, but rather the shared liability, together with the need to exercise influence over as many ships as possible, the better to insure the trade itself. At all events, these joint ventures, as well as the trading companies, tended to reinforce the bonds between merchants, and impelled them towards the cartelization which would probably have ensued in any case. In this cartelization, moreover, we can detect one of the functions of foreign trade in the economy as a potential generator of profits and capital accumulation.

A special obstacle to the free movement of capital was posed by the monetary system, which was both underdeveloped and over-complicated. The foundation of the *Riksbank* brought no notable improvement in this respect for several decades. Indeed its founding may be viewed as a step leading away from greater flexibility as it was the result of Palmstruch's disastrous failure in the issue of paper money.

One thing must be borne in mind in regard to the monetary difficulties of that time: they did not greatly impede trade, the formation of capital, the movement of capital to new sectors, or business transactions in general. A tendency to exaggerate their effects is very common in literature; indeed the contemporary annals complain constantly over the inability of money to replace the widespread practice of payment in kind. Actually the business world established its own monetary system with a very close equivalent of our cheque account and current endorsement system. Thus a merchant would cancel a debt for goods bought or for credits obtained by admitting a claim for goods sold. This system made it possible to set off claim against counter-claim by way of third and fourth parties, and the use of promissory notes and similar documents further lubricated the machinery. Although this system grew more widespread in the eighteenth century, it was already fully developed in the seventeenth. It was an important part of the Dutch and English commercial and financial systems and it was through her connections with those countries that it came to develop in Sweden.

Space does not admit of a detailed analysis of the intricacies of the monetary system or of the different relations which ensued from rapid changes in the system. A brief description of the essential features must suffice. One of these was the use of two special coins for foreign trade, the ducat and the *riksdaler*. The value of the former was determined by the Dutch ducat, while the *riksdaler* stayed close to the German *reichstaler* and retained a constant value in silver. Its chief purpose was to facilitate the control of foreign exchange and its rate fluctuated with the ups and downs in the balance of payments. The *riksdaler* was hardly ever used as legal tender within Sweden, even though its value *vis-à-vis* the domestic currency kept rising as the latter was almost continuously debased in value. *Daler* silver and *daler* copper, the two domestic units of currency, served purely as moneys of account; they were never actually coined. Coins were struck only for fractional denominations. Thus a coin of four marks or 32 *öre* was called one *daler*. When copper coinage was introduced in 1624, the intention was to have a *daler* copper match a *daler* silver. But since the price of copper had been figured far above its market value, a difference in the exchange rate arose, so that it eventually took three copper units to equal one silver. An attempt was made in 1644 to restore the value of copper by stamping the words 'daler silver' on the new issue of copper pieces. The object sought was a double monetary standard with a fixed relationship—and preferably equivalance—between *daler* silver and *daler* copper as moneys of account, and hence between mark and *öre* in silver and copper as coins of substance. But the scheme misfired. Instead, there developed parallel systems of several currencies in which none of the currencies had a fixed value, was interchangeable with the others, or could be measured against a common denominator. The Palmstruch bank had to have four columns in all its books of account: one for ducats, one for *riksdaler*, one for *daler* silver and one for *daler* copper. A fifth column for carolines was inflicted on the *Riksbank*; this was the name given from 1664 to two marks or one-half *daler* silver.

In 1644 the rule was laid down that all debts were to be settled in the currency for which they had originally been contracted. If a debtor sought to pay in another currency, the amount would first have to be evaluated by a court.

It goes without saying that this confusion was scarcely calculated to promote well-functioning capital and money markets. The credit system had no choice but to disregard these 'regular' channels. If a reasonably well organized monetary system had existed, the emphasis on household self-sufficiency, barter trade, and the ploughing back of profits into fixed property would not have persisted as long as it did. If any consolation could be derived from this sad picture, it was that most other countries were beset by similar troubles.

According to one school of thought—in Sweden chiefly represented by Eli F. Heckscher (1879–1952), the leading pioneer in modern Swedish economic history—government economic policy prior to the 'liberal emancipation' played two roles only: to impede healthy growth, or to tilt at windmills. This notion is reinforced by the conviction that economic policy almost always originated on the wrong premises, that its administrators misjudged the conditions they sought to alter and improve. They had not read their Adam Smith properly—a sin of omission that could not be forgiven even those active before 1776.

The above opinion is emphatically not adhered to in this book which proceeds from quite different assumptions. To be sure, economic policy could fall short of its purpose or fail completely: because it was too ambitious in relation to the administrative and technical apparatus then available; or because the wrong methods were used; or because it was contradictory, often deliberately so, certain objectives being irreconcilable; or because it encountered too powerful social and political resistance. Nevertheless, it was successful often enough, even if its instigators themselves complained, having desired even better results—and even when policy misfired, it did not prove futile. The very aspirations of policy often throw light on the factors to be contended with, showing what these really were like, and not merely how they were interpreted by contemporaries. Economic policy was certainly never conducted in a vacuum. Even when it happened to fall short of some purely economic criterion of performance (and where, outside the model workshops of a thought-provoking but fictitious world, do such criteria operate?), it proceeded from and sought to influence actual and ideological social and political factors. It had its own intrinsic logic and necessity, even if it does not win the approval of latter-day economic thought.

If we try to examine the economic and political aspirations of the seventeenth century in the light of these other premises, a different and probably more accurate picture will emerge.

Broadly speaking, economic policy dealt with two main tasks: to enrich the national economy generally, and to do so by means and in forms which permitted a freer distribution of resources to cope with the new and increasing political military commitments. In the pursuit of these endeavours it was only natural to draw lessons from other, more advanced economies, chiefly the Dutch, French and British. So Sweden became heir to the political-economic ideas which prevailed in these countries. Certain correlations seemed plain: wealth went hand in hand with a well-developed foreign trade and merchant navy, with a nation-state form of polity, with industrial growth, with a favourable balance of payments, and with a uniform public administration. However, the political aims were not rooted merely in imitations and the drawing of simple parallels. The short-comings which held Sweden back in the emergent phase of the age—the paucity of non-agricultural business, a poorly developed manufacturing industry, the lack of a more uniform administration, almost total foreign control of trade and shipping, the perpetual difficulties of keeping government finances solvent—all these things indicated the points at which measures had to be applied to strengthen the Swedish economy, quite apart from the lessons which could be learned abroad and from the 'mercantilistic' ideas of the time. The plans and hopes which went into this work could occasionally be faulted for their excessive grandeur, not to mention chauvinistic zeal. But that did not prevent the adoption of practical and pragmatic approaches in essential respects; nor, on the whole, did it prejudice rational action, given the necessary prerequisites.

In so far as this policy was directly dictated by the new or unfulfilled government needs, it naturally acquired special direction and character. The main concern here was to allocate existing resources and to create new ones which could be more readily deployed to desired purposes. However it is impossible to isolate these endeavours from general trade and industrial policy, whose aim was to improve the economy as a whole. The policies coincided: it is scarcely possible to single out any specific case where one was wilfully pursued at the expense of another.

On the other hand, certain developments of profound social and power-political consequences were permitted to occur, creating serious internal conflicts and, possibly, if we take the longer view, imposing certain barriers on growth. Powerful vested interests were being built into the system. This became necessary because the political and other aims could not be achieved unless endorsed, or preferably, sustained by important group interests in Swedish society, and because this policy was in the interests of such groups to a large, if not greater degree than the state's own. The authorities

47

had to ride along with group interests, be influenced by these interests, and try to balance them against one another and against what was believed to be the public weal.

We have earlier observed that the success of the government policy for the development of the iron industry was so great precisely because it coincided so well with the interests of the new iron mill-owners. That does not mean that the entrepreneurs had things all their own way. Rather, the policies paid due regard both to the new technology and to the economic climate which had to be created to stimulate the iron industry, and so gained a solid base promoting a high degree of harmony between government and business in this sector. This also holds true of urban policy, which has often been criticized and even ridiculed in historical literature. It did not, to be sure, produce a long line of flourishing and expanding cities: but if there had been no urban policy what would have been the result in such important cases as Stockholm, Göteborg, Norrköping, Uppsala, Gävle and Borås? Irrespective of the difficulties encountered, which made the results fall far short of the aspirations, the line of approach must be regarded as rationally justified, and not as a vain imitation of foreign conditions with but artificial relevance for the Swedish economy. By any reasonable criterion, a modernized, more expansive economy could not be fashioned from the existing subsistence type of agrarian society unless a higher degree of specialization and division of labour was achieved. As various communities were converted into towns with the conferral of charter privileges, they attracted tradesmen and artisans who became deeply committed to the improvement of the urban economies. Nor should we forget that the Government gave its greatest support to those towns which had already proved their vitality, such as those cited above. Further, this policy was to undergo major modifications, especially during the Carolean era.

Similar observations apply to the manufacturing system and to the encouragement of external trade and a nationally-based merchant marine. It was by way of external trade that a growing share of the capital to finance new ventures would be obtained for one hundred and fifty years to come. This appraisal also holds, and perhaps with even greater force, for imports and the adoption of foreign entrepreneurs and specialists, many of whom came from newly annexed subject provinces. Even though it is easy to overestimate the value of individual contributions, for example those of Louis De Geer, the phenomenon itself was undoubtedly important as a result of an extremely purposeful policy.

A similar intentness of purpose was manifested by the steps taken to improve the machinery of public administration—a fundamental necessity if other aspects of policy were to be conducted with any degree of success. Actually, the organization of this machinery was a crucial prerequisite for great-power status and, for all the serious weaknesses which developed, made it possible for Sweden to retain her position as long as she did.

The efforts to create an effective central administration loyally served by local administrations were of long standing. It was a problem which had been a special challenge to the Stures and Gustavus Vasa. The latter had managed to solve it, with an efficiency unique in his time, by introducing a system of bailiffs who were made responsible to the central government. This work was continued by Charles IX, though somewhat marred by his unstable temperament. More enduring reforms were enacted under Gustavus Adolphus and implemented two years after his death by Axel Oxenstierna. He gave the executive authority a more definite form by institutionalizing the Council into a fairly close equivalent of today's cabinet government. The 'collegiums' or administrative boards he introduced functioned as an intermediary between the equivalent of today's ministries and the central government. These boards were directly responsible to five high officers of state, who in addition to forming the core of the Council served as an inner cabinet: the 'supreme government' under the king. Each of the five officers of state had under him two or three privy councillors, assistant ministers as it were, plus a 'secretary of state'. A fixed form was also given to provincial government by the creation of governors to administer the counties and to assert the authority of central government at the local level.

This organization became a focal point of the constant struggle between crown and nobility; but whichever faction ran the central government at any one time, the system of public administration prevailed over all vicissitudes from Gustavus Adolphus onwards, upholding the interests of state and nation against every form of particularism and dissolution. Kings and nobles never fought one another over the issue of a strong central government—both parties wanted it—but over who was going to hold the reins. Should supreme power be vested in the regent, the Council, or in the officers of state? Naturally the strength of the central government was dependent upon whoever was in charge and on the varying internal distributions of power. The stable administrative apparatus meant that the nation's public business could be transacted with strength and firmness in spite of such changes at the helm. Without it, Sweden's great-power

status, outwardly impressive yet inwardly weak, would have disinte-
grated much sooner, assuming it could have been established at all
after the death of Gustavus Adolphus.

In one very important respect, however, the position of centralized
authority under the kings differed from that under the Council or
officers of state. This related to the ownership and rental of land,
which in turn bore upon what might be called the domestic portion
in financing the political and military establishments. Our terms of
reference here require explanation. As noted earlier, the financing of
wars and the administration of conquered territories was dependent
on the availability of foreign currencies—currencies which were
obtained by the exporting of copper, iron and tar products. However,
it was only from the sale of copper that the bulk of these earnings
accrued directly to the state, which owned considerable interests in
Stora Kopparberg, the chief mining site. Revenues flowing in from
the other exports went to private entrepreneurs. In one way or
another, therefore, the crown had to purchase the holdings of foreign
exchange in private hands. By the same token, the state was con-
strained to rely mainly on 'ordinary' tax revenues to finance domestic
administration. Ever since the first years of rule under the young
Gustavus Adolphus, impelled as he was by the need to placate the
leading titled families and to win their support, the taxation system
had been caught in a vicious circle, involving large-scale transfers of
crown lands and revenues to the nobility. It would take us too far
afield to give a detailed account of the legal and financial means by
which landholdings and tax-levying rights were alienated. The actual
conveyancing took two main forms: as donations or enfeoffments,
and as payment for services rendered, usually to liquidate debts
incurred by the crown. Either the conveyances pertained directly to
previously state-owned property, in general the crown lands which
Gustavus Vasa so meticulously had confiscated from the Church; or
they embraced the 'rents' (taxes) payable to the crown by the independent owners of 'tax peasants'. In the former case, the nobility
acquired title to land by enfeoffments or outright purchase, the
peasants who had worked this land becoming tenants under the
nobility (*frälsebönder*). In the latter case, the peasants remained the
proper owners of their lands though the crown's right to impose taxes
had been taken over by a nobleman. This alienation process inevitably caused legal confusions. Distinctions between employees and
other categories were observed by the nobility only on the manorial
estates (*säterier*), which were operated under special privileges and
on a large scale immediately under the landlord's management. In

50

the long run, tenants and owners paying taxes to the nobility came to be lumped in the same category. What the one paid in rentals for his tenancy of a nobleman's land, the other paid in taxes ̄ or the use of his own land.

Whatever the social and legal consequences, the state was only too painfully aware of their meaning. It had been thrust into something like a gigantic building contractor's swindle, where incessantly pressing needs for money forced the alienation of more and more property, together with the fiscal powers which permitted the collection of this money. So extensive was this process that crown and freehold peasant land amounted to less than 30 per cent of the total at around the time the *Riksbank* was founded; the nobility had increased its holdings twofold since the accession of Gustavus Adolphus.

This vast transformation may be expressed in another way. With the methods now in use, the financing of wars and conquered lands led to a tremendous shift of wealth, the greater part of it to a handful of higher noble families. It stands to reason that this situation also had social and power-political consequences, both of which in turn were closely interrelated.

A small number of families, often allied by marriage, not only owned a disproportionately large part of the country's riches. Their possession of wealth in itself made them into a social and political power factor of unprecedented force. This position of power was reinforced by the fact that so much of the formal political and administrative power lay in the hands of these families. It was from them that the five high officers of state and the Council members were recruited, as well as virtually all the high-ranking civil servants and military officers. At the same time, the economic power and political influence these families exercised posed a threat to the legal position of the great majority, namely the peasants.

A great deal has been written about how the tenants were affected by the changeover of land ownership from the crown to the nobility. Was it also a change for the worse from a material point of view, as has often been suggested? The question cannot be answered with absolute certainty. According to Kurt Ågren, who studied the conditions in Uppland province from 1650 to 1680, with particular reference to the estates owned by Bielke and De la Gardie, the peasants did not suffer material losses. To some extent their position actually improved, in that they were exempted from obligations which the crown had exacted of tax-peasants and tenants under the crown, without always having to pay new imposts to their new masters.

51

Indeed, it could be said with some justification that their material lot had also improved, since the large landowners were usually better at agricultural management than the crown.

The legal and political impact, however, was detrimental. If a nobleman wished to weaken their legal and political position there was very little the peasants could do about it. As subjects of nobility rather than of the crown, they were more dependent on the personality of their lord and master. It can be argued that the conversion of tax peasants and tenants from the crown to the nobility did no more than substitute one tax burden or rent due to the state, for another due to a titled family: but in view of the blurred distinctions between different categories of peasants, not to mention the ill-defined standards of equity in general, there were ample grounds for fearing that the nobility would try to gain feudal rights over these peasants, too—something which the crown had never attempted. A particularly acute situation appears to have developed over the labour services (*dagsverk*) which the peasants were required to perform on the large manorial estates and for the ironworks. Here again, however, conclusions should be drawn cautiously. Examples can be cited to prove both the inordinate exaction of labour service and the conversion of peasants from freeholders to tenants or even hired hands on the manorial estates (a process often accelerated by the indebtedness accumulating from non-payment of taxes or rents). However, Ågren's investigations suggest that this tendency, where it did occur, was neither general nor widespread.

In any event, the perils were sensed to be serious enough even if one discounted the exaggerations of peasants in their complaints. Here and there, a number of precedents had in fact been set which, if more widely applied, could easily have led to a general stifling of peasant freedoms.

These tendencies were all the more natural in that foreign influences on Swedish thinking manifested themselves in two ways. First of all, owing to the wars and the general increase in international contacts, the nobles had formed different conceptions of their status. The social order prevailing elsewhere in Europe, they came to feel, was the 'right' one. In other countries the peasants, if they were not actually serfs, enjoyed far less freedom. Swedish nobles who acquired estates in the conquered provinces also acquired title to 'subjects' who were attached to the soil. Secondly, the ranks of nobility were swelled during the century with a higher proportion of foreigners: nobles from the conquered territories, mercenary officers who had signed up permanently in Swedish service, and immigrant businessmen and industrialists. These people obviously brought with them ideas of social order which prevailed in their countries of origin. The existence of a free, proprietary peasant class with curtailments of noble prerogatives was anathema to many of them. Prejudices of this kind were bound to be highly infectious. Axel Oxenstierna, for instance, was in the habit of referring to 'his' peasants as 'our subjects'; and Per Brahe once told Queen Christina that 'we are all subjects of the crown, the peasants indirectly and we directly'.

In the light of the foregoing observations, there would appear to be good reason to question the thumbnail description of this period as one of 'power dreams and peasant hardships'. As far as the non-material conditions are concerned the characterization has a great deal to be said for it. The creation and maintenance of great-power status led, partly because of the above-described methods of financing it, to severe restrictions of the rights of the peasantry; to put the case in an extreme form, the largest section of the Swedish population was threatened with the loss of its traditional freedom. We may well ask what would have happened if the chain of events set in motion with the extension of noble privileges in 1617 under Gustavus Adolphus, and intensified by the Nobility Organic Law of 1626 and the new privileges conferred in 1644, had continued unchecked. When Charles XI finally called a halt, his measures did not set everything right, but they definitely reversed the direction of the developments described.

The stage was now set for one of the major events of Swedish history: the reversion of alienated lands to the crown, called by historians the 'reduction'. First, however, a few more words of background. That the peasant class was not more rigorously suppressed than it actually was, given the conditions before the reversion, is due to two reasons. There was, first, the strength of long-standing tradition. Secondly, the Riksdag Organic Law of 1617, with its provision for 'checks and balances', served in its way to reinforce this tradition. The Organic Law defined the powers of the four Estates: nobility, clergy, burghers and peasants; the free owners comprised the membership of this last group. It also defined the tax-levying powers of the Riksdag. Although the Estates were denied the right of submitting motions, they could protest against measures they considered unfair or contrary to law. The exact age of the parliamentary tradition itself is a matter of dispute. Officially the founding of the Swedish Riksdag is set in 1435, when a great meeting was held at Arboga. However, scholars have also cited the written summons by Magnus Eriksson of a 'Riksdag' which convened at Kalmar in 1359. At all events, it is generally agreed that the tradition was firmly established under Gustavus Vasa and conclusively affirmed in 1597 at Arboga where Duke Charles effectively seized power with the help of what he called the 'grey mob' (from his point of view not at all a contemptuous reference). The Organic Law of 1617 furnished final proof that the Riksdag had been institutionalized in the country's political life. When one considers the role of countervailing power which the Riksdag came to play in the social upheavals during the seventeenth century, its firm establishment can truly be said to have taken place in the nick of time to prevent the great-power dream from reducing the peasants to serfs. However, it would be an oversimplification to view the alignments of political and social conflict as essentially confined to peasantry on the one side and nobility on the other. The pattern was far more complicated than that. The nobility was not a totally homogeneous class. A class unto itself was formed by the 'high' nobles or *haute aristocratie*, whose leading representatives were the Oxenstiernas, Brahes, De la Gardies, Wrangels, and De Geers. Another class comprised the military officers, civil servants and the owners of small estates, who came close to what the English call 'gentry'. The two classes of nobility did not mix much. As Sten Carlsson observed in his books on the stratification of Swedish society, counts and barons almost always married the daughters of counts and barons. The gentry also intermarried, though their group increased more rapidly owing to the many ennoblements of officers and civil servants, which probably reached record heights during the reversion under Charles XI. To a great extent, the interests of the gentry diverged from those of the richest families, both economically and politically. Its members readily begrudged the 'greats' their princely wealth. But perhaps above all, the gentry, of whom many occupied the lower rungs of the public career ladder, envied the others' monopoly of the highest civilian and military posts in the realm. Monarchs at loggerheads with the Council and its circles were not averse to looking to the gentry for support. The gentry, in turn, would often find it in their interests to ally themselves with the 'commoner' Estates of clergy and burghers; the latter were recruited from the ranks of merchants and ironmasters, and though of lower social rank, enjoyed the power that goes with money.

When these various interests could be fused with those of the peasantry into a compact opposition to the Council and high nobility, as Duke Charles succeeded in doing in 1597, Queen Christina in 1650 and Charles XI in 1680, the key to power lay securely in the monarch's hands. Without drawing the parallel too far, a comparable technique was applied in France, where sovereigns played off their titled civil servants against the landowning nobility to promote their absolute rule; in that struggle, the landowners retained the trappings of upper-class status but were shorn of political power. The relevance of this example for Sweden is that, until the Age of Liberty began in 1720, a Riksdag opposition which was more than a match for the high nobility never led to increased authority for parliament, but always to more power for the king. Indeed, the greater this opposition was, the more absolute the power of the monarch. The struggle between crown and aristocracy may have been decided by the 'will of the people', but having once won, the people let the king reap the spoils.

It should not be concluded from the foregoing that conflicts of interest always followed the same alignments. Beneath the surface of any one conflict, social, political and ideological factors would be fermenting and interacting in various ways. Power constellations altered from time to time, and it would probably come closest to the truth to say that the royal power stood the best chance of carrying the day whenever the struggle between social groups reached a particularly critical phase. This pattern of history was to repeat itself when Gustavus III ended the Age of Liberty in 1772. As several scholars have pointed out, it was the kind of history that a more resolute king might have been able to repeat in France and thereby prevent the revolution from taking the forms it did.

These limited shifts in the balance of power were deeply rooted in the past and in contemporary ideological, political, social and economic conditions. A full account of the factors involved is beyond the scope of the present volume. However, a few intimations seem necessary in order to understand the seventeenth-century problems and the development which followed.

Swedish discussion on constitutional law was strongly influenced by foreign sources. Various schools of thought gained prominence, particularly concerning the interpretation of sovereign powers and the relation of the sovereign to his subjects, i.e. the different classes and the privileges and influence which should belong to the Estates who represented them. Antique and medieval streams of thought were becoming 'secularized' into different conceptions of natural rights and theories of contract. The king was granted sovereign power, but not unconditionally. He had to fulfil his part of the contract, comply with the laws and pledges of his predecessor, and safeguard the rights of different groups. Should he depart from these guide lines, he was no longer a 'good king' but a tyrant and the people were in full right to rise against him. It was not unusual that a displacement of meaning occurred between royal power as represented by the king personally and royal power as synonymous with sovereign power. In the latter case, the king's personal exercise of power could be restricted, or even transferred to the Cabinet or Council or, to speak in more social terms, the aristocracy. This permitted fairly broad oscillations in the distribution of actual power within one and the same constitutional framework, depending on which interpretation held sway. Thus when Gustavus Adolphus acceded to the throne, the leading circles could strongly uphold the supremacy of royal power, yet at the same time demand that the young king be bound not only by certain 'fundamental laws' but also in the day-to-day conduct of business by the Council's advice and, as regards the major decisions such as declarations of war and the making of peace, by the power of the Estates. As Per Banér explained in 1633, a new king had to acknowledge and sanction the existing polity 'if he wants ever to have the crown upon his head'.

These words expressed a line of thought which had great import-ance for maintaining the balance against a monarch's personal pre-tensions to royal power. There were foreign prototypes to draw on, of course, but by virtue of uniquely Swedish conditions that line of thought had acquired a particular emphasis in Sweden. Even though an hereditary monarchy had gained acceptance since Gustavus Vasa established it in 1544 at the Riksdag of Västerås, the former tradition of elected kings lived on, and had undoubtedly received ample nourishment from royalty itself, first by the depositions of Erik XIV and later of Sigismund, and by the Estates' election of Duke John and later of Duke Charles to royal office. The heir of a king had a right to the throne, but the right was not absolute. Power was vested in the Estates to confirm his legacy or to transfer it to another 'elect' if the former refused to meet the demands imposed.

The distribution-of-powers problem recurred in constitutional debate throughout the century in regard to the right of the Council and the five officers of state to reach independent decisions, i.e. decisions taken in the king's name, but without his having been consulted. Was the highest executive body an agency of the king or was it an autonomous part of the supreme body, to which specified authority was delegated? Two long regencies, the first after Gustavus Adolphus and the second after Charles X Gustavus, made this a burning issue. The Italian diplomat Lorenzo Magalotti, who has left us vivid descriptions of Sweden in the year 1674, noted that while the king contended that the Council had no more than an advisory function, the Council insisted that the king comply with its decisions;

56

if not, it argued, what was the sense of his being required to learn the Council's opinion in the first place?

The ability of the nobles to assert their claims against royal power and the Estates derived from their position as landowners and as the holders of posts vital to the running of the kingdom. The situation was rather paradoxical. The development of Sweden as a national state (which politically destroyed the medieval feudal positions) in combination with the new tasks necessary to create and maintain the country's position as a great power, made it possible for the great families to transfer their power from the local to the national level, and they strengthened their hold on power in spite of upheavals, revolutions, purges and beheadings. This they could do for the simple reason that the new dynamic state could not manage without them. Efforts were made to keep the high nobility in check by offering competition from commoner secretaries. Thus Göran Persson served under Erik XIV, and Erik Jöransson Tegel and Chesnecopherus under Charles IX and Gustavus Adolphus. These men were, of course, regarded as upstarts, and as such were heartily despised by the aristocrats. But the availability of talents outside the aristocratic circle was never great, and the most successful upstarts would themselves join the First Estate before long, whereupon they fairly soon adopted the notions and pretensions of their class.

It required wealth and connections to obtain the sort of education that really qualified a man for the higher callings of the realm. Since the end of the sixteenth century, the great families had been in the habit of purposefully giving their sons a higher education, often sending them to foreign universities, as well as on long trips abroad, where they could assimilate the cream of contemporary knowledge in languages, philosophy, political science and diplomacy. Charles IX's solicitude for Uppsala University was wilfully tied up with the demands that less energy be devoted to the training of priests and more to the production of capable civil servants. With the enlarged machinery of public administration aggravated by the constant demands of war, the shortage of capable hands became increasingly acute. The young nobles would climb up the career ladder at an accelerated rate—and the promotions were particularly rapid for those belonging to the high nobility. It is surely revealing that the great 'reduction' should have been carried out while Sweden was enjoying its longest spell of peace in the seventeenth century. The king was then less dependent on the services rendered by the great families; besides, he had at his disposal an ambitious but frustrated 'young' nobility longing to demonstrate its talents.

Proud of their birth and more than ordinarily aware of their status and rights, the high nobles were also intensely conscious of their obligations to serve the nation. Some almost moving stories are told of the Chancellor Axel Oxenstierna who would try to get a few weeks off (sometimes only a few days) to rest up at one of his estates along Lake Mälaren, only to be constantly reminded by Gustavus Adolphus that his presence was urgently needed in Stockholm or wherever the itinerant monarch happened to be at the time. And fierce was the royal displeasure if Oxenstierna could not prove more serious illness for his 'evasion of duty'. But, of course, rights and duties were apt to be confused. A nobleman could line his own purse with good conscience, since he felt that he was furthering the interests of his country at the same time.

The Nobility Organic Law of 1626 established not only the constitutional position of the nobility, with the right to vote in Estate deliberations vested in the heads of leading families. It also underlined the special position of titled noblemen by dividing the House of Nobility into three classes, endowed with equal decision-making power: a first class of counts and barons, a second of privy councillor descendants (in so far as these did not belong to the first), and a third class of gentry. Some idea both of the size of incorporated nobility and of its internal distribution of power may be formed if we mention that, of the 127 registered noble families at that time, only three were countly, nine baronial, and twenty-three were of the privy-councillor class. Twelve counts and barons thus possessed the same number of votes as ninety-two heads of gentry. Although this system encountered some opposition, it could be put into effect because of the actual distribution of power which then existed. The system was to remain in force for almost a century.

For all the conflicts which frequently erupted between high nobility and peasantry, they were far from being the only power groups in Swedish society. Several references have already been made to the importance of the gentry. However, the clergy and burghers also had roles to play. The priests enjoyed strong propagandistic influence by virtue of their twofold connections: with the universities and education on the one hand, and directly with the laity on the other. As communicators of opinion they presumably held an advantage. Although the chief problem for the Government was to keep the more strictly ecclesiastic demands of the clergy within reasonable bounds, this class represented a latent political power not to be ignored.

From all indications, the burgher Estate was less important and more malleable. This was to change, however, during the Age of Liberty. The interests of burghers were limited to co-operation in economic matters, such as full or partial exemptions from the rule which required that Swedish-built and Swedish-owned vessels engaged in Bothnian traffic put in at Stockholm; and the regulations of guilds and trades. These matters were important enough. However, the social and political struggles of the day did not affect them as directly as, for instance, the peasantry was affected by the alienation of crown lands to the nobility. In addition, the burghers were prevented from acting as a class by their own motley composition. The Estate majority consisted of legally trained magistrates, who were inordinately overrepresented at Riksdag sessions; their actual number in the country at large was no more than a few hundred. The minority, representing virtually all economic pursuits except agriculture, consisted of franchised merchants and artisans, manufacturers and some other groups. By acquiring magistracies this minority could, however, overrepresent itself to some extent in the Riksdag at the expense of the 'true' magistrates. By and large, too, the burghers appear to have been kept in fairly good humour politically; though teeth might grate when efforts were made to break the closed oligopolistic character of the handicrafts by liberalizing the guilds. Then, too, the spokesmen for different industries and towns could disagree on things like the Bothnian trade regulations, and the ranking of inland cities and staples in respect of their trading rights.

Given the position as described above for the high nobility, dominated as it was by a handful of families with strong ties of kinship, the countervailing power imparted to the commoner Estates by the Riksdag sessions took on special importance. Of crucial weight was the fact that the tax-levying power lay with this Riksdag. The nobility, itself exempt from tax on a large part of its holdings, could not impose levies on other citizens, whether in partnership with the king or in his name, without the consent of the Riksdag. Yet the result was also the paradoxical one already noted: the strength of high nobility reinforced the king's personal authority, in that the commoner Estates came to regard the monarch as their ultimate protection against aristocratic domination. In this way the concentration of social and economic power, together with the political position in the consultative constitutionalism attained by the high nobility, bore the seeds of its own countervailing through monarchical power. Over long periods this system could function in a reasonable equilibrium or, to quote the contemporary verdict, as a happy blend of 'monarchy, aristocracy and democracy' (the last term was in reference to the commoner Estates). That was undoubtedly the case under Gustavus Adolphus and Axel Oxenstierna, in no small measure due to the former's skill in exploiting the broad scope permitted by the system, as well as to the latter's flexibility and discretion.

However, the system could easily be upset—which it undoubtedly had been by 1668, the year we have taken as a starting point for this survey.

One cause was the shifting basis of constitutional theory, both internationally and nationally against the background of changed political conditions elsewhere in Europe: the entrenchment of absolute rule in France under Louis XIV; in England the never acknowledged but strongly contended claims of the Stuarts to dictatorial exercise of royal power; and in Denmark 'the royal law' as finally formulated in 1666. The divine right of kings was upheld in France and England especially. In Denmark, the social contract was the prevailing theory: the king ruled because power had been transferred to him by the people. After the upheaval of 1680, Sweden came closer to the contract school of thought, even though the divine right theory was far from being excluded; both in theory and in the political machinery employed, the change was looked upon as constitutionally correct, as a more proper interpretation of the basic laws in so far as the king's assumption of the Council's duties was involved, and as a social contract when the authority of the Estates was transferred to the king.

This pivotal shift in constitutional theory occurred gradually, during and after the *de facto* change, and thus was perhaps as much an ideological confirmation of it as a spur towards it. That it acquired practical political consequences was due to the results of the old system, which had become brazenly provocative in the social and economic spheres.

For the king the matter of state finances was of special importance. The alienation of land and taxation powers to the nobility had reached a stage at which state revenues had long since seriously suffered; to the extent these revenues derived from land, the state was getting perhaps less than half of the total. It is clear that this financial problem also bore an inverse relationship to the political. If the political power of the nobility was to be broken or at least substantially curtailed, its financial resources would also have to be reduced. Further, the royal power would have to be given the wherewithal to build up a partly new public administration, if not its actual structure then at least in its staffing.

For the commoner Estates, the consequence of the crown's dwindling tax base was that many more levies had to be imposed on those who remained taxable. Here a complicated situation had arisen for the peasants. The greatest objection to conversion of crown tenants into tenants under the nobility, and of freeholders from tax-payers to the crown into taxpayers to the nobility, did not come from those personally involved, but from those who were not. After all it was on them the burden fell when enfeoffments encroached on the total tax base. To be sure, even the freeholders 'belonging' to the nobility did win some representation in the Riksdag, in spite of occasional demands to exclude them; but the bulk of the Fourth Estate consisted of freeholders who still paid their taxes to the crown, and they were the ones who were complaining the loudest. On the other hand, the 'feudalized' were not moved by the material considerations alone. Both the tenants and the freeholders under the nobility strongly feared that their feudal lords would ultimately take their land away from them and increase the formation of manorial estates.

On top of everything else, the Council aristocracy had mismanaged the state's affairs, perhaps especially so during the regency which preceded Charles XI—or at least a strong propaganda case could be made out for mismanagement when the so-called Regency Inquisition was carried out as a precursor to and part of the Reduction (that is, the resumption of the crown estates). Here a large part of the gentry, joined by high nobles who felt themselves snubbed by the ruling families, supported royal ambitions and the commoner Estates in their criticism of a real or supposed misgovernment. If one could only get rid of the 'old men', the doors would be opened to new, enticing careers. The critics were not entirely motivated by self-interest: they honestly thought a renaissance was needed badly. As they saw it, the 'old men' had mismanaged the nation's affairs. The time had come for new blood and new policies—and many of the formerly neglected gentry saw themselves among the chosen few.

There followed a long period of redistribution of property titles, though it fell far short of depriving the nobles of their positions as great landowners. It was a period marked by a policy in which royal absolutism replaced constitutionalism in the division of power. The end product was a fairly conservative consolidation of government finances and state power, but it also confirmed the establishment of the separate Estates and nobility as legal and social institutions. It was a period of setback for internationalism and culture, ushering in the emergence of orthodox Lutheranism, with conformism and witch

61

trials in its train, all against a background of peace and relative prosperity. This period would be followed in its turn by the great Northern War, which put an end to the great power era. The building up of a brand new Sweden was to begin fifty years after the events which culminated in the founding of the *Riksbank*.

Before we proceed to describe this new Sweden, a few words should be said about the everyday lives of the people in the seventeenth century, the material standards they achieved, and the ways of life they chose or were forced to choose.

IV

Axel Strindberg has referred to this period as a combination of great-power dreams and peasant hardships. According to the results of modern research, mentioned above, this was an oversimplification of the situation. The alienation of crown lands cannot be said to have materially deprived the peasant: indeed many of the peasants under the nobles were in a better position than the freeholders and tenants under the crown.

This does not mean that life was not hard for the vast majority. To begin with, times were hard, given the harsh nature and rudimentary technology for coping with it. That wars and the administration of empire should subject the Swedish people to severe strains was inevitable. Conscriptions and heavy contributions were exacted recurrently during the long campaigns, even though mercenaries were largely used and the wars were partly made to pay for themselves by the taxation of occupied territories. The burdens would ease considerably in periods of peace, yet not to the extent of altering the basic conditions. The military establishment had to be kept in perpetual war readiness. Administration, diplomacy and the other trappings of great power status incurred huge expenses, even though the foreign possessions were made to contribute substantial amounts. The many noble castles demanded their tribute of deliveries and labour services. The great nobles had large retinues to support.

Class differences were great, but so were the differences within each class. If the nobility as a whole could be said to be reasonably well-off, a handful of families possessed enormous wealth. If merchants and artisans as a class could be said to earn a fairly good livelihood, they still fell far short of the gentry. However, a few leading wholesale merchants, manufacturers and highly specialized artisans managed to create large fortunes. A colonel received ten times the salary of a captain, and a bishop earned ten times as much as a clergyman in the lowest grade. Similar disparities must certainly have held true for the peasants, as regards both the size and the fertility of their holdings. Geographical location was no doubt a determining factor.

Perhaps the differences can be most graphically illustrated if we mentally juxtapose the castles owned by De la Gardie, Brahe and Wrangel, the ordinary manor houses owned by the gentry, and the normal peasant dwellings. According to Lorenzo Magalotti, the Italian ambassador to Stockholm during the 1670s, these last were built of unplaned grey logs and roofed over with strips of birch-bark topped by tufts of grass. The room, and usually there was no more than one, contained an open fireplace and functioned as a kitchen too. A more 'affluent' peasant might add an extra room or two.

Differences of diet were similarly conspicuous. For the peasantry at large, hunting and fishing supplemented and embellished a drab dinner table. Given the existing state of agriculture, however, the everyday diet could not be other than monotonous; for many it was also extremely meagre, even during good years. Mixing bark in the bread was more than a popular literary allusion to the poverty which existed: it was a stark reality for large groups of the population. The efforts of noblemen to reserve hunting rights to themselves on their own domains were not completely successful, since woodlands had by long tradition been regarded as common property. Yet these efforts did impose a restriction; above all, the well-organized hunts of the wealthy, usually conducted as highly gregarious activities, imparted a different look to the nobleman's dinner table than to the peasant's. The nobility also had a penchant for foods that could only be supplied over long distances, an alternative that was quite out of the question for the masses. An illuminating example is given by the pains Axel Oxenstierna's wife went to in order to provide her husband with salmon from his northern Swedish domains while he was taking part in the German campaign; and a diplomatic crisis nearly erupted when it was feared that wartime blockades might prevent the free transportation of wines and food across Germany to meet the needs of the royal court.

The outer symbols of status also indicated differences of class. Noblemen, burghers and peasants could be readily distinguished by the clothes they wore. Ambassador Magalotti reports his astonishment at seeing a number of burgher wives in Stockholm who were beginning to dress almost like ladies of the nobility. The high-born and wealthy often wore fine foreign-made fabrics with a preference for gaudy colour schemes; the peasantry had to make do with grey homespun from the wool yielded by black sheep.

There is no dearth of literature to tell us how the men and women of nobility spent their lives. The leading families owned a large number of estates with castles and manor houses. Although it was usual to establish a 'headquarters' at one of these places, the itinerant life was greatly favoured. It was always possible to get away to celebrate some special occasion on another estate or to visit family relations on their properties. Members of the nobility who held public office or worked at the royal court spent a large part of the year in Stockholm. The richest families, such as the Oxenstiernas, Wrangels, Brahes and Bondes, also built stately mansions in the capital and maintained large retinues there.

Perhaps it was all this construction activity which plagued the peasants most. It would appear to have appropriated a greater share of labour services than did the maintenance needed to keep the estates and their households in good order. In any case it is clear that this service requirement, particularly if exacted during the sowing and harvesting periods, imposed a heavy burden, the more so since the peasant was usually told to bring his horse with him. Vilhelm Moberg has described the peasant's lot in his historical novel, *Ride This Night!* Of course Moberg is dramatizing; his book is literature, not history. Yet there is no doubt that he has captured the essence of the labour-services system and the strains it imposed, even though the differences between the claims of nobility and crown show the latter in far too favourable a light. However, it is not difficult to imagine the burden of the sacrifices demanded from the peasants of say, Wrangel, when they were commandeered away from their farms to build his castle at Skokloster or his palace on Riddarholmen island in Stockholm.

The most serious aspect of the labour-services system, even after the official regulations of 1650 which were meant to check its further development, was that the peasants and their hired hands were placed under the direct command of the nobleman and his bailiffs. Since this manpower could hardly be expected to shoulder unwanted tasks with enthusiasm, conflicts and rows frequently erupted. The nobles and bailiffs could if they wished harshly enforce their disciplinary authority over 'recalcitrant labour'. The trial of more serious offences was left to the courts of law, but the judges made it only too plain where their sympathies lay. Working discipline was to be maintained at all costs, and the punishments inflicted were often severe, ranging from stiff fines and imprisonment on bread and water, to whippings, running the gauntlet, and 'riding' the wooden horse with weights attached to the feet.

On estates owned by nobles with better economic sense, a built-in protection against excesses existed. A nobleman would best assure himself of a regular income of rents and labour services if the peasants were fairly treated and allowed to run their farms properly. Then, too, many of these men, though stern and demanding, had a strong sense of justice and decency. It was not considered quite *comme il faut* to play the role of notorious peasant-tormenter. Indeed, there was a kind of pride in being able to show off happy, flourishing peasants on one's own domains, as testified by Per Brahe. But it was also human nature that noblemen who seldom visited their estates extorted as much as they could in order to finance missions elsewhere. Misery they did not see with their own eyes was easily forgotten, as long as the resources demanded were collected and made available.

That the general tendencies were unpleasant, that class oppression existed everywhere and often functioned in a harsh and humiliating manner, should not tempt us to make generalizations based on those features only. There were certainly important variations operating within the broad framework we have described.

Whatever the hardships of the peasants, conditions were worse for the people who had nothing but their labour to offer. Labourers were subject as a class not only to harsh legislation, which in effect made it a crime to be out of work, but also to the stern authority of employers and to a discriminating penal law. It is also clear that employed hands were the first to suffer whenever people were conscripted for military service, or when belts had to be tightened in famine years. Nor did a labourer stand much chance of standing on his own feet. Such opportunities did not exist in the mines and the mills. An avenue of escape might be offered by the cultivation of new land, if only in the form of crofting, but this opportunity was usually limited to the children of peasants. In the handicrafts there was stubborn resistance against journeymen who wanted to establish themselves as masters. The government regulation of guilds to ease this restrictive practice encountered embittered opposition, especially in the old German crafts with their tradition of *numerus clausus*, the closed system. To paraphrase the oft-quoted words of privy councillor Klas Fleming, spoken at a Council discussion on the guild rules, a man of the people might become king, but he could never become a master in the trade of chamois dressing.

During the latter part of the seventeenth century the problems of

C
65

the labouring, landless class did not assume quantitative significance. Population grew at too slow a rate; the demands of war acted as a brake; and any surplus of labour that did arise was more or less readily absorbed by noblemen on their estates and ironmasters in their mills. When Charles XI released the peasants from conscription on the condition that they support assigned troops on their land (*indelningsverk*), the peasants no longer had the same incentive to discharge their obligations by working for the nobility, and the nobles began to complain of a labour shortage.

To all appearances, a considerable increase in population began to set in at the same time. This development was to alter the picture substantially within another hundred years: and after the lapse of yet another century it would shatter totally the social canvas of seventeenth-century Sweden.

2

IMPOTENCE AND PROGRESS

I

IN December 1768 the conflict between King Adolphus Frederick and the ruling party of 'Caps' took an acute turn.[1] The King tendered his resignation in order to force the Council to summon the Riksdag. Since most of the high administrative officials belonged to the opposing party of 'Hats' and refused, either on grounds of principle or political tactics, to serve a government without a king, the Caps were forced to yield. The Riksdag in session from 1769 to 1770 voted them out of power, and the Hats once again took over.

The Caps were returned to office by the special Riksdag convened in 1771 to confirm the accession of the new king, Gustavus III. However, the Caps did not enjoy their new power for very long. In August 1772 Gustavus III staged the *coup d'état* which put an end to the Age of Liberty and its parliamentarism and ushered in a period of monarchical constitutionalism. Gustavus was to make his rule absolute seventeen years later. Royal autocracy was to last until 1809, when it was replaced by the constitution which has since remained the basis of Sweden's polity even though much of it has no more than nominal value today.

We have no reason to evaluate the various judgments that have been passed on the Age of Liberty and the *coup d'état* which ended it. We are not interested here in the merits or imperfections of any one form of government, but rather in the underlying economic and social factors and in how these affected the struggles for power—or vice versa.

In certain respects the links with the past, in particular with the Carolean era which immediately preceded the Age of Liberty, were clearly defined, even though these links were contained within a

[1] *Translator's note:* The Caps and Hats were the names of the two parliamentary parties during the Age of Liberty.

67

framework of far-reaching changes. The constitutional change was essential, of course. All the same, common fundamental features of the political, economic, and social structure remained. Developments occurring during the period of Carolean absolutism go a long way towards explaining the conditions and problems in the Age of Liberty. As we had occasion to observe earlier, the Sweden of 1768 was not the Sweden of 1718. But the Sweden of 1768 could not conceivably have emerged if events had not unfolded the way they did, especially in the social sphere, during the three to four decades which preceded the Age of Liberty. In terms of social history, the changes that took place, often involving the creation of something new, do not signify a rupture with the past, even if that is what many would like to think. On the contrary, changes usually, fundamentally perhaps always, become comprehensible only if the links with the past are taken into account. It is in the past that the conditions for change have arisen and largely acquired their character.

Obviously, this legacy from the previous epoch applies in great measure to the field of foreign policy—here defined both in the more limited sense and in the wider one of Sweden's position in the world. The loss of great-power status meant fewer commitments and obligations, but that certainly did not render Sweden devoid of interest in a Europe of wars and intrigues during this period of 'cabinet politics', when alliances and lines of march could change overnight. Although the country could no longer decisively tip the scales with imperial weight, in the fluctuating, delicate balance-of-power systems of eighteenth-century Europe, Sweden could still perform a marginally important role. It was therefore tempting for the different contestants to compete for Swedish support and to exert influence on Swedish domestic affairs to achieve this aim.

During the first period of the Age of Liberty, lasting until the end of the 1730s, when the prudent Count Arvid Horn, leader of the Caps, was in charge of the country's fortunes, nothing came of these foreign attempts to get Sweden back into the international cockpit; although Horn was later harshly criticized for showing partiality to the Russians. Foreigners had an easier time afterwards, partly in consequence of the struggle between the Hats and the Caps. The different great powers, chiefly France and Russia, but also England, could then play one party off against the other, and work on the need of both for money.

The power constellations out in Europe were not identical with those which had prevailed during Sweden's great-power era. They were bound to change if for no other reason than that Sweden had played out her imperial role. Swedish hero kings, feared by actual and presumptive enemies and exposed to ingratiating overtures from alliance-seeking states, were no longer turning Europe's political geography topsy-turvy.

Throughout its course, the Age of Liberty bore two remarkable resemblances to the European world of the seventeenth century: the quest of France for supremacy, and English efforts to maintain the balance of power (England having assumed the Dutch tradition). The differences, however, were also striking. Russia, no longer impelled by the dynamism of Peter the Great, was admittedly weakened by internal strife up to 1741, when the Empress Elizabeth seized power. Despite this, a strong external position had been achieved through the treaty with Sweden at Nystad in 1721, which gave Russia Ingermanland, Esthonia, Livonia, and a part of Karelia, including Viborg, the old Swedish border fortress to the east. The pervading characteristic of Russian foreign policy was the continued advance of the czardom's positions *vis-à-vis* the three important neighbouring states: Sweden, Poland and Turkey.

A new state, Prussia, emerged as a power factor of major importance. The treaty of 1720 with Sweden had given Prussia most of the Swedish possessions in Germany. Under Frederick the Great, Prussia achieved the same reputation for military prowess in Europe which had been Sweden's from the middle of Gustavus Adolphus' reign up to the death of Charles XII. At the same time the imperial authority of the Hapsburgs had been further weakened. Europe lived in a combination of two great power-political conflicts: the emergence of Russia, and the Central European drama with Prussia as the leading actor, France as the rapacious Cerberus—and, as the balancing factor, England, which through the personal union with Hanover in 1714 had also acquired a direct interest in Central European affairs. Added to these two was a third factor: the struggle for the supremacy over overseas colonies in which France, Spain, and England were chiefly embroiled. It was a struggle which intimately affected the European power balance, further accelerating its variable register of change.

Sweden twice let herself be drawn into foreign ventures, failing miserably each time. On both occasions she was ill-prepared, misguided by incorrect estimates of the actual situation, and unable to muster strength for a concentrated effort. It was as if the country were perversely bent on demonstrating to the whole world the utter and final ruin of a once effective war machine.

The first venture was the Hat-inspired war against Russia. The desire to revenge the losses of war under Charles XII; a growing adulation of the great hero king, especially by the younger nobility; a chauvinism which began to regard Horn's prudence and isolationism with contempt; a French interest in a change at the helm so that Sweden could be exploited to French political gain: here was a blend of sentiments and interests just waiting for an opportune moment. A reshuffle at the top came during the Riksdag of 1738–39. Horn resigned when the Riksdag, ignoring the Council, took over the conduct of foreign policy and ordered the removal of his fellow councillors from office. Sweden was now given her first purely parliamentary government formed by an organized party.

At that time Russia was involved in a war with Turkey and with internal strife over the throne. What opportunity could be more suitable? The Russians made it even more so when they murdered a Swedish envoy on his way home from Turkey, thereby providing both a formal excuse for declaring war and a welcome subject matter for agitation. The victim, Major Malcolm Sinclair, became a national hero; his fate was mourned in a song demanding vengeance. France added incitement. A Swedish attack would prevent Russia from intervening on behalf of Maria Theresa in the War of the Austrian Succession.

Sweden attacked. By then, however, the time was no longer opportune, if it ever had been. Russia had made peace with Turkey, and Elizabeth had installed herself on the throne, turning Russia's resources against the Swedish arms which had been sent to support her claims to the crown. Within a year Sweden's defeat became a fact. Finland was occupied by Russian troops. Peace could be obtained at a relatively low but humiliating price. Where Sweden had failed to impose her will on the Russian succession, Russia could impose hers on the Swedish: Duke Adolphus Frederick of Holstein and Lovisa Ulrika of Prussia, sister of Frederick the Great, were installed in the royal palace in Stockholm.

Luck proved no better in the second exploit. Once again the motives were mixed. Sweden's old ally, France, applied the pressure. The Hats sought retaliation against the royal couple for a *coup* planned to take place in 1756 but exposed beforehand, in which the queen was made to play the role of scapegoat. At the same time the Hats hoped that by taking part in the coalition against Prussia, they could share in the rich booty which was expected. But the inferior Swedish troops accomplished nothing, except be beaten by Prussia's war-hardened armies, and in 1762 Sweden was forced to seek a separate peace through the mediation of Lovisa Ulrika. The country

70

managed to save itself only with the help of a queen whom the war was meant to humiliate mortally.

The days of heroic deeds were definitely over as far as Sweden was concerned. Gustavus III and Gustavus IV Adolphus were to try again in their time, but the annals of faded glory were not brightened by their endeavours.

For all the ignominy of these military adventures, and the further strain they imposed on an already sorely tried treasury, the agony was short-lived on both occasions. The actual campaigns were brief. For the most part Sweden's armies were either encamped or in retreat. Very little of the enormous display of force which had been manifested during long periods of war under Gustavus Adolphus, Charles X and Charles XII, was required when the Age of Liberty tried to imitate 'the age of greatness'.

Nevertheless, throughout the whole of the Age of Liberty Russia posed a threat—or at least was believed to do so. Yet when we compare the great-power era with the Age of Liberty, there is a striking contrast between all the commitments and demands of an empire and the situation of a small country favoured by a general prevalence of peace—a country, moreover, that was spared foreign attack. There is no doubt but that this difference was of great importance in the internal rehabilitation during the Age of Liberty, in shaping social and economic conditions, and in the distribution of power. Essentially, during this age the foundations of present-day Sweden were laid. In the midst of political discords at home and shorn of power abroad, Sweden could still advance and achieve progress of imposing dimensions, certainly in the economic sphere.

II

Links with the past were unmistakable in the country's economic situation. The general structure of the Swedish economy remained unchanged in one very important respect: between 80 and 85 per cent of the population still depended directly on agriculture and allied occupations for their livelihood. As before, ironworking was the most important industry. However, the mining and processing of copper had suffered a serious decline. Of the forest products, the exports of tar diminished while sawn timber became more important. Imports retained their former composition, with grain as a leading addition.

The new import was a consequence of the great increase in population, which was followed also by other changes, in particular the geographic expansion of agriculture through new cultivation. This was accompanied by greater emphasis on domestic grain production and a relative decline in animal husbandry, since most of the new land appropriated for cultivation was in areas which had formerly provided the best pasturage. We may say that the growing population was accommodated by lowering the standard of living, in that meat products, which required more processing, were replaced by grain products: in other words, quality had to give way to quantity. The country faced the law of diminishing returns. Certain organizational changes were also begun, no doubt caused in part by the pressure of population. Under this head comes the enclosure movement initiated by Jacob Faggot in 1757. Fields were to be repartitioned so that each peasant could work a single consolidated holding, or, failing that, as few separate fields as possible. In practice the reform proceeded very slowly; since its implementation was voluntary, the peasants had first to be convinced, and that was a very gradual process. Where the reform was carried out, however, there is no doubt that it exerted a considerable influence on agricultural productivity. Another significant barometer of structural change was the digging of ditches on a near-national scale. Ditching, of course, was essential to cope with the often waterlogged areas where most of the new cultivation was concentrated, but it was of great importance even in the old farming areas.

An innovation that was to prove of momentous import was the cultivation of the potato. Its more widespread adoption had to wait, however. The long struggle to teach the Swedish people to include this important article of food in their diets provides a perfect illustration of how fear of the unknown can hold back progress. Not until the potato had proved its worth for distillation into liquor did it come to be cultivated on an appreciable scale; and many more years were to elapse before the potato gained general acceptance as human nourishment in its more natural form, so to speak. Even so, its initial use in distilling spirits had the advantage of reserving grain for food products.

As indicated earlier, the incentive to cultivate new land was a rapid increase in population. It has been estimated that Sweden had about 1·4 million inhabitants at the beginning of the Age of Liberty. The population rose to nearly two million by 1770, and by the end of the century had increased further to between 2·3 and 2·4 million. The rate of increase was particularly great in the 1720s and 1730s, signifying a recovery from the incessant warfare of previous decades.

It was noted in Chapter I that exact figures on urban–rural distribution are lacking prior to 1805. However, all the available evidence indicates that the towns increased their share of the total population at a very slow pace. By 1805, certainly, they did not account for even 10 per cent, nor did they until 1850. This means that at least 90 per cent of the population stayed on the farms. If we choose to ignore the increase in imports, Swedish agriculture was thereby called upon to feed 600,000 more mouths during the Age of Liberty, and an additional 300,000 to 400,000 up to the beginning of the nineteenth century. In short, the farming population increased by about 75 per cent within the space of eighty years. Between 1800 and 1860 the total population was to increase by another $1 \cdot 5$ million, of whom $1 \cdot 3$ million were rural, with the greater part living on agriculture and related occupations.

It stands to reason that a population increase of this magnitude could not occur without radically altering the old agrarian society. The exact sequence of events in this transformation is unknown; nor can a general pattern for the country as a whole be discerned, since the process differed in character from one region to another. In the main, however, the following facts can be established. When more children were born (and survived the first critical years), that not only meant having more mouths to feed, it also meant the division of land among more heirs. An extensive subdivision of farms began, which certainly contributed to a lowered agricultural productivity, especially as long as the system of open-field strips predominated. This indirectly stimulated a gradually increasing interest in the redistribution of holdings. As subdivision was intensified it became necessary to obtain new land. Meadows and other 'outlying land' were the first to be brought under the plough. Next in order was the ploughing of virgin soil lying outside the settled districts. These new areas presumably compensated to some extent for the cultivation of meadowland in the old districts because natural pasture grounds were often available in proximity to the newly ploughed soil. This meant that the population was spreading out over areas once sparsely settled or not at all, first and foremost to the wooded districts. Both subdivision and extended cultivation of land were most extensively practised in Norrland, Värmland, Dalsland, Bohuslän, Västergötland and Småland. In these parts of Sweden population was growing most vigorously. The ancient plain country around Lake Mälaren and in Östergötland exhibited the lowest rates of subdivision and reclamation, and population growth there was substantially slower as well. The explanation, of course, is that there was

C*   73

little new land left in these areas. Further, the prevalence there of large-scale agriculture impeded such a development, and such sub-division as did occur nevertheless did not weigh in the statistics, since it was more or less balanced by amalgamations of holdings.

A regional pattern of specialization began to emerge. The old farming districts were converted to 'granaries'. In the new areas, livestock raising retained its earlier importance and character. There the pursuit of agriculture—in so far as it was not in itself regarded as a subsidiary rather than principal economic activity—would be supplemented by livestock raising, logging, home *sloyd* and cartage. Värmland had already become the great ironworking province during the seventeenth century. In the eighteenth century it would also become the leading timber province, at the same time as new cultivation and subdivision greatly increased the number of proprie-tor peasants.

Sweeping changes took place in the pattern of land ownership, partly in consequence of reversion and partly of legislation which permitted tenants on crown and noble estates to buy land they had previously rented. By mid-century it is estimated that half the country's arable land was owned by peasants as compared with less than 25 per cent before the Reduction. This transfer of land to the peasants had no effect on the actual farming methods then in use, as was observed earlier. On the other hand, the increase in freeholds may well have checked a further trend towards the formation of manorial estates and large farms. If so, the indirect result would have been to hamper agricultural productivity. Socially, however, the effects of these conversions were great. The conditions which had threatened the very existence of a free peasant class had been elimin-ated.

A new social phenomenon now posed serious problems: because land subdivision and reclamation could not keep pace with the grow-ing population, a large rural proletariat developed. Even though the really large groups of propertyless did not begin to form until the end of the eighteenth century, the trend was well-established before the Age of Liberty had ended. A large increase in the number of proprietor peasants occurred concurrently with a large increase in the number of those who owned nothing. This dichotomy in the structure of Sweden's agrarian society was to have far-reaching economic consequences one hundred years after the period which concerns us here. It was to become a basic determinant of that society's disintegration and of the rapid industrialization which accompanied it. It was also a basic cause of the emigration which was to take one million Swedes to a new life in America in the years 1860 to 1910.

None of this could be even dimly perceived when the Age of Liberty drew to a close. However, another change was first noted at this time: the transformation of southern Sweden, and Skåne province in particular, into the country's largest granary. As Jacob Faggot pointed out in a report written in 1755, Skåne was by nature 'a perfect breadbasket for Sweden'. It was not for that reason, however, that Charles X wrested Skåne from Denmark in the Treaty of Roskilde (1658). The chief importance of Skåne at that time lay in its command of Öresund, the strait between Sweden and Denmark; the treaty put an end to Danish sovereignty over the strait. As yet Skåne had hardly developed agriculturally; indeed it was underdeveloped. Intermixed ownership had gone further here than in the rest of Sweden, and the large estates were almost exclusively run as peasant farms. Skåne did not attain its position as the country's leading agricultural district until after the enclosure movement. Once attained, its position was striking. Mention has often been made of the single-handed achievement of a Scanian landowner, Baron Rutger Maclean (1742–1816), who made it mandatory for his peasants to consolidate their strip holdings into single parcels in 1785. This experiment turned out so well that Maclean's fellow landlords and the peasants themselves in Skåne were moved to follow suit. The legal supremacy enjoyed by large landowners over the peasantry was put to good use in this instance. It is from that time that the large Scanian estates and the province's peasant-run farms could begin to count their riches. That Skåne should have become so fertile is due not so much to the mildness of nature as to the organizational ability and skill of man.

These developments were to have even greater impact later on as the trade in grain began to assume increasing sophistication. Areas of surplus and deficit could be equalized, which was important not only because certain areas constantly had a very low food-producing potential, but also because poor harvests were a recurring problem. It was only very seldom that there was a nation-wide crop failure. However, inadequate transportation facilities and poorly developed trade distribution had always made it difficult to equate supply and demand. A perfect balance would still be wanting even after the distribution system had improved and large granaries had been established, as happened in Skåne and also to a certain extent on the plains of Uppland and Östergötland. Yet even if the improvement was incomplete, it had a far-reaching effect,

There were three kinds of specialization which formed the basis of this shift towards greater mobility of farm produce: the already mentioned concentration on grain production in certain regions; the formation of manorial estates, whose higher productivity created surpluses for sale; and, by contrast with the seventeenth century, the large and growing importation of grains. So Livonia did not really become a 'Swedish breadbasket' until after its cession to Russia in 1721.

Interesting factors come to light in relation to grain imports. During the great-power era it had been the cardinal task of exports to finance wars and expansionism. The claims on Sweden's resources were of a much more modest order after the loss of empire—or, as many people might put it, after Sweden had been relieved of the burden of empire. Revenues from exports could now be used in quite a different way, towards providing sustenance, and the chief emphasis was to be put on imports of grain. It is tempting to speculate whether Sweden would have been able to cope with her prolific birth-rate in the eighteenth century if the wars of Charles XII had ended with the retention of an empire with its vastly expensive foreign commitments.

In spite of imports and a growing domestic food trade, harvest fluctuations could still strike hard. Years of poor harvests could tax the population by higher death-rates. Nevertheless, the conclusion drawn by some earlier historians, that the country was thereby caught in a 'Malthusian situation', has been proved wrong in the light of recent research. Even though many people did starve to death during some of the most severe famine years, misfortunes, usually an epidemic or a particularly severe winter, were necessary to produce such terrible consequences. When this did happen it seems to have struck almost exclusively those who already were enfeebled for other reasons: the aged, the ill, and infant children. The effect on population figures was markedly moderate and temporary: it could not check the long-range trend of constantly increasing numbers. For all its drabness, life was dramatic enough for most people, requiring no Malthusian spice. Besides, the lack of storage facilities made it impossible to compensate for bad years with the surplus from good. The advice given by Joseph to the Pharaoh, that the land lay up corn in seven years of plenty against seven years of famine, could be followed only to a limited extent.

The effects of population growth were not confined to the agricultural changes just mentioned. Apart from the effects on animal

76

husbandry discussed above, the traditional sidelines of an agrarian society also felt the impact. Most conspicuous was a sharp upsurge in different forms of *sloyd* or homecraft. The last Riksdag session of the Age of Liberty virtually equated *sloyd* and agriculture in importance. As one spokesman put it, they were 'the two sources from which all labour and earnings derive'. The authorities, once hesitant, if not outrightly hostile, gave increasing support and encouragement.

The growing scope and significance of *sloyd* was connected with population growth in several different ways, both directly and indirectly. The mounting numbers of landless persons who were unemployed over long periods had to support themselves or work for their employers in tasks unrelated to farming. It seemed natural, especially in areas with long-standing traditions of *sloyd*, to strive for an artisan's or even an industrial scale of production. At the same time, in the new agricultural districts with their relatively low yields, the peasants were compelled to find supplements which not infrequently turned out to be the main sources of livelihood. This need probably explains the geographic dispersion of the more sophisticated homecrafts, which were to be found in Norrland, Dalsland, Bohuslän Västergötland and Småland, to name the most important areas. *Sloyd* did not make much headway on the fertile plains; contemporary annals include many complaints that the peasants were inclined to idleness whenever they were not forced to work by the seasonal demands of their calling. This form of comfortable leisure was not caused solely by idleness, however. There was a more weighty reason for it: the shortage of wood on the plains for heating and lighting. When wood was lacking for these purposes, wrote the provincial medical officer of Mariestad in 1765, the peasant and his household preferred to sleep as long as it was dark outside. 'Having sufficiently of corn for his bread and aquavit, he considers it unnecessary to work and cloaks his negligence with the excuse that he can undertake nothing of practical value in the darkness.'

Although the observant doctor of Mariestad was exaggerating, he did expose the heart of the matter, which was simply that the opportunities and incentives for developing *sloyd* varied from one part of the country to another. Here the specialization we discussed earlier comes into the picture. The areas of poor yields needed currency to pay for grain from richer areas. Since these were generally those most recently brought under the plough and in richly forested areas, they often paid with the earnings from *sloyd* products and from carting and lumbering for the iron and timber mills.

Circumstances of this kind have often been taken as a premise for the theory, still widely held, that economic progress would not be possible without the incentive of poverty, which was supposed to compel the development of new lines of activity, such as shipping, trade and manufacturing, as well as initiate inventions and set in motion momentous processes. This argument has often been made to 'explain', for instance, the early and successful industrialization of the northern United States.

As the history of Swedish *sloyd* demonstrates, the theory has some validity. But it should not be simply and wholly interpreted to mean that poverty is the mother of wealth. A great many preconditions are needed to set such a process in motion: so if nature stints agriculture, she must be more generous in other things, such as raw materials, transport facilities, harbours and sources of energy; the process also requires men who under fortunate circumstances are inspired by tradition, vitality, and resourcefulness to get activities under way and induce others to join them. Also it requires markets that can absorb what is being produced, areas of prosperous farms for instance, whose owners can afford to buy crafted produce but lack the time to make such things themselves; or a broad upper and middle class interested in this business; or opportunities for exports to other and perhaps more affluent countries. These three markets, at any rate, existed in Sweden during the eighteenth century. To use a twentieth-century term, Sweden was anything but an 'under-developed' country in this respect.

The predominant form of *sloyd* in the eighteenth century was textile making. It was based in part of foreign raw materials; the importing records make frequent mention of flax. Gradually, however, domestic sources of flax came to account for an increased share of the linen used. Flax cultivation in close proximity to textile manufacture was common in the north, particularly in Ångerman-land province. These areas had certain traditions to build on, but a further incentive was provided by a marginal agriculture and a sharp rise in population. Although flax seems to have been cultivated primarily on the least fertile soils, there is no doubt that Noorland's typical incarnation of the old-time farming-cum-forestry society also played a role. Norrland was well endowed with cattle and horses, and flax required reasonably good manuring in order to thrive. It has been contended that the textile manufactories, which enjoyed eager official support and encouragement during this period, had no more than an indirect impact on the homecrafted product, in that they did not offer more serious competition. They were much too quality-conscious or, perhaps more accurately, 'genteel' in their

78

production, and accordingly catered almost exclusively to the rich, or in any case to the more prosperous noblemen, gentry and burghers. This observation is essentially correct, but it does not go far enough. The manufactories certainly exerted a direct technical stimulus on the *sloyd* trades. The new methods and tools they devised were adopted by the more successful and ambitious *sloyd* entrepreneurs. Here, too, the contrast with the seventeenth century is striking.

Various methods were used to market products made in the home. According to theory and legislation, which was, however, eventually relaxed almost beyond recognition, specialization should also apply in trade. Peasants were to offer their products in the markets or directly to retailers in the towns, and it was then up to the latter to look after the further distribution and sale of these products. The system looked tidy on paper, with certain inland towns authorized to handle domestic trade and others designated as centres for foreign trade, and with the so-called Bothnian trade compulsion, whereby all foreign trade to and from ports along the Gulf of Bothnia had to call in at Stockholm. As far as the *sloyd* products were concerned, however, this well-ordered theory of specialization appears to have found only partial application. Many producers were in the habit of embarking on long business trips within the country, or they would send their employees on selling and buying rounds, reminiscent of the Västergötland pedlar's trade described in the previous chapter. Peasants of the Sjuhärads region around Borås seem to have been on good trading terms with the townspeople. The local merchants bought much of the *sloyd* production for their trade, and ardently backed the Västergötland pedlars against other towns which sought to impede their commercial wanderings. Nevertheless, in the eighteenth century the citizens of Borås started complaining: too much of the trade in *sloyd* wares was bypassing their town. At other places in West Sweden, along the Bothnian coast, and between Finland and Sweden, a bitter struggle raged between the devotees of specialization and the lively peasant-sponsored maritime trade. The peasants operated their own vessels for their trade, thereby destroying the carefully planned division of labour principle in the domain of shipping. To some extent the peasants were helped by urban merchants and others who advanced credit, but we have no means of knowing how far this practice went. The suppliers of credit could in any case minimize their risks by acting as agents on commission. At the same time this system, where it was applied, provided the peasants with a larger, and presumably surer turnover, and it ought to have favoured the tendencies towards specialization and larger-scale operation in *sloyd* which undoubtedly manifested themselves here and there. From there the step towards a sort of industrialization was not great, even though considerable time might elapse before it was taken. Large regions could work for a single merchant, co-ordinate their production with his needs, and use his advance payments to eke out an income which was otherwise seasonally determined by agricultural activities. It is interesting to note that in one Riksdag after the other, many of the burghers supported the peasants in their demands for the free exercise of *sloyd* and the right to market its products; this suggests that the two groups had some common interests in spite of many differences. Other villages co-ordinated their handicrafted production with the pedlar's trade, eliminating outside merchants: a method that was quite common in Dalarna.

A similar community of interests was not possible between the workers at peasant *sloyd* and those engaged in the regular handicrafts. It was not only a question of professional rivalry, but also of other antagonisms. Competition was not serious since peasants and artisans primarily catered for different markets; but such competition as did arise could be bitter enough. Some of the handicraftsmen may well have felt the stronger resentment, since every form of outside competition, no matter how slight, had a negative effect on the attempt to keep the handicrafts as a closed system, a *numerus clausus*. It will be recalled that this system had, besides, met with a degree of official opposition.

Actually the official attitude towards the cartelist-oligopolist tendencies in the handicrafts was ambiguous. There are a number of problems (some of which were occasioned by economic and social policies), that we must understand in order to form an idea of the general situation of the handicrafts during this period.

During both the great-power era and the Age of Liberty, government economic policy specifically encouraged the handicrafts as a vital component of urban industry. This policy was a fusion of different, and not necessarily compatible, elements. There were numerous goals: increased specialization; the setting of prices favourable to consumers; guarantees of high quality; a diversification of crafts; and many artisans. All this was desired, plus a strict, regulated control over developments.

If the demands for specialization, reasonable prices and more crafts militated in favour of free, or at least keen competition, the demands for quality and price-control required a greater degree of trade-licensing. A compromise might have been possible if this ambivalence had been the sole problem. However, the authorities were hampered in that they alone could not make decisions. The artisans were organized in powerful guilds. If the community at large wanted a quality-conscious and reasonably flourishing handicraft trade, it was necessary to humour the guilds to a great extent.

The authorities, as we said, were of two minds on the subject. When the guilds behaved as pressure groups, they could cause a lot of embarrassment; but they could also be very useful to the Government. From time to time, when the right balance was struck, there would be admirable co-operation in the spirit of give and take. The guilds were given wide latitude to follow up on their special economic and political aspirations, in return for committing themselves to enforce government controls on their members—all in accordance with the pattern of a corporative society.

This system had ancient roots in Western European culture, reaching its full flower in the late medieval period: it was then that the Estates had carved out their social and political positions; the Church had emerged as a state within the state; the independent trading towns had attained the height of their commercial prosperity; the craft guilds had perfected techniques for exercising command over their special spheres.

In no other sector did the traditions then developed live on with such vitality as in the handicrafts. It is not hard to see why. The reason is chiefly economic. The basis of handicrafted production and marketing had undergone little or no change. Improved technology was limited to a few very modest advances. Within the finer crafts, whose organizations remained the strongest and most stable, the term of apprenticeship was necessarily long, and various strategems were devised to make it even longer. Geographically and socially the markets remained fairly limited. The authorities were continually dependent on a supply of skilled manpower to meet the needs of the army and civil administration, as well as to satisfy lavish upper-class tastes. In consequence, they wished to maintain a good relationship with the guilds; indeed, they occasionally felt it proper to give the guilds active support in their cartelist aspirations.

Economic and social motives were here closely interwoven. To understand how the guilds functioned as cartels, a few words must first be said about how they were organized. Membership of a guild comprised the master craftsmen and, usually, the journeymen, though the latter lacked voting privileges. At the top of the hierarchy was an alderman and usually two associates in office known as assessors. In earlier days the members of this governing body had been appointed for life, but during the seventeenth and eighteenth centuries they appear to have been replaced at regular intervals, generally every tenth year. Major decisions, such as assessment of dues and the admission of new masters, were reserved for assembly meetings. If a guild wished, it could and did avoid the presentation of mastership diplomas by postponing the assemblies for long periods.

The guilds came to operate as social institutions as well as economic cartels. They provided needy members and their families with financial assistance, and sometimes conducted a regular kind of insurance business. They also regulated the wages of journeymen and apprentices to prevent bidding for manpower; spelled out regulations on prices of raw materials which were binding on suppliers in cases where the guilds themselves did not act as wholesale purchasers; and set prices and other terms of sale for finished goods—a practice that had to be carried out under cover, since it was frowned upon by the authorities. The opportunities for cartelization would have existed in any case owing to a strong tradition of solidarity in the handicrafts. However, the decisive impulse towards solidarity lay in the guilds' power over the establishment of new enterprises. Without the consent of his guild, no one could become a master craftsman, i.e. an independent artisan. The trade-licensing power, in addition to limiting new enterprise, tended to favour the sons and relatives of old members. Numerous examples can be cited of journeymen who for lack of the right connections were stopped from becoming masters by means of extra-long probationary periods and meaningless, expensive, even impossible mastership tests. Thus a journeyman bookbinder would be assigned to bind a book which was not obtainable, or could only be procured abroad at prohibitive expense. From time to time the authorities tried to break the cartels by conferring masterships outside the regulated crafts, but these encroachments did not accomplish much. Men of manual skill were in short supply, and a frustrated journeyman was loth to by-pass his guild for fear of reprisals; even if he did take the step, and made the grade, he would sooner or later be hounded into the guild anyway. Besides, the 'freemaster', as the publicly licensed were called, quickly enough sided with the guild members in opposing an increase in membership. The authorities had to take care not to appoint too many freemasters, lest excessive competition make the trade unattractive. The various free-mastership decrees, dated 1669, 1672, 1719, 1724 and 1772, proved largely futile owing to these factors, and also to the strong political opposition by the burghers against every 'liberalization' of economic policy—a trend which certainly, in this respect, was favoured by the nobility and gentry, as large consumers of handcrafted products. The result was a see-saw pattern in which every move to liberalize the guild system was followed by crown regulations that gave preference to the guilds.

Part of the guild policy (aside from the control over trade licensing), was a limitation on the number of employees, a stand which received fairly consistent approval from the authorities. At first glance, it might be concluded from this that the different handicrafts would tend to stagnate with regard both to their labour force and production volume. Yet eighteenth-century statistics disclose a fairly sharp rise in the numbers of masters and employees. This contradiction is only apparent, however. What happened was that the number of artisans increased at the same rate as the total urban population, and by a process that ensured a greater differentiation of handicrafts in the larger provincial towns. More trades were represented than had been in the past. This development was quite compatible with the guild's licensing control. The guilds, of course, could not prevent new masters from establishing themselves in towns where their trade had not existed previously, and where a larger population base had generated new needs. Besides, an increase in the number of masters could hardly be contained when a larger population created an expansive market. By mid-century, at any rate, the provincial towns had about 6,000 masters, 4,000 journeymen and 5,000 apprentices, making a total of 15,000 artisans. In Stockholm between 7,000 and 8,000 persons were engaged in handicrafts, and of these about 1,000 were masters and the remainder more or less evenly distributed between journeymen and apprentices. The scale of operations continued to be much larger in the capital. Although the number of masters appears to have increased only slightly, the average number of employees had risen from 1·6 or 1·7 per master to between 6 and 7. The chief explanation lies in the expansion of the baking, brewing, shoemaking and hatting trades, as well as in building construction.

Summing up developments from the end of the seventeenth century to the 1750s, the handicrafts had roughly tripled the size of their labour force. They now employed between 5 and 6 per cent of the adult male population as compared with 2 to 3 per cent earlier.

Their contribution to the supply of national requirements had grown in corresponding degree, or, when one considers the increased productivity in larger enterprises with their fifteen to twenty employees, may even have grown on a more progressive scale. However, if one also considers that the rural crafts may have employed as many as 20,000 persons at this time, it becomes clear that *sloyd* was of far greater importance than the handicrafts for the 90 per cent of the population which lived outside the towns. This impression still holds even if the zealously supported manufactories are added to the handicrafts.

The manufacturing policy of eighteenth-century Sweden closely resembled that of the great-power era. Manufactories were treated like pampered pets. Their advancement was fostered by various means, such as generous state credits and a body of legislation that conferred great benefits on entrepreneurs in relation to labour, not to mention other privileges.

According to earlier verdicts on this policy, especially Eli F. Heckscher's, it was a complete failure. Manufactories were equated with hothouse plants, doomed to wither away once the politicians withdrew their artificial irrigation. Per Nyström's research findings have essentially moderated this view, if they have not changed it entirely. As the beneficiaries of government support, the manufacturers could admittedly enforce legislation marked by a distinctive class bias. Even so, the manufactories should be seen not as artificial products but as natural components of that day's economy, possessing considerable stability and financial soundness. There is no evidence for the argument that government credits were crucial to these enterprises, even though manufactories were given first consideration; nor were manufacturers any more negligent than other entrepreneurs in honouring their debts. The fairly constant production maintained throughout the century also suggests that they could find markets for their products, even allowing for fluctuation in business conditions. As from 1760, the labour force diminished, especially in the textile branch; but since production volume remained constant, this should not be interpreted as proof of stagnation and decline. It is more likely an indication that production costs could be lowered, and efficiency increased. Improved production was essential for the manufactories which, even though they required little in the way of capital investment, incurred heavy expenses in regard to labour, raw materials and the long-term selling credits they usually had to grant.

As in the previous century, textiles predominated in the manufactories. Approximately 80 to 85 per cent of all manufactory workers were employed in the textile branch; the proportion for wool manufacturing alone seems to have been about 60 per cent of the total. Next in size came the tobacco industry with about 10 per cent, while the remaining 5 to 10 per cent were distributed among a number of small manufactories. All in all, the manufactories appear to have employed about 20,000 people in the 1760s. The urban handicrafts engaged 37,000 at the same time, and perhaps 50,000 earned their living from rural crafts. Including family members, the number employed in mining and ironworking amounted to 57,000. The so-called soldier families, including soldiers, ex-soldiers and their dependants, numbered around 150,000. The agrarian population at the same time numbered around 1·3 million.

These figures clearly show that the manufactories were of limited importance in the national economy, ranking even below the handicrafts. But that is not to suggest that they were totally insignificant or of no interest apart from their contemporary role as receptacles of political hopes and expectations. For the manufactories had two interesting features: the technique of business management they embodied, and the novel element they introduced in that day's economic and political environment.

The manufactories contributed to the economy by broadening the scale of producing and selling activities. This in itself was a major departure from the old corporative business methods. It was therefore necessary for the state to put them in a class by themselves, which to a great extent meant granting the manufactories a privileged position. A path had to be cleared through the jungle of vested interests which the corporate organizations had built up in the cities and towns. This could only be done by state concessions, combined with huge credits and favours, such as free grants of land, exemption from taxes and customs duties, and privileges for manpower: manufactory employees were exempted from military service and subjected to special legal regulations which favoured the employer. Many of the prerogatives enjoyed by the nobility were taken as prototypes. The entrepreneurs became a class of aristocrats in their own right, and in that capacity aroused the same resentment in artisans and tradesmen as did the nobility.

It was only in a limited sense that manufactories were run on lines that today would classify them as 'factories'. Their particular kind of large-scale production derived from such operations as purchase of raw materials, organization of work, and marketing. Defined thus, a manufactory could be dispersed among several workshops in the same town, where production was conducted on a handicraft basis and often directed by master craftsmen in the manner of the ordinary handicrafts. To some extent, too, work was assigned

85

to employees to do at home. In Stockholm, for example, the sprawl-
ing facilities occupied by Barnängen, a textile firm, did not house
any of the large machine halls that we associate with today's factory.
Its buildings were given over in part to dwellings for employees,
while the rest contained small production units in which work was
done strictly by hand.

There existed a mixture of what can be called centralized and decentralized enterprises. The decentralized type was the older. At first,
the entrepreneur handled no more than the financing and selling.
He would provide self-employed suppliers, artisans or homeworkers
with raw materials and semi-manufactures, and then attend to the
disposal of the finished products. Gradually the entrepreneur
brought an increasingly larger share of the production under his
direct control. He was forced to supervise each step of the manufacturing process and organize it so that the different suppliers
could be fitted flexibly into a common production schedule. The
logical step from there was to hire these suppliers as full-time
employees, find working premises for them, and provide the tools
and equipment. Even though the old system of remuneration might
be retained, with master craftsmen regarded as self-employed and
responsible for seeing that their employees were paid, the masters
became in effect entirely dependent on the entrepreneur. They
worked only for him and at his command. This centralization process
was most widespread in the textile industry. There the suppliers
were not so much their own businessmen as they were department
heads, though the departments themselves might be scattered in
different places. That type of organization and relationship between
manufacturing enterprise and suppliers may well be likened to the
petrol station in our motorized age. The oil company puts up the
capital, defines the work to be done, and makes all decisions of
importance. The petrol-station owner runs the business in his own
name and earns his income directly from it, but is bound by a contract which effectually makes him a hired hand.

If the manufactories are understood as, basically, something new
and partly alien in the corporative society, and as representing the
quest for better coordination of production and marketing, it is easy
to grasp why they were the object of so much official solicitude. They
constituted a venture into the new and untried, and as such imparted
a vital spark to a commercial and industrial life that was stagnating
in so many respects. Consequently, it is unfair to criticize the results
for falling short of what they should have been. Nor can the manufactories be faulted because they did not harbour the seeds of the

industrialism which was radically to transform the Swedish economy in the following century. Since they worked under quite different conditions—technical, economic and social—from the factories of industrialism, it would be wrong to blame them because for failing to further the development of this industrialism.

As members of a corporative society the manufactories of necessity reflected corporate trends which proved to be ill-suited to the innovations of a century later. In regard to working methods and organization, the manufactories relied largely on the traditions of the craft guilds. In addition, although they were subject to special legislation, they remained legally bound by contemporary concepts of justice. The class bias which informed other legislation, such as the Law of Master and Servant and the special regulations for handicraft employees, was applied also to the manufactories, to some extent even more stringently. Exemption from military service was not an unmixed blessing: the crown granted it as a privilege to entrepreneurs to help them recruit labour, but to employees it became a threat. Workers who did not perform what was demanded of them could be dismissed and punished by losing their exemption from military service, which almost always propelled them straight into a soldier's uniform. Also in other respects special ordinances for the manufactories tightened the grip of entrepreneurs over the master craftsmen they employed—who in their turn were vested with great power over their employees.

If the manufactories represented a willingness to take risks and to try something new, the same thing could hardly be said of the most important 'industry': ironworking. Naturally it was affected by the current trends, as we shall see later; but throughout the eighteenth century ironworking stagnated almost totally in terms of production volume and exports.

This stagnation was the result of a deliberate policy which had two explicit aims: to keep down the cost and consumption of fuel, and to keep prices up by limiting supplies to the international market. The first objective, as we noted earlier, was part of ironworking policy in the seventeenth century. The second was the application to iron of what had been official policy on copper during the great-power era. This extension to cover iron was an eighteenth-century innovation which, after certain experiments beginning in 1725, became a matter of practical politics as from 1748.

The controls imposed were of two kinds: firstly, limits were put on output by fixing sales quotas for different ironworks; and second-

ly the mills were restricted in the amount of pig iron they could buy
when they did not produce this themselves, as well as in their procurement of coal and wood. In principle, their rights both on the purchasing and selling side were governed by the conditions existing in
1748. Even so, a considerable elasticity was permitted. When old
mills shut down or reduced their output, new ones could be established or those in operation could increase their output. Great
variations were also allowed from year to year, so that underfulfilled
quotas in one or more years could be carried over into subsequent
years. This elasticity, however, was seldom so great that the prescribed ceiling could be exceeded, with the result that export figures
could be held remarkably steady from year to year. Computed in
five-year averages from 1735 to 1780, they were never below 40,000
tons or above 45,000 tons.

The supervision of exports posed no serious problem, since between
85 and 90 per cent of them passed through Stockholm and Göteborg,
with the capital alone accounting for about 60 per cent.

That this restrictive policy succeeded so well was not due primarily
to the relative ease of enforcement, however. The iron mill owners
obviously had an incentive to comply, in that the controls guaranteed
protection against poaching of one owner on markets developed
by another. Basically the controls were originated and operated
wholly in what were understood to be the interests of the mill owners
themselves. It was quite simply *their* cartel policy, and the government controls did no more than give it official sanction.

The policy could have been highly successful if Swedish iron had
retained its strong seventeenth century position; it will be recalled
that quality iron at that time enjoyed almost a virtual monopoly. In
the new century, however, its position weakened, and it continued
to deteriorate during the century's course. The main reason for this
was the appearance of Russian iron on the world market. Up to
mid-century, Britain imported from 75 to 90 per cent of her bar-iron
tonnage from Sweden; but then the proportion dwindled in the
1750s to below 65 per cent and in the ensuing decades to between
35 and 40 per cent; in the meantime, the Russian share gradually
rose to around 60 per cent. Actually, Sweden was not exporting less
bar iron to Britain, but the British market had been continually
expanding, and it was the Russians who benefited from the expansion. At the same time Britain was increasing her own production
of iron, with the result that Sweden's position in the total British
consumption decreased more than her share of the British import
of iron.

Thus Sweden failed to profit from a great boom in British demands for iron. During the eighteenth century the population of Britain rose from between five and six million to about nine million, an increase of roughly 80 per cent. A gradual industrialization had begun and the new factory system was well established before the end of the century. The development of towns was rapid. British maritime supremacy was reinforced by a fast-growing naval fleet and merchant marine. Important iron manufactures were founded, which produced a large volume of exports, especially for the Latin countries. Agriculture was transformed by the enclosure system, and with large-scale operation came the use of new implements. The demand for iron mounted in every sector. Yet the former chief supplier, Sweden's iron industry, stood still.

To some extent this development, and the Swedish policy which underlay it, can be explained by saying that the industry could not have done anything else even if it had wanted to. What had once been the industry's mainstay, hard iron bars, ran a poor second to the soft bars and cast iron which were increasingly preferred for the new types of structures devised to meet contemporary needs. Swedish concentration on quality iron limited the scope for expansion, since purchasers could be satisfied with inferior and hence cheaper materials.

It has been suggested that Swedish pricing policy facilitated the takeover of various markets (especially the British), by Russian iron. In other words, Sweden, by limiting her production in order to maintain high prices, enabled the Russians to step up their supplies.

Nevertheless, we must not be over-hasty in condemning Swedish policy. True, when Russian iron first appeared in volume during the 1730s, the Russians were clearly speculating on the high Swedish prices which made it possible for them to 'spoil the market' for the Swedes by undercutting their prices. From the Swedish point of view, the Russians were 'dumping'. However, while the supply of Swedish iron was admittedly curtailed to keep prices up, there is a great deal of evidence to indicate that the Swedish government was actually making a virtue of necessity. Swedish iron, in comparison to Russian and some British iron, was expensive to produce. Further, because the cost of fuel rose steeply with increasing demand, average costs rose to such an extent that the iron mills had virtually no choice but to limit output. Despite the new market conditions, however, Swedish iron was still in demand because of its quality.

Viewed in this light, the pricing policy becomes more comprehensible. From the viewpoint of the ironmasters and the iron exporters (often one and the same person, since the large exporters were gradually assuming ownership of iron mills), this policy, dictated by harsh necessity was far from incomprehensible. Apart from the deflation engendered by the Caps in the 1760s, the eighteenth century was a period of good business for the Swedish iron industry— a period of stability and consolidation in the midst of all the stagnation. It is most unlikely that policy of low prices to boost sales would have proved a better-paying proposition. Indeed, the indications are that the implementation of such a plan, which was even then recommended by certain writers, would have imposed far worse conditions on Swedish ironworking.

We must not conclude that Sweden had no interest in gaining new markets. She was most definitely interested: efforts made to promote sales were crowned with partial success, especially in the Latin markets, where significant gains, in particular during the 1780s and 1790s, which explain the increase in exports noted earlier. At least three explanations can be advanced for the shift or interest away from Britain. Difficulties on the British market had created the need for new outlets. Unlike Britain, the Latin countries wanted hardware products from the Swedish iron manufactories, which were as much the object of official solicitude in the eighteenth century as in the seventeenth. The third reason involved official concern for Swedish shipping, as exemplified by the Commodity Act of 1724—equivalent to the English Navigation Acts. Both the government and the merchants engaged in foreign trade, who were also shipowners, had an interest in ensuring that Swedish vessels were used to carry both exports and imports. Thus direct exports to the Latin countries were meant to counter the extensive imports from these countries (given the preferred status of Swedish shipping). These ideas also influenced the business policy pursued by Sweden's foreign-trade merchants towards the end of the century; there was then a marked shift from specialization in either exports or imports to a greater diversity of operations. As we shall see, the political ramifications of this shift were quite interesting.

The most stable of the Latin markets, and also the most important, during all but a very few years, was Portugal, which from 1740 onwards imported from 2,000 to 4,000 tons of Swedish iron annually. From the 1770s the French market assumed almost equal importance, and towards the latter 1780s absorbed no less than an annual average of 10,000 tons.

All in all, exports to the Latin countries were steady at between 4,000 and 5,000 tons up to 1770; hovered between 8,000 and 13,000 tons thereafter; and soared up to 16,000 tons in the closing years of the 1780s. The British market, up to 1770, absorbed between 10,000 and 20,000 tons; and thereafter from a minimum of 15,300 tons to a maximum of 19,600 tons. Thus Britain remained the leading customer, despite the factors discussed above. Below is a summary table showing the distribution of Swedish exports of bar iron from 1738 to 1799. It should be borne in mind that the table does not present a full picture, since the exports of hardware products to the Latin American countries were particularly important and carried greater weight as earners of export revenue because of their higher prices.

SWEDISH EXPORTS OF BAR IRON, by countries of destination,1738–99, in percentage of total volume.

Year	Britain	Netherlands	Baltic countries	Latin countries
1738–39	60·5	10	19·5	10
1745–49	57	9	24	10
1755–59	62	7	21	10
1765–69	56·5	8·5	22·5	12·5
1775–79	53	6	19·5	21·5
1785–89	48	4·5	15·5	32
1795–99	50	3	27	20

Over and above the observations already made, two further points are revealed by the table: the great reduction in trade with the Netherlands, corresponding almost exactly with the rise in exports to the Latin countries; and the fairly stable volume of exports to countries on the Baltic littoral.

However, if account is taken of the price differences for different commodities, we are given, according to the calculations of Eli F. Heckscher, a different picture of the relative weights of these markets. The Latin share then works out at 34·5 per cent for 1781–85 and 39·1 per cent for the next five-year period, as compared with Britain's 35·4 and 37·7 per cent respectively. Strictly speaking, this means that Swedish iron exports, and hence the country's foreign trade, had greatly changed their essential character. Swedish trade was branching out into new markets, and had achieved what contemporaries, at any rate, understood to be an increased measure of independence.

When we speak of ironworking as the only genuine 'industry' of the time, it must not be forgotten that the enterprises involved were very small units by modern standards. Their total output seldom exceeded 50,000 tons in any one year. Furthermore, this limited production was divided among so many mills that Leufsta, by far the largest of them, did not account for more than 1 to 2 per cent of the total. The following table shows that more than two hundred mills were in operation in 1777. During certain periods of ownership, however, some of these units were combined into relatively large aggregates.

NUMBER OF IRON MILLS IN 1777, by province, exporting via Stockholm.

Province	Number of mills	Total licenced output in tons
Västmanland	74	9050
Närke	21	2950
Dalarna	20	3150
Södermanland	18	1400
Östergötland	17	1500
Uppland	14	5850
Gästrikland	15	2700
Finland	13	1600
Hälsingland	11	1900
Småland	8	850
Värmland	6	900
Medelpad	4	510
Ångermanland	3	600
Västerbotten	2	150
Västergötland	1	190
Totals	227	33,300

Although these iron mills obviously had important common interests, they displayed a diversity of structures and problems. Conditions differed from one area to another. Large mills were operated differently from small, and traditions and ownership patterns varied from mill to mill. Several of the largest mills belonged to old noble domains and were run as part of an extensive business under estate management. The majority of smaller mills were owned by commoners or by families newly ennobled in recognition of their services to the iron industry; ownership of an iron mill gained for them an important rung on the social ladder. During the eighteenth century some of the leading mills, as well as a few of the smaller ones, passed into the hands of the large exporting houses, and at least for a time were deliberately merged into a structure of vertical integration between trade and production.

According to one school of thought, of which the chief exponent is Karl-Gustaf Hildebrand, the stagnation of ironworking in the eighteenth century was due in part to the emergence of a new general

tion of mill owners, less expansive and dynamic, and concerned more with stability and security than were the pioneering ironmasters of the seventeenth century. Undoubtedly there was this change in outlook; not, however, as the cause of a new phase in ironworking, but rather as a result of it. The industry no longer operated under conditions which allowed its leading practitioners room for dynamic expansion. They had to make the best of what lay to hand or find an outlet for their dynamism in other spheres. When several of the most eminent and progressive merchants of Stockholm and Göteborg became ironmasters, it was in the combination of commerce and ironworking (which often involved the merging of several mills under one management) that they could give free rein to their ambitions. Within the iron industry itself, these men were not technical, economic or social innovators. They could not be for the simple reason that the previously described market situation for Swedish iron left no room for innovation.

Having dealt in more detail with the iron industry, we can, appropriately, proceed with a more general account of Swedish international trade and the role played by the great merchant houses in the eighteenth century. To begin with, the only true dynamism imparted to the Swedish economy during the eighteenth century and into the beginning of the nineteenth came from these firms, which were concentrated in Stockholm and Göteborg. This was because of their ability to accumulate capital and to make it available both domestically and internationally. Many of these merchant houses were to contribute significantly to the industrial development of the nineteenth century as company founders, financiers and exporters, especially within the forestry industries.

The 'commercial capitalism' associated with merchant houses was not unique to Sweden. Its *raison d'être* was the nature of the pre-industrial economy. Investment in the dominant sector of economic activity, agriculture, was made possible by direct investment savings. Land clearance and construction were largely attended to by a household's own labour resources. In these cases the savings were achieved by what might be called a curtailed consumption of leisure, and took the form of an increase in production in proportion to the investment. Apart from the construction work which went on in the cities and on the larger estates, and which was never extensive in proportion to the total of new investment, the only sectors that required heavy capital outlays for fixed assets were ironworking, shipping and the manufactories, as well as some of the handicrafts.

The day-to-day requirements of capital for industrial purposes applied not so much to production as to the marketing of products. It was often a question of distributing bulky and heavy articles by means of a poor transport system. It took considerable amounts of capital to finance the delay between the time an article left the production site until it reached the buyer, and even more time would elapse before he paid for it.

This state of affairs was not confined to foreign trade, of course. But since the specialization which existed was overwhelmingly a specialization *vis-à-vis* the outside world, it was in foreign trade that 'capitalism' became especially imperative. The cardinal task for Sweden here was to finance the output of the iron industry. Since the main responsibility for marketing iron rested with the merchant houses of Stockholm and Göteborg, it was logical that they should also underwrite the financing. In many cases the financing came to include the actual production process as well. In due course the houses also acquired the ownership of many mills, and as we noted earlier, some of the most important iron mills thus passed into merchant hands. In addition, these houses became involved in the foreign marketing process, with the result that much of the shipping business was run by them. Several houses also branched out into other industries, sometimes to the extent of building and operating their own plants; though compared with their interests in iron-working, these activities were of minor scope. The merchant houses also functioned as banks, doing large-scale business with the general public in deposits and loans, which were usually granted under short-term notes.

Naturally, the fact that so much of the need for capital lay within the trade sector did not mean that independent commercial enterprises had to fill the bill to the exclusion of other sources. That this nevertheless happened was chiefly due to the impossibility of achieving complete integration between production and trade. The units of production were small. On an average, the output of any one mill was not a paying proposition for any one merchant house, which of course had to transact business in volume in order to flourish. In so far as there was integration between the two, it therefore tended to proceed in a reversed order, that is from distribution to production. This does not mean that such integration was widespread, nor does it suggest that the merchant houses acquired a dominating hold over the whole iron industry by way of the money they put up for the sale of output and, very often, for its processing. Nonetheless, the system did operate so as to give them control of certain important iron mills; in these cases, moreover, the merchant houses had evidently striven to gain control, if for no other reason than to consolidate their hold on an industry which, after all, constituted the very core of their mercantile calling.

The merchant houses were family businesses, usually owned and managed by two or three partners, sometimes four. They were organized as general partnerships. According to legal theory each member of a general partnership carried full personal liability for all partnership debts regardless of the amount of his investment. But as this form of business organization was applied in the merchant houses, all non-mercantile business could escape partnership liability by being written in the individual names of the partners. In many cases, moreover, the formal joint capital was limited to a certain basic amount shared equally between the partners. Any increment of capital beyond this sum was entered in the books as a loan advanced by one of the partners, and was left to run indefinitely at a fixed rate of interest. The apparent flimsiness in company partnerships should not be overestimated. It was often balanced by the close ties of the partners not only through business, but also in family matters. The partners were almost without exception related, being fathers and sons, brothers-in-law, sons-in-law, cousins and other next-of-kin. Taken as a whole these circumstances were important in at least two ways:

(1) The capital put up to start a partnership could never be very large, since it usually combined the fortunes of no more than one, two or three families. When a new name appeared on the company signboard, it did not necessarily signify the infusion of outside blood: it was not uncommon for a young man on the staff to promote his career by the well-known technique of 'marrying the boss's daughter'. On the other hand—and this was the more significant consequence— the extra name did not dilute the original family fortune; this could be kept intact within the firm by having the daughter's share assigned to her partner husband. Further, the presence of several partners, who were each liable for partnership debts in full, tended to enhance the firm's credit rating. In the event of a bankruptcy, creditors could be excused for believing that they stood a better chance of recovery if more than one person was liable.

(2) The close family ties were not limited to one firm alone. They had ramifications which not only criss-crossed virtually every merchant house in Stockholm and Göteborg, but also branched out to enterprises in London, Amsterdam, Riga, Danzig, and Marseilles. Many of the leading Swedish merchants were immigrants of the first

or second generation, as revealed by their French, English, Irish, Scottish, Dutch, German and Baltic names: Grill, Jennings, Lefebure, Alnoor, Tottie, Schön, Wahrendorff, Pauli, Bescow, Hebbe, von Bippen, Worster, Montgomery, Deneke, Pommeresche, and so on. By the same token a number of Swedish families had established themselves as merchants in other countries. Obviously, the close personal and business associations built into these relationships could not help but have tremendous importance. They facilitated contacts and inspired trust. Given the handicap of long distances, the difficulties of transport, and the intricate and insecure legal machinery for enforcing claims in other countries, the element of purely personal confidence was absolutely crucial if a credit and trading system was to function at all. It had as one of its results the development of a particular form of mercantile specialization, namely the growing preference of merchants to transact business with the countries from which they came, or with which they had intimate personal ties. Firms with Irish, Scottish and English names concentrated on shipments to British ports, especially of bar iron. Merchant houses with roots in Baltic or German areas opted for imports of grains, salt and textiles from Baltic and German ports. This does not mean that merchant houses came to specialize exclusively as exporters or importers, or that they focused all their attention on specific countries or products. Nevertheless, the general tendency was clear enough, even though it gradually became less pronounced than it was at first. It has been indicated above that this specialization, as far as it went, acquired a singular, though anything but incomprehensible political significance as the Age of Liberty drew to a close. We shall have reason to study this development in the next section of this book.

How did the merchant houses finance their extensive operations? Or, phrasing the question differently, how did the system of credit, for which these firms were the chief service agencies, function?

In order to provide a reasonably detailed, even if schematic answer to these questions, it is necessary first to look at the international credit system during the eighteenth century.

The principal centre of credit for most of the century was Amsterdam, which, however, began to lose this position towards the 1800s when London and to some extent Hamburg, took over. The shift of financial power to Britain was a natural consequence of her having taken over the Dutch role of world trade entrepôt a century earlier.

The development of an international credit system can be roughly traced as follows. As an entrepôt country, the Netherlands controlled a large share of European trade and shipping from the end of the sixteenth century until well into the eighteenth. Consequently the country also became the focal point of international financial operations and, in the absence of heavy demands on savings for domestic investment, the principal exporter of capital in Western Europe. In the long run, however, this position could not be maintained without corresponding dominance of trade and shipping. The erosion of Dutch financial hegemony was accelerated by wars and crises. 'Venice and Holland, where they were in times past, and England where it is today, should suffice to prove the value of such commerce,' wrote the Swedish Convoy Commissariat in 1801, in an account which assessed the importance of transit trade and shipping. Incidentally, this observation has served as an argument in the controversial question as to when the economic decline of the Netherlands set in; around 1800, at any rate, the evidence of decline had been noted by contemporaries.

Though no longer supreme, the Netherlands did not completely lose its influence on trade and finance. Together with London and Hamburg, Amsterdam lived on as a clearing-house of international business until well into the nineteenth century, and there is no question but that Amsterdam was *the* clearing-house up to the 1780s.

The Netherlands was able to maintain its eminence in the field of international payments even long after the country had lost its corresponding entrepôt position. This suggests that a high degree of multilateralism prevailed in trade. In the long run, with a more highly developed general bilateralism, it would not have been necessary or possible to even out each country's balance of payments in relation to the others. As far as Sweden is concerned, the statistics kept by the Board of Commerce provide incontrovertible proof of multilateralism. During the period from 1741 to 1805 Sweden admittedly maintained a fairly well-balanced trade with the Netherlands, France, Portugal, Spain, and the Mediterranean area. At the same time Sweden had a heavy export surplus in relation to Britain —still by far the most important market, though dwindling in relative terms—as well as to Hamburg, Lübeck and several other German cities. A heavy predominance of imports was shown in the trade with Russia, the Baltic states, and the German Baltic areas. Whatever role smuggling may have played, it was likely to increase imbalance on the import side. In the final settlement of accounts, the excess of exports to Britain paid for the excess of imports from the Baltic countries.

Up to 1870 at any rate, Sweden was more interested in the exchange rates quoted in Amsterdam and Hamburg than in London. This indicates that payments were made chiefly by way of Amsterdam, followed by Hamburg. British importers also did business in Amsterdam and Hamburg, honouring their obligations by bills of exchange drawn on banking and merchant houses in these cities. Swedish interest in London greatly increased towards the end of the century, when payments were often made more directly, so to speak. As yet, however, Amsterdam and Hamburg were more important as 'Swedish' financial centres.

The ability to accumulate what then was considered as enormous quantities of capital explains why the Dutch merchant houses could move from the forwarding and shipping of goods to the financing of international trade on a longer-term basis. However, it is unlikely that they could have fully acted the role of merchant bankers without the facilities which permitted the free exportation of both minted and unminted metal from the country—a Dutch speciality that is well worth bearing in mind in this century of mercantilism. Here, too, an important role was played by the Bank of Amsterdam: it did not issue notes, but operated strictly as a bank of deposit, a practice that enhanced its reputation and eventually helped to create a money market that was better organized than that of any other country. Price movements in the Netherlands, and hence the rates of exchange in Amsterdam, held fairly stable; or it would be more accurate to say that the former held stable while the latter fluctuated according to the price movements and balances of payments of each country quoted. In this way the exchange rates varied less in the Netherlands than they did elsewhere, which immediately pinpoints the key reason why international payments were so willingly transacted through Amsterdam.

Britain emerges as the most important recipient of Dutch capital exports. Indeed, an ironical observer might say that the Dutch, in financing the explosive growth of both public and private sectors in the British economy, sacrificed their own. Towards the end of the century the Dutch also invested heavily, though less extensively, in France. And from the beginning of the nineteenth century, Dutch money became increasingly tied to the fortunes of the United States. In 1818 it is estimated that the Netherlands held about 11,000 million dollars in United States securities, a sum equivalent to half of the American national debt.

The channelling of so much capital to Britain during the eighteenth century—in the form of government loans, loans to the large trading companies and other credits—can no doubt be explained in large part by the special method of trade financing which the British employed. (They were able to employ this method of financing precisely because Dutch credits were available.) The British consistently appear to have followed the practice of exporting on credit but paying for their imports in cash. This method had great advantages: it earned income from interest but avoided payment of interest, and maintained a strong bargaining position on both sides of the trading equation. The low rates of interest on money borrowed from the Netherlands afforded an agreeable interim space for these transactions, which of course ultimately owed their existence to the great confidence enjoyed by the British merchant houses. This in turn derived in no small measure from the complex family ties between these houses and those in the Netherland. In effect, the contracting parties did not regard themselves as citizens of countries with different and sometimes conflicting interests, but as members of a commercial community, united by personal as well as practical bonds.

How did the Swedish merchant houses and the financing of Swedish trade and industry fit into this picture? Part of the answer is already implicit in the above account, but some further elaboration may be of value.

On the whole, the Swedish merchant houses can be said to have reversed the British trade-financing methods as described above: the British paid promptly in cash for imports and sold exports on credit. Swedish importers bought on credit, while the exporters tried to collect from the buyer even before their goods left port. In financial terms, the Swedes conducted a distinctly passive trade, whereas the British were markedly active in theirs.

By and large, the procedure used was as follows. The Swedish importers usually obtained credit from their foreign suppliers. As a general rule, however, the suppliers did not leave their credits outstanding for very long, but drew on a merchant house in Amsterdam or Hamburg, depending on the instructions issued by the Swedish importers. An importer would then pay the merchant house by delivering goods, performing a service or, perhaps the most common procedure, by tendering a bill of exchange received for commodities he had himself exported or purchased from some Swedish exporter. The Swedish exporters would actually be paid for their goods in whole or in part, either at the time of despatch or shortly thereafter, by drawing bills on the foreign importer of the goods or on a banking house in Amsterdam or Hamburg. They would then use the bills in selling to Swedish importers or perhaps directly to a foreign country. When they themselves had imports to pay for, they could employ the bills as a money of account for paying the supplier or the bank they instructed him to draw on. In effect, these transactions meant that trade was financed by imports. It was the relatively long credits on that side, ultimately (and usually quickly enough) assumed by the banking houses in Amsterdam and Hamburg, which, in consequence of the bills of exchange purchased by Swedish importers from the exporters, also 'advanced' the payments for exports. In the final analysis, however, the essential aspect of the whole system was a smoothly functioning exchange business, with the banking houses of Amsterdam and Hamburg as its central agencies.

Naturally, a system where importers relied on credits and exporters were in a hurry to be paid had disadvantages. In any event, it was a system calculated to favour the foreign party whenever business agreements were negotiated. That it was nevertheless retained is due to several circumstances. In the first place, necessity knows no law: Sweden had no capital market of her own to finance her foreign trade, and the capital of her merchant houses was either inadequate or sluiced into projects which looked more promising. Then again, necessity may not have been all that pressing; the use of foreign facilities appeared to be both cheaper and more flexible than what a domestic source could offer—if such a source had been available. Besides, business relationships were so intimate and intermingled with personal ties that foreign creditors were not likely to indulge in high-handed behaviour. In its actual operation, the bill of exchange system, where credits and payments eventually converged on the great banking houses in Amsterdam and Hamburg, also imparted an air of anonymity and impartiality to the transactions—of 'institutionalization', as it were—which greatly reduced direct dependence on one's trading partner, even if he happened to be the ultimate source of credit-granting power. Fundamentally it was merely a matter of using the same bank, which arranged 'clearances'.

While the above description cannot tell us exactly what proportion of their capital needs the large merchant houses of Sweden obtained abroad, we can still draw some general conclusions. The chief role played by foreign banking houses was to finance the period of waiting and transportation costs from the time the goods left Sweden until they were sold abroad; and, conversely, from the purchase of goods abroad until some time between their arrival and sale in Sweden. The latter date depended on when the Swedish importer sent his remittance or performed other services in lieu of cash. The inference to be drawn from the usual practice of transferring credit from the foreign supplier to some banking house is that the term of credit must often have been extended.

The importance of foreign financing for international trade must not eclipse the fact that Sweden did have a domestic credit market and that tremendous exertions were expended to develop it. Here again the merchant houses were involved, since they to some extent functioned as banks. At the same time, however, a more institutional market made its appearance.

Thus the merchant houses of Stockholm regularly advanced credit to domestic producers to finance their production and stock-in-trade; this was the Swedish credit system, *förlag*, described earlier. In addition they sold on credit to a certain extent by borrowing on the domestic market. This market was divided into two fairly distinct sectors, the one comprising what might be called institutional credit organizations and the other a free market of private firms and individuals.

The institutional credit market was represented by the different discount companies which appeared at or near the end of the eighteenth and beginning of the nineteenth centuries. These companies became especially popular as depositaries, inasmuch as a certificate of deposit could be used as a circulating currency (these certificates being made out as promissory notes payable to the bearer, and carrying an interest at 3 per cent which was paid on redemption). By granting loans against personal security, they represented an advance in banking technique, even in comparison with the *manufacturdiskont* founded in 1757. As the name suggests, this firm discounted bills issued for industrial products. Its operation had created a more flexible system than the loans against fixed securities and stocks which characterized the activities of the *Riksbank* and the Ironmasters' Association (*Jernkontoret*) as lenders. However, the discount companies were not exactly innovators in lending money on the strength of a borrowers' name. The Ironmasters' Association had been doing that ever since 1769. Since the *Riksbank* and the Association actually were more important than the discount companies in this field, their activities ought to be dealt with at greater length.

On February 18, 1735, a crown ordinance was issued authorizing the *Riksbank* to lend money on fixed property and iron. The ordinance was amended on May 8, 1739, to extend to a wider list of commodities, including steel, copper, brass, lead, grains, aquavit, wine, sugar, salt, tobacco, hemp and 'sundry manufactured goods'. The granting of loans under these conditions continued until 1762, and was resumed after the end of the 1760s in regard to metals.

As far as the large merchant houses were concerned, and thereby all the exporting industries, the most important part of the *Riksbank*'s lending activities was in the class of stock headed 'steel, iron, etc.'.

The general ledgers for loans present a very clear picture not only of the extent to which exporters were borrowing on their stock, but also a date-by-date sequence in the fluctuations of this stock. The seasons of the year impressed a distinctive rhythm on operations. Borrowing took place in January–March and October–December and repayments in April–September, with shifts in one or other direction in some years depending on whether the springs and winters were early or late. Most of the repayments were spread over several instalments. Sales were made in smaller units than the replenishment of stock. Apart from the obvious fact that a shipment comprised a large number of consignments, this was because the merchant houses did not begin to accumulate their pledgeable inventories as from the time the goods were weighed in customs in Stockholm, but upon their arrival at the weighhouses in those towns through which the iron had to pass on its way from the mills to Stockholm.

This prolonged the stock-keeping time during which goods could be pledged with the *Riksbank*. Iron could be put up as security very soon after it was delivered from the mills.

It is difficult to gauge the significance of this lending for merchant-house and export-industry financing. If iron prices are taken as a yardstick, the total advances by the *Riksbank* in 1755, then amounting to 400,000 riksdaler, would have paid for between one-third and one-half the iron exported via Stockholm. It should be noted here, however, that lending operations pertained to the country as a whole and to more commodities than iron. In relation to overall exports of iron, the advances accounted for a proportion of between one-fourth and one-fifth, but they probably varied in importance from year to year in accordance with market fluctuations. Thus during the years 1806–10, which were difficult ones for the iron export trade, the loans advanced were particularly large.

The business of financing trade in iron was also conducted by the Ironmasters' Association, though its activities in this branch were generally less important than those of the *Riksbank*. It was originally founded to protect ironmill owners against the price-reduction policy of exporters. This it did by placing supporting orders with the mills.

The money for this purpose came from a fund to which mill owners contributed annual dues at the rate of one daler copper for every *skeppund* (375 pounds) of iron forged. This method later came to be applied for other purposes, among them the financing of the salt company and its stock.

However the growth of this fund soon compelled the Ironmasters' Association to enter the lending business so as to earn interest on its investments.

Efforts were made from the very beginning to cloak these operations in secrecy, with the result that it was mostly an inner circle of the Association which benefited from the loans. Since these borrowers included some of the leading Stockholm merchants of the 1750s, the Association's loans were chiefly granted to iron exporters in the capital and not to the mill owners in the countryside. According to the new rules adopted in 1769, loans to tradesmen would not be approved unless these persons were also mill owners, and as such were in a position to grant credits to productive enterprises. As this was true of many of the large merchant houses in Stockholm, they naturally qualified as high-priority borrowers. For the most part, however, the houses availed themselves of this facility to only a very small extent; this is true of the very largest mill owners among them, such as Tottie & Arfwedson and Bohman, Hassel & Görges. In regard both to amounts of loans and their frequency, the Ironmasters' Association lagged behind the *Riksbank* as a source of capital for the large merchant houses, and hence for the financing of the iron industry and foreign trade; a possible exception may be made for the 1790s.

As for the free credit market consisting of private firms and individuals, there is not much to add, beyond the observations made concerning the merchant houses and the promissory notes they accepted for their loans. At the same time, however, they were active on the money-receiving end, and here some things should be noted. In this capacity they functioned as banks, and in some cases even as savings banks. The money deposited with these banks was placed with the merchant houses to yield sufficient return to pay for their own outgoing interest plus a margin or profit. Although most of the money involved came from relatively large fortunes, not a few of the depositors appear to have been small savers. When bankruptcies occurred, as happened to the large House of Finlay in 1772, anxious investors could stage the kind of run familiar from many bank crises. On the other hand, it cannot be said that any merchant house was ever directly brought to ruin by blind public fear, which was the fate suffered by Palmstruch's bank. This deposit business was certainly far too small in relation to the often tremendous volume of business transacted by the large merchant houses to provoke such a result.

All these activities took place against a background of confusion and disorder in the monetary system. To tell this story is also to unfold the history of the *Riksbank*, not only because the national management of money was entrusted to it, but also because, subsequently, it never performed as important a role in the total economic policy as it did during the eighteenth century. That stemmed from the basic pattern of government during the Age of Liberty, which was virtually synonymous with the Riksdag, or, more exactly, its secret committee. The Riksdag could exploit the *Riksbank* for general economic and political ends in a way that was impossible during the periods of more dualistic government—and, owing to the Bank's position as an agency of the Riksdag—was also impossible during the periods of absolute monarchy. During the Age of Liberty the *Riksbank* and its management of the monetary system became an instrument in the hands of whoever happened to be in power. For good or ill, the Bank's services became an indivisible part of the total political scene.

During the period of reconstruction up to 1739, coinciding with the ministry of Arvid Horn, it was admittedly out of the question to harness the Bank to such ends. To begin with, this was a period of general wariness in politics. Moreover, the Bank had its hands full cleaning up the mess left behind by Charles XII, entailing measures to deal with emergency coinage, growing state credits in the bank, and other irregularities. The fall of Horn made it possible to try a different policy.

Actually, the basis for a new banking and monetary policy was not so much provided by the *Riksbank* or by the politicians as by the general public, which had shown a remarkably flexible talent for circumventing inflexible regulations. After the brief paper-money experiment of the Palmstruch bank, still a vivid and frightening memory, the *Riksbank* did not issue bank notes on a regular basis; however, that did not prevent the existence of a *de facto* paper-money system. As evidence of the deposits and other debts placed with it, the *Riksbank* had issued different types of receipts; one of these, the so-called assignment note, was to be converted to a bank note in the proper sense when the Age of Liberty had grown a few years older. These notes were supposed to be endorsed every time they changed hands, but that requirement was conveniently forgotten by the general public. The practice which evolved was simply that the first bearer signed his name and made an endorsement in blank. In this way the assignment notes could circulate as paper money. Their position was further enhanced when the Crown began to accept them for tax collection and in other transactions with private persons and firms. In effect, they were thus raised to the level of legal tender; but since the assignment notes represented actual deposits, they could not be issued in amounts larger than the Bank's reserves of coining metal, that is copper.

A purely inflationary issue of notes was thereby delayed. However, the obligation was not totally binding. Assignment notes could also be authorized without deposits by means of different transactions between the twin branches of the *Riksbank*: the discount bank and the loan office. Actually, it was possible to exceed the holdings of copper metal by fairly large amounts. Owing to the awkwardness of copper coins and the difficulty of moving them about, the value of notes in relation to copper would have had to plummet for a run on copper to start. Since the price of copper also fell for various reasons, the latitude for note issue was further expanded. In any case, the withdrawal of copper coins to melt into metal for export was no tempting proposition.

The Hats made it deliberate policy to exploit note issue as a means to promote economic ends. They assumed that lack of capital and credits retarded the country's industries, and since many of the leading Hats were noblemen and burghers engaged in the running or promotion of various enterprises, this scarcity obsessed them.

On this score, the Hats were alleged to have committed the 'common mercantilist error' of confusing money and credit with real capital. Even so, they were right in believing that a more abundant supply of credit would greatly stimulate the industrial sector of the economy. As a corollary of this argument, a more abundant money supply would also create real capital. The inflationary mechanism was itself an asset for this purpose. Money was easy to borrow, and when this ease was combined with increased profits in relation to liabilities it provided an exceptional stimulus for new projects and investments. In view of the politically strong position held by so many entrepreneurs, both the titled and the burghers, this connection came to play a principal role in the formulation of *Riksbank* policy.

At first, however, another circumstance was also operative: the unfortunate war with Russia. The compulsion to finance this war set the note printing presses in motion. By the end of the war there was twice as much paper money in circulation as at the beginning. Reversion to a more restrictive policy after the war was impossible, or in any case not considered to be in the best interests of the national economy. Sweden abandoned the copper standard in 1745 and maintained a pure paper standard up to 1777. During this period the field was left fairly open to continuous inflation, except for an externally inspired but deliberate, even stubborn policy of deflation during the 1760s.

The implementers of this inflationary policy had doubts, not so much about the falling value of money, as about its effects on rates of foreign exchange. They were quite correct in interpreting the rise in these rates, that is the depreciation of Swedish currency, as a consequence not of trends in the domestic monetary system, but of import surpluses and deficits in the balance of payments. What was overlooked, however, was that a surplus of imports could also derive in part from a depreciated currency and may even have operated with a two-pronged effect: that is, exports were hampered at the same time by an inflation of costs. As we had occasion to observe earlier, the stagnation of iron exports was certainly related to these high costs, which moreover had a tendency to rise with increases in production, particularly on account of the important marginal role played by fuel costs. However, these difficulties hardly manifested themselves in the early stages. The efforts made by different exchange offices to keep the currency under control succeeded fairly well during the 1740s, which in effect meant that imports were stimulated even more. In the absence of automatic devaluations of Swedish currency, imports were prevented from soaring in price. On the other hand, the manipulations of the exchange offices probably had little fundamental effect on developments. The primary counter to domestic inflation came from a sharp rise in international prices, which among other things affected Swedish iron prices throughout the 1740s. As soon as prices stopped rising abroad, the efforts of the exchange offices were of no avail. The exchange rate rose from about 30 copper marks per thaler Hamburger banco in 1740 to about 70 copper marks in 1760, and hit a ceiling of 108 only a couple of years later.

Things came to a head with the international commercial crisis of 1763, whose immediate, though not basic, cause was the sudden bankruptcy of de Neufvilles, one of the most eminent banking houses in the Netherlands. The result was a crisis in international trade and payments, with many failures in different financial centres, a general fall in prices, and industrial depression in its wake. Swedish

106

monetary policy proved untenable in this situation. The choice was now between stabilization at the existing level; retained inflation and additional sweeping depreciations of the currency; and a resolutely pursued restabilization of the domestic monetary system, in other words a clear policy of deflation. Just how far the first two of these three alternatives were at all feasible is difficult to say. In any event, on grounds of monetary theory and even more for political reasons, it was decided to adopt the third alternative, even though it took two years before it was put into practice properly.

The crisis precipitated the Hats' downfall in the 1765 Riksdag and put the new Cap party into power. Although views on monetary policy at a more theoretical level hardly followed party lines, there can be no doubt that the alignments were decisively clear-cut in the arena of politics and entrenched interests. It was the importing sector which chiefly informed the Caps' economic policy. Just as the Hat party came to represent the large exporting, ironworking and manu-factory interests, so the other 'industries' had found a vehicle for their opposition in the Cap party. As long as inflationism had been permitted to continue for purposes of foreign exchange control, it had favoured exporters at the expense of importers by raising the prices in Swedish money of the currencies importers had to pay for their purchases. The success achieved by the exchange offices with their manipulations during the 1740s could not prevent the final consequences as the later developments, described above, evidenced.

In adopting a strategy of deflation, the Caps embarked on what they thought was a cautious policy, even though events were to decree otherwise. They envisioned a drop in the exchange rates, paralleled by tighter restrictions on domestic rates, by four points a year so as to achieve the former parity of 36 copper marks to one thaler Hamburger banco within nine years. But the plan was thwarted by two strokes of bad luck: the one should have been anticipated, the other hit unexpectedly. This latter development was that prices on the international market generally, and in Britain particularly, suddenly rose after a long decline, at the same time as Swedish prices were being forced down. This alone was enough to speed up the Swedish deflationary sequence—and the recovery of the exchange rates. What one would have expected was domestic speculation in recovery on the exchange rate and falling prices. Speculation did occur; indeed before the devaluation plan had been made public its broad outlines were well known. It was no doubt accelerated by price movements in Britain. This speculation took two forms. While waiting for further fall in the exchange rate, importers sought to reduce the prices which exporters charged for their bills of exchange; as a result, exportation received less payment in Swedish money. The general public began to hoard bank notes in the expectation of a rise in their value later on, thus sharply reducing their circulation and making it much more difficult to obtain credit. Debtors went into bankruptcy, one after the other: they were supposed to service their debts at values, which, though nominally unchanged, had risen sharply in real terms. At the same time the values of fixed property on current account dropped rapidly, so that prices would often end up below the amounts of mortgages: this meant that debts could not be discharged in full even by sale of property. That a large number of mill owners and merchant houses suffered from this development has already been partly demonstrated. For instance, the Finlay collapse, while admittedly deferred until 1772, can be seen as stemming from the deflation of the previous decade. Deflation also set in motion the changes in ownership of leading exporting firms and ironworks which took place at the end of the 1760s and beginning of the 1770s, though here the outcome also hinged in large measure on the political purges simultaneously launched by the Caps against some of the most prominent Hat merchants. Also hard hit were a large group of landlords in the cities and estate owners in the countryside, which development was reflected in an unusually high rate of title transfers during the years immediately after 1766. This in turn had important social and political consequences, notably the king's refusal in 1768 to carry out his royal duties, which brought the Hats back to power; and 1772, when Gustavus III staged his *coup d'etat*.

On the whole, however, the deflationary crisis turned out to be far briefer and less pervasive than might have been surmised from its rapid, feverish course. For in the midst of misfortune Sweden was blessed, and in two ways. Firstly, three consecutive years of unusually good harvests began in 1767; and secondly, foreign prices recovered, with Britain and her iron prices once again taking the lead. Accordingly, the means were provided for a reasonably smooth switch from the policy of deflation to what for a time could almost be called a new but better-balanced inflationism, for which the Hat party, reinstated in 1768, was responsible. The *Riksbank*'s stubborn refusal to ease the situation by granting credits could now be followed by a decidedly more generous credit policy. The new policy made itself felt in 1769, when the Bank resumed the granting of loans against metals, stopped in 1762; in the Ironmasters' Association's revision of its lending rules in 1769; and in the founding of the Discount Company in 1773.

The Discount Company and its successors exerted an unintentional influence on monetary policy. For gradually the *Riksbank* was divested of much of the control over what had been its primary function, and this led to a new general confusion which was highly reminiscent of the seventeenth century with its double monetary standard.

The special popularity enjoyed by the promissory notes at 3 per cent interest, issued by the discount companies as deposit receipts, in that they could be used as legal tender, has already been noted. At the same time their practice of lending against personal security made it much easier to borrow money from them than from other credit institutions, which demanded substantial securities. One of these companies, the General Discount Office (1787–1803) provided an extra service, the so-called assignments, which were issued on the strength of its assets—that is to say, the credit the company held with the *Riksbank*. Since, however, the assignments were not limited to the actual amount of this credit, it being felt that the credit need cover only the redemptions expected at any one time, assignments for amounts over and above actual cover could be issued. In effect, the General Discount Office had set itself up in business alongside the *Riksbank* as issuer of notes.

A way was thus found to circumvent the *Riksbank* for supplies of, if not formal, then at least practical credit, and this expedient was found very useful by Gustavus III in 1789. This date marks the commencement of a new confused epoch in the history of Swedish money, already so rich in confusions. It would also spoil the attempts at stability which had been made by the monarch's former minister of finance, Johan Liljencrantz, with his coinage devaluation and the adoption of a silver standard in 1777. Both these measures were technically successful but, in terms of economic policy, imposed the same kinds of strains as had the Cap deflation ten years earlier.

What happened in 1789 was that Gustavus III wanted to finance his Russian war without having to ask the *Riksbank* for help, and thereby risk becoming dependent on the Riksdag. Instead he borrowed money on the open market. For the purpose of administering these loans, he prevailed on the Riksdag to set up a special government agency, the National Debt Office, which is still in existence today. The agency was to be managed by commissioners appointed by the parliament, with a status similar to that of the Board of Governors who had been managing the affairs of the *Riksbank* for the past 120 years.

Had the debts contracted by the National Debt Office corresponded

109

to what it actually borrowed on the market, the result would not have been more than an increase in the national debt and as such not very serious. However, the Office, like the Discount Company and General Discount Office before it, became another bank of issue, and to a far greater extent than either of these two. Its treasury notes (*riksgälds*), which bore 3 per cent interest for the first two years, were declared noninterest-bearing in 1791. They were accepted as legal tender and, owing to the fast rate at which they were printed, quickly depreciated in relation to the *Riksbank*'s notes (*banco*). In consequence, the latter, being of safer value, disappeared from circulation. Not only that, the total sum of Bank notes in circulation fell from more than six million riksdaler in 1788 to barely one million in 1802. Inasmuch as the difference between *banco* and *riksgälds* was strictly maintained, so that all payments agreed upon in the former had to be paid with Bank notes, the result was an increasing shortage of 'sound' currency, together with general difficulties of the same nature which bedevilled the seventeenth century system with its awkward calculations in different monies of account. To a very great extent it became the task of the National Debt Office and of the Discount Office established in 1798 to redeem state loans from other countries by borrowing at home. This served to set the printing presses yet more furiously to work. The Discount Office issued assignments at several times the amount of its credits with the National Debt Office. Since these assignments circulated as notes (precisely as noted earlier for corresponding issues from the General Discount Office in relation to its credit balance with the *Riksbank*), the quantity of paper money outstanding shot up even further. At the end of the eighteenth and beginning of the nineteenth century there were at least three times as many assignments in circulation as in 1789; or twice as many if we allow for the depreciation of treasury notes to two-thirds the value of Bank notes. This was the ratio fixed by the currency reform of 1803, when one-and-a-half riksdaler in *riksgäld* was made equivalent to one riksdaler in *banco*. Even though the treasury notes continued to circulate for a long time thereafter, albeit they were supposed to be redeemable in *banco*, the parallel standard of currency went out of operation. The Bank notes had retained their value in silver from the currency reform of 1777, and by virtue of the ratio then established, the treasury notes were tied to the silver standard as denominations in a more uniform monetary system. This uniformity was lasting, though the silver standard itself was not.

The war with Russia in 1808–09 was to alter the Swedish monetary system for a third time. New demands for financing compelled a new changeover to a paper standard, thus spoiling the reforms of 1777 and 1803. The paper standard remained in force until 1834, when a new currency reform was enacted.

III

Behind the change of government after Charles' XII death lay not only the defeat and impoverishment of the Great Northern War. The new distribution of political power also stemmed from changes in economic conditions and in the social structure. These changes continued to make themselves felt throughout the Age of Liberty, and in their turn explain the upheaval which took place in consequence of Gustavus' III *coup d'etat* in 1772.

Sweden was unquestionably ripe for political reform after the Northern War. It would have come in one form or another even if that fatal shot at Fredrikshald had missed or never been fired. The tendencies in this direction had been obvious in the years before the king's death. They were revealed in the apocryphal story attributed to Charles XII himself, who upon returning home from his adventures in Turkey is said to have remarked that Count Arvid Horn had grown a head taller since they last met. The Count's added stature symbolized important social changes: changes induced or reinforced in part by the war, and in part for reasons certainly unrelated to the war. Paradoxically, some of the changes were engendered by the very absolutism which they were to nullify so completely later on.

These changes were far from homogeneous in character; on the contrary, they were quite diverse and contradictory. Indeed, the political transformation they wrought did not at all appear to follow a logical cause-and-effect progression. It would be much truer to say that the changes signified a regression to pre-war days, or even to the period before the Reduction. This applied with particular force to the nobility. In the new constitution, and even more on the strength of unwritten laws, the nobles were again greatly reinforced in their political power. Although their ranks now consisted in large part of other families, the nobles of 1719 regained the authority their ancestors had lost in 1680. In addition, they were clearly bent on recovering their economic and social position. Among other things, they sought to reserve anew for themselves the exclusive rights of manor ownership, rights which had devolved upon many commoners during the Northern War. The nobles also entertained plans to

111

revoke the confiscations of estates carried out earlier under the Reduction. However, a counter-reversion on this scale was bitterly opposed by the commoner estates and the gentry, who had managed to gain an equal position with the high nobles when class distinctions were abolished in the House of Nobility.

The high nobles who gained power under the constitution of 1719 were men of a different stamp than their counterparts during the great-power era. True, the old dynasties, with traditions and wealth dating back to medieval times, remained. Almost without exception, however, they had been edged out of political leadership by new titled families, who owed their eminence to careers in the higher ranks of military service and public administration. Under Charles XII the newcomers had represented the steadily mounting opposition of higher civil service nobility to a system which to a great extent was the prerequisite for their own rise to the highest positions in office and society. If anything this dependence aggravated their opposition and emboldened them in their demands for power as pre-emptive by right of birth. Certainly some of the newcomers were men of wealth, having married into the old families, or aggrandized their fortunes by inheritances from commoner relatives. Yet in no instance could their wealth really be compared with that of the seventeenth century landowners—and this made them all the more dependent on office and political power in order to assert themselves in society. For people who do not own much privately, the ownership of the state is of special importance.

The new nobles reacted not only against royal power, but also against the other Estates, and not least against their fellow brothers in the same Estate: the gentry and the more recently ennobled members of the officer and civil service corps. Whatever portion of the economic wealth of the nobility had been left untouched by the Reduction, had been ravaged by the Northern War. No other group had suffered so much from the strains and casualties which the war inflicted. Most of the officers recruited for campaign duty came from the nobility. Many families had lost all their sons and their lines were thus doomed to extinction. In the absence of fathers and sons many families had seen their estates decay and their fortunes ruined. For lack of eligible suitors, many titled women had married commoners. Titled estates and manors thus passed into other hands. Commoners had become the incumbents of high civil and military office to a degree unprecedented in Swedish history. Moved by his own conception of the public weal, Charles XII had filled vacancies without the slightest regard for birth: as he put it, an appointee had merely to

112

be a 'good fellow' in order to qualify. In consequence, the composition of the ruling establishment had been greatly altered. In contrast to his father, moreover, Charles XII was not inclined automatically to ennoble new holders of more distinguished offices. Partial amends for this neglect (in the eyes of the rank-ordered society) were made during the initial years of the Age of Liberty, when the new wielders of power conferred noble titles on a large scale. They were undoubtedly prompted to do so for two reasons: to win support from the gentry, on whom the House of Nobility reform had conferred greater power; and to offset the discrepancy between social position and civil service rank which had arisen from the increased number of untitled officers and civil servants.

The infusion of new blood in the aristocratic ranks was nothing new as such, even though it was of special importance in the year following the end of the war. Charles XII had actually granted ennoblements and promoted existing nobles to higher rank. Charles XI had been even more generous, showing no little partiality for the officials who had most zealously enforced his Reduction. At one and the same time, he had thus politically diluted the old nobility, fixed the social ranking of all nobility, and in the process decimated its political power and its economic positions. Earlier during the great-power era, too, ennoblement had also been a frequent reward. Some of the eminent privy councillors at that time, such as Johan Skytte (1577–1645) and Schering Rosenhane (1609–1713), were 'upstarts'. For that matter, not a few of the nobles had themselves promoted such advancements: by taking a talented youth under their wing and generously sponsoring his career, they inevitably paved the way for his advance, thereby adding life-giving new blood to the old dynasties.

The fact that political, social and economic advancement led to titled rank in an increased number of cases shows how deeply rooted the pattern of social stratification actually was. As the Age of Liberty opened, Sweden was further away than ever from any tendency towards egalitarianism. Indeed, the new rulers emphasized the distinctions of rank even more with their wholesale ennoblements. They formally declared that appointments to low-ranking offices would be made on the basis of merit and proficiency alone. But that was no more than lip service: measures could be and were taken in practice to prevent commoners in the lower grades from climbing too high in the administrative hierarchy. As for the highest offices, they were reserved exclusively for the nobility.

The end of the war made such manipulations even easier. A large part of the war machine could be put in mothballs, and a great many officers had to be relieved from active duty. A formal application of the seniority rule—whereby the names of officers with the fewest years of service were struck off first from the active roster—thereby eliminated the greater number of commoner officers. The nobles, who had usually become officers more quickly, held longer seniorities. Merit and proficiency were similarly interpreted in the civil service. The nobles, having usually started their studies earlier and formed their connections in younger years, could always be placed ahead of commoners at promotion time.

In addition, what might be called the purely social rules were tightened with a revival of the former prohibition against marriages beneath one's station. Once the nobles had absorbed the most recent additions to their numbers, they were supposed to keep their ranks closed. This attitude is also evidenced in their enjoinder upon the monarch to exercise economy in the induction of new members into the nobility, and also later, in 1762, when the House of Nobility refused to accept new members. These moves deprived the newly ennobled of their political rights and jeopardized their other privileges.

Thus both the aim and the reality of parliamentarism in the Age of Liberty was reflected not in democratic government, but rather in the rule of aristocracy: and this aim was largely shared by the parties in power, whether Hats or Caps.

In the pursuit of this aim, however, the parties came to build their positions on shifting sands. The economic and social conditions scarcely harmonized with the political distribution of power which Sweden's leaders sought to achieve. Sooner or later, therefore, this distribution could not be wholly maintained. A number of compromises proved necessary and, as the Age of Liberty drew to a close, the trend away from the original power grouping acquired such momentum that it was anything but surprising that the whole system should eventually topple. Even so, a few words are in order to explain just why the system toppled as it did and just why it was succeeded by the type of monarchy which Gustavus III represented.

The first compromise came as early as 1723, when the commoners forced through two major curtailments of aristocratic privilege: first, that already mentioned rule for promotions based on merit and proficiency, with exceptions made for the highest offices only; and second, the vesting of commoners with rights to purchase scattered freeholdings and to retain title to those lands which the nobility had already lost. In these sectors, at any rate, there could be no question of a successful reactionary policy. On the other hand, the compromise did no more than establish the *status quo*. The commoners

114

did not gain any new rights at the expense of the nobility. Not only that, even some of the old rights they retained were mere formalities; they looked good on paper, but could not be fully implemented in practice.

The course of events throughout the Age of Liberty was marked by a number of divergent tendencies in the social and political spheres. On the one hand, the nobility entrenched their privileges and political advantages. On the other, great changes were generating new aspirations, especially within the ranks of the burghers. Further to this latter point, we must note the emergence of important groups who did not belong to any of the Estates, and were therefore excluded from the political rights which parliamentary representation entailed. These groups comprised some of those whose social position was usually identified by the term 'untitled gentlefolk'. They existed, they grew in numbers and influence, they had to be accepted; but as people 'beyond the pale', they could be classified as neither fish nor fowl. With a growing awareness of their worth and power, and a cumulative resentment that they should nevertheless be shut out from the machinery of government, they represented potential dynamite: they were the harbingers of a social revolution that might also readily enlist political revolutionaries in its cause. To some extent these groups also included men of title, who had either been refused induction into the House of Nobility, or who had come so far down on the family ranking list for the exercise of representative functions that membership seemed hardly worthwhile. These nobles were the 'Jacobins' of their class: they figured prominently in the opposition built up around Adolphus Frederick and Lovisa Ulrika; played a role in the coup engineered by Gustavus III; recruited insurgents at Anjala in 1788; joined the conspirators who assassinated Gustavus III at the opera-house masquerade in 1792; were among the young hotheads who renounced their titles at the Riksdag of 1800 in Norrköping; and in alliance with other powerful groups, spearheaded Sweden's last political revolution in 1809.

The most important social changes within the bourgeoisie, considered as an Estate, were scarcely calculated to foment a revolutionary frame of mind. None the less, they were evidence that revolutionary material was accumulating. In the previous section we dealt with the economic foundations of these changes: the advent of a group of great merchants, shippers, manufacturers and ironmasters, who were far above their peers in wealth and power. Taken as a group, they controlled substantial portions of the country's economic power. Though the group included some nobles, it formed what might be called a 'higher' bourgeoisie. It was a perplexing situation, aggravated by the fact that many of them, in particular those who were ironworks owners only, had no political rights, being untitled gentlefolk. This group came to play a special role in politics because of the great importance attached to trade and industrial policy in eighteenth century government. A kind of double function asserted itself. The support of leading merchants and industrialists was needed in order to realize economic and political policy; and precisely because their support was needed, these men were in a very strong position to formulate this policy and to dictate its conditions. The upshot was a policy favouring these groups' interests alongside and in alliance with the aims of the nobles. In the process, however, the same groups became competitors of the ruling nobility for power, influence and political-social position. Socially, they were at first regarded with contempt as upstarts. There was, however, no overlooking their possession of money, and many distinguished families saw no other way of rescuing their estates and acquiring new capital than by marriage ties with the 'Skeppsbro nobility', as the newcomers were called in Stockholm and Göteborg (in reference to the merchant houses strung out along the waterfront), and the 'mill nobility' the name given to them in the ironmaking districts of Närke, Västmanland and Värmland.

Another characteristic feature of the period, a huge bureaucracy, also played its part. No matter how jealously the nobles guarded their right to higher office, and no matter how hard they tried to usurp the lower posts as well, they were forced to let more and more commoners come in. The sparseness of new ennoblements was an indication of their dilemma. It was no longer possible, as during the first years of the Age of Liberty, to incorporate the higher ranks of officeholders in the Establishment by ennobling them. Thus social and political dynamite was planted in the corridors of Sweden's civil service.

At the same time new ideas of social organization had gained ground. The importance of the universities increased with the demands for higher academic standards in the civil service. A number of writers became engaged in social criticism. The ideas of the Enlightenment reached Sweden around the early 1730s. Its ideas signified not only an appeal to reason—and what reason could be cited to justify the ranking of birth above competence? The Enlightenment also spoke of equality, favoured the abolition of privileges and hierarchical classifications, stressed the equal rights and worth of all men—indeed, these ideas could even be misinterpreted to mean that all men in fact were equal. It also intellectualized the position of important strata of society who stood outside the inner sanctum of political power. This was a far cry from the days of Carolean absolutism, when intellectual pursuits largely were conspicuous by their absence, or from the earlier part of the great-power era when such pursuits were limited to an elite, as typified by names like Erik Sparre, Hogenskild Bielke, Johan Skytte, Axel Oxenstierna and Magnus Gabriel De la Gardie; in that time, moreover, these men stood at the vanguard not only of politics, but also of social thought, the formulation of constitutional theory, and contemporary political ideology. The political leaders of the Age of Liberty certainly included men of scholarship and intellectual training. However, the most important and highest level of debate was sustained not by them, but by new groups: the scientists and writers. The newcomers did not try to defend and ideologically justify the existing order, as leading social thinkers had done during the great-power era. They rattled its chains and tore at them, trying to burst through. Nothing was so sacred that it could not be scourged and questioned.

In the midst of all these changes, the constitutional machinery ground on. But it too, was exposed to a slow but sure transformation, which followed, but still corresponded fairly well with, the tendencies towards the dissolution of the various enactments dating from the 1720s. The decisive turn came with Horn's resignation in 1738, his Cap ministers' loss of office (although they were not formally dismissed), and the formation of a first Hat ministry in 1739. The conduct of executive government was based on the privy-council concept, that is, the monarch was to govern in accordance with the advice of his councillors; the king commanded two votes in Council deliberations. The Council was supposed to be appointed by the king upon the recommendation of a special Riksdag committee consisting of representatives from the three highest Estates: nobles, clergy and burghers.

The Council was responsible to the Riksdag, which examined the minutes of its meetings and could dismiss any councillor on the ground that he had not followed its ordained policy. This prerogative was exercised with the wholesale dismissal of Horn's ministry in 1739. In due course the Age of Liberty evolved from Council-conducted government under an aristocracy, which it was in substance under Horn, to a parliamentary system, where the Council in effect became an executive arm of the Riksdag, acting between its sessions—and specifically a branch of its powerful secret committee, which consisted of 50 nobles, 25 clergymen and 25 burghers.

117

Throughout this period the peasants remained formally excluded, though from time to time they were in practice allowed a real role in the committee's deliberations. Actually, the secret committee developed into a kind of super-government, which often had the decisive voice in all matters alongside the Council, though its more important business had to do with foreign policy, government finances and the administration of justice. To a large extent, too, the appointments of civil servants came to be handled by this committee.

The distribution of power within the Riksdag can be partly gauged from the numbers in the different Estates. About 300 nobles, representing approximately 1,000 families, usually attended the Riksdag sessions. The clergy numbered 75, including all the bishops, with the archbishop presiding *ex-officio*. Some 100 members represented the burghers. The peasantry (or rather the freeholders and crown tenants only) numbered around 150 who were usually selected by district on the basis of indirect elections. Obviously, the nobles enjoyed disproportionate influence through sheer numbers; if needed they could mobilize close to 1,000 members. Moreover, by virtue of their control of high administrative offices, the nobles could lay special claims to representing the Establishment. However, the privy councillors were not permitted to take part in the House of Nobility decisions: hence the 'deference' shown by the Hats in 1739 when they refrained from formally dismissing the opposition.

The change of parties in 1738–39, while it entrenched parliamentary rule and allied Hat nobles and leading merchants, produced another unintended result. The composition of the opposition to the new regime changed too. It came to consist less of the newly ousted, who of course represented the Council aristocracy and the upper ranks of nobility, and more of various disappointed groups within the lower Estates. The Caps, when they finally managed to recover from their fall, took on a more radical, almost revolutionary tinge: to their banner had flocked malcontents from all the four Estates, especially from the burghers and clergy.

Although it would be a rash generalization to say that the two parties had divided along 'class' lines, a flavour of class conflict was certainly added to the elections for burgher seats in the Riksdag of 1765, when the Caps returned to power and promptly launched the policy of deflation described in the previous section. In his thesis *Hattar och mössor i borgarståndet 1760–1766* (Hats and Caps in the Burgher Estate (1760–1766), Per Erik Brolin has clarified the social and economic backgrounds of both parties. His findings provide clear evidence for the differences hinted at above concerning social stratification, interest groupings, the general attitude to trade and industrial policy, and the degree of political radicalism in response to the Enlightenment. Other structural differences were also apparent. By the mid-1760s, the Caps had grown into a national party, which employed propaganda and agitation to influence the election of Riksdag members, especially to the Estate of Burghers, and could thus act in organized form not only in the Riksdag but also out in the field. This process of democratization undoubtedly affected the party in two other ways. The opportunities for corruption, once so great, now evaporated: a politician could no longer be bought as readily for a new opinion when he was dependent on a constituency, and was elected with reference to a programme or platform, as when he obtained his seat automatically by right of birth, office or other social position. Party-political emotions reached a higher pitch. This may have been because those minded to agitate tended to let their zeal get the better of them; or it may have been that men who took to the hustings were moved by a holier wrath when they felt their interests to be betrayed by the incompetence and selfishness of earlier officeholders. The anti-Hat agitation whipped up by the opposition among the clergy certainly seems to have contributed to the bitterly moralizing tone which infused debate, and to the later prosecution of the ousted Hat leaders within the burgher Estate.

Be that as it may, the differences in social stratification were clear enough. The large exporters and the very largest import houses—often one and the same—were Hats. The great majority of small-scale importers, and indeed small tradesmen generally, were Caps. They were suffering from the inflation and the way it was exploited by the greats. They were disfavoured or overlooked in the official regulations of trade and industry. They were socially underprivileged. As elections to the burgher Estate were made more democratic, allowing franchised merchants and craftsmen more seats at the expense of the magistrates, these underprivileged groups increased their representation—and gave the Caps their chance. The crisis of 1763 inflamed passions even more, and in 1765 the time was ripe for another change at the helm.

It has been argued that the Caps, once restored to power, rapidly dropped their radicalism. If it be granted that their deflation policy was a radical measure, they allegedly turned their backs on con-stitutional reforms, the quest for social equality, and what might be termed 'economic liberalism'. This interpretation, which is the most common, is so oversimplified as to be erroneous, however. Naturally, the practical problems thrust upon the Caps in the midst of severe economic crisis were bound to deter any implementation of a more radical economic programme; but it is not equally obvious that the Caps lost interest in such a programme. Had Adolphus Frederick never staged his royal 'strike' in 1768, it is possible that the Cap ministry would have made serious practical politics of its liberalization plans.

In any event, the Caps had a consistent grasp of where, essentially, they were headed, even though they changed their minds in important respects, as in their attitude to the monarchy. In the first place, they were 'anti-Establishment' in the sense that they wanted to curtail the powers of civil servants. They also sought to enlarge the scope of local government and generally to have a larger number of administrative posts filled by elected officials rather than crown appointees. In the second place, the Caps wanted to curtail Council power in favour of parliamentary power, and within the Riksdag they preferred to have plenary assemblies handle more of the decision-making process than the secret committee. Thirdly, they aimed at wider latitude for the 'natural industries' which meant depriving the manufactories of all or part of their government protection, as well as the removal of other controls, such as staple rights, the Bothnian trade compulsion, and the Commodity Act of 1724. Fourthly, the Caps strongly opposed inflation, which they interpreted with reference to the quantity theory of money; this led to demands for restrictions in state expenditures and a lessening of the almost uncontrolled inflation of the paper money printed to finance these expenditures. Fifthly, impelled by views that could almost be said to reflect Rousseau-ist doctrine of the general will as the basis of government, the Caps wanted to liberalize elections to the Riksdag and make this body more directly accountable to the people. For this purpose they recommended the virtually unfettered freedom of the press and, somewhat more hesitantly, the enforcement of binding election mandates in the Riksdag.

The Cap ideology—for it was that in a very real sense—was articulated by a number of writers in the best spirit of Enlightenment. Many arguments advanced in the economic sphere were inspired by the Physiocrats. The most eminent of these writers, Anders Bachmanson Nordencrantz (1697–1772) and Anders Chydenius (1729–1803), deserve note for the light they shed on the radically new world of ideas which the Caps represented in the 1760s, not so much because they were outstanding economic theorists—there are more distinguished names—but because of their influence on contemporary political thinking.

Nordencrantz had an unusually broad range of experience and ability to draw on. In his youth he had worked several years as a merchant in England. He entered the Riksdag in 1726 and served thereafter for a time as consul in Lisbon. By the time he became a director of the Board of Trade in 1743, he had spent several years as ironmaster in Roslagen and Finland. It would appear that his philosophy was greatly influenced by a heavy financial loss he suffered from a property transaction. His loss was aggravated as inflation had drastically reduced the real value of the assets created by the sale, and with every year that passed he nourished increasingly bitter suspicions that the real villain of this drama was the merchant house of Jennings & Finlay. Whatever the significance of his first-hand contact with the debit side of inflationism, his writings clearly shifted during the 1750s from 'mercantilism' to outspoken 'anti-mercantilism' and to a criticism of the Hat policy towards trade and industry. In due course Nordencrantz adopted a decidedly 'liberal' philosophy. Economics was far from being his only concern, however. Social institutions and public affairs in general interested him too. He was well-read in Enlightenment philosophy, frequently quoting its leading exponents such as Montesquieu, Rousseau, Hume, Locke, Helvetius, Voltaire and the elder Mirabeau. He was a convinced believer in the supremacy of reason: that it was by relying on his ability to reason that Man could progress. Nordencrantz was not hostile to religion; on the contrary he frequently marshalled support for his arguments from the Bible; but he advocated religious freedom and on the whole sided with the deist wing of the Enlightenment.

In constitutional law theory, Nordencrantz pleaded formally for the distribution of sovereign powers as advocated by Montesquieu, but the practical shape he gave this doctrine made it look distinctly more like Rousseau's. All power belonged to the people. Civil servants should be elected, and as long as they held office should not be allowed to sit in the Riksdag. Freedom of the press ought to be complete: that was the ultimate guarantee of the liberty and power of the general will. Privileges should be abolished; to retain them would be to betray the general public, just as it was a betrayal to let civil servants enjoy lifetime tenure. For the same reason strong economic interest groups, such as the exporters, should not be allowed to have parliamentary representation.

Given these theories, 'liberalism' in the economic sphere followed with almost logical necessity, just as Adam Smith was later impelled by his dislike of privileges, guild interests and private exploitation of government, to demand free competition and to imagine the guidance of an unseen hand. In his demands for economic freedom it was natural for Nordencrantz to begin with the role played by the bureaucracy. The civil servants, he observed, held the real power in a mercantilist society: they determined who should produce, what they should produce, how they should sell, and who was going to be rich or poor. As he saw it, the most glaring example of their rule was the favouritism shown to manufactories and the neglect of agriculture. A free trade and industrial policy would wrest control from the hands of a few and even out economic differences; a 'liberal' economic policy was understood by Nordencrantz in terms which would characterize the classical liberalism as more 'democratic' than the policy of controls under mercantilism.

Nor was the liberal conviction lacking that a free economy would yield a better total result. Anders Chydenius expressed this idea eleven years before Adam Smith in the following words: 'Every individual voluntarily seeks out the place and trade where he best increases the national profit.' The principal targets of his ire were the Commodity Act and the Bothnian trade compulsion. As regards the latter, anyone disposed to speculate on the influence of environment over ideas can look for evidence in Chydenius' occupation. He started out as chaplain in a tiny parish in Ostrobothnia and later became a rural dean in Gamla Karleby. In contrast to Nordencrantz who often vacillated, Chydenius never altered opinions once formulated. He was also more radical, allowing no scope for doubts and compromises. No modifications of the regulations he attacked would do: everything had to be swept away. This radical approach was paired with strong social pathos. He focussed always on the circumstances of the broad masses and the improvement of their lot. In his descriptions of the harsh and unfair conditions under which the poor lived and worked in consequence of prerogatives, trade regulations, and labour legislation, he could sometimes employ turns of phrase which for indignation and brilliance are not eclipsed by the Communist Manifesto published eighty years later. Thus: 'To toil for others' gain as long as he bears up, to be thrown into wretchedness in old age and die in beggary, such are the laurels which are to inspire the working man to love his country.'

Chydenius was far from alone in his liberalism, but he was the most radical. In his social pathos, his sympathy for 'the toiling masses' in their distress, and in his demands for justice, equality and emancipation, he was not only a radical, but indeed a unique figure in the Sweden of his time. Owing to the wide distribution of his writings and the position conferred by his performances in the

122

Riksdags of 1765, 1772 and 1789, he came to exercise a tremendous influence on patterns of thought—an influence which later appears to have been underestimated. Actually much of the liberalization that was to follow in a more humane and tolerant spirit under Gustavus' III 'enlightened despotism', and later under Oscar I, could be traced to Chydenius; although many other sources, often foreign (particularly in the time of Gustavus III), served as inspiration. In any event Chydenius demonstrated that new ways of thinking about man and society could make headway in a country where aristocracy, rank and special privilege were so firmly entrenched.

The Cap regime of the 1760s was brief, and a failure in many important respects. The radicalism which imbued the Caps upon entering office was eventually narrowly restricted. They fought against the interest groups identified with the earlier regime; but they lacked the political vision or could not command enough support to begin tearing down the very foundations of a rank-ordered society, and the 'outsiders' were granted no new political rights. Existing tensions were thus aggravated and disaffection stronger than before. As so often happens the political result was upheaval, a revolution supported by diverse, incongruous, conflicting interests which, given the situation, were able to unite around a common idea. It was not a revolution for the implementation of some new theory upon which all were agreed; the rallying point was a feeling that the existing state of affairs was out of date—plus a common fear that if all disaffected groups did not stand together, one of them might gain at the expense of the rest. Thus was built, on the most feeble of foundations, a new epoch of transformation and rebirth—infused, in the midst of strife, with the charm and enchantment that a dark background could bestow on one of the most bewildering and brilliant personages in Swedish history. In the minds of most, Gustavus III was rescuing them *from* something which threatened them.

And virtually all groups felt themselves threatened—or frustrated in hopes once ardently held. The nobles and civil servants feared the radical turn that the Riksdag was taking with its attacks on rank and privilege. Were not events drifting towards a new Cap régime, perhaps one more permanent and radical? The Hat councillors deposed in the spring of 1772 were, together with their supporters, driven to seek help from the newly enthroned monarch. The Caps, freshly returned to power, feared Hat countermoves, doubting their ability to cope with the social and political pressures they themselves had generated. Would they be able to control the situation? As many saw it, the only way out of a perilous situation was royal support. The commoners and the untitled gentlefolk feared that the nobility and bureaucracy would regain dominance, or failing that, that the Caps would never dare to carry out the reforms they desired. Many, both within the parties and without, regarded the politicians and their feuds in particular, with a weariness verging on contempt. Had not the time come for unity and concerted action? Who then, could provide this if not the twenty-five-year-old Gustavus, who at least constitutionally stood above and beyond party?

In addition to these sentiments, all calculated to urge the king towards revolution, there was a general unrest in the country at large in the wake of crop failures and famine. Now and then, perhaps, desperation instils courage. More often it begets demands for something new, an acceptance of virtually any kind of change.

The international situation was also favourable. France eagerly encouraged a *coup d'etat*, offering diplomatic support and large subsidies for the purpose. Russia was preoccupied with the war against Turkey and the partition of Poland, in which Prussia also was involved. Denmark was not prepared to undertake any action alone. In other words, the guarantors of the earlier constitution remained passive. Besides, everything happened too fast for any outside intervention to be effective. A few arrests, Gustavus' ride through the jubilant streets of Stockholm on August 19, 1772, his speech before the Estates, the confirmation of the revolution two days later—and that was it. The king had presented his subjects with a *fai accompli*, and theirs was only to accept. Few mourned the Age of Liberty which had so suddenly been relegated to the annals of history.

It was an elegantly engineered coup: not a single drop of blood was spilled. However, the adoption of a new constitution did not —and could not—dispel the complex of social and political problems that had been basically instrumental in ending the Age of Liberty. The same problems were to haunt Gustavus III in his twenty-year reign, and were the deepest political reasons for the bullet at the opera masquerade on March 16, 1792, which led to his death.

It is beyond the scope of this book to unfold the whole drama from the shouts of jubilation in August 1772 until the final act at the masquerade ball twenty years later. We will confine our account to the broad outlines of the social and political struggle for power. As far as this struggle was concerned, the transition from parliamentary rule to royal absolutism did not represent any watershed. Gustavus had buttressed his revolution largely with support from the nobility. He could not, however, reward the nobles with enlarged or at least preserved privileges, though in principle, he favoured the nobility, and described himself as the realm's foremost nobleman. He could not because the coup, or rather the discontent which made it possible, had also been sustained by commoner demands for the abolition of existing privileges. The initial solution was simply to let the whole question of privileges rest where it was. This expedient was feasible because there were so many other reforms to consider. Although some of these caused anxiety, they could on the whole be carried out to the general satisfaction: improved control over the civil service; ratification of the 1776 Freedom of the Press Act; a more humane Penal Code, which among other things abolished torture in prison; and the currency reform of 1777. However, the Riksdag of 1786 proved that the old antagonisms persisted: arrayed on opposite sides were the nobles, unhappy because their privileges were not improved, and the commoners, unhappy because the same privileges were not curtailed or abolished altogether. Many of the burghers felt apprehensive over the relaxation of regulations for trade and industry, while the clergy did not take kindly to the introduction of religious freedom. A release from frustrations came with the war against Russia from 1788 to 1790. Gustavus III started it to divert attention from domestic discontents, hoping that victory would restore him to popular favour. But the course of the war upset all his plans, and disatisfaction at home grew. The King was saved in the eleventh hour, by the rebellion of a group of officers, the so-called Anjala League, and a declaration of war by Denmark. Mustering all the skills of propaganda, Gustavus exploited both events to rally the majority of his people around him; patriotism, anti-nobility, and hatred of traitors were the emotional strings he played on. In 1789 he summoned the Riksdag. In the face of a compactly hostile nobility, the commoners and the King entered into the so-called Act of Union and Security: the king retained sole authority in matters of war and peace (the essence of absolute rule), while the Riksdag retained its role as a legislative body, which meant that it held the power of the purse. The price, if indeed Gustavus III considered it a price any longer, was the reduction of noble privileges. Commoners were given the right to hold more public offices and to own titled land, that is land enjoying exemption from crown imposts. Conversions of leaseholds to freeholds were again permitted; they had been banned since 1773. Restrictions on the rights of peasants to hunt and fish, and to have their own servants were abolished.

A great step had been taken towards a definite weakening of noble power, especially since the king's right to appoint his own civil

officials equipped him with a sharp weapon against the nobles. Once
again a conflict between the titled and untitled ended with an increase in the royal power. But the trend towards the early dissolution
of the stratified society that might have resulted was checked by an
assassin's bullet three years later. That event froze the status quo of
1789. For fear of the nobles, no further attempt was made towards
the equalization of the Estates. The nobles on the other hand, fearing
the violent reaction against the King's murder, did not venture to
alter the constitution which otherwise might have been tempting
with a minor on the throne. A sort of armistice was concluded, followed by nearly two decades of stagnation and conservatism. The
fears inspired by the French revolution first among the nobility, and
later the whole 'Establishment', reinforced that rigid conservatism.

In the meantime, the stratified society continued to decay, as the
economic foundation for its existence increasingly weakened. One
was not only confronted with the end of a changing economic and
social structure that had been in progress for almost two hundred
years, but also with changes that were even more far-reaching and
rapid. Because of these changes, the new political order, however
well it may have reflected the transformation that had taken place,
corresponded poorly with what lay ahead. Thus a new process of
adjustment, extending far into the twentieth century, became more
difficult and painful than it need have been. It was as if political
development were doomed to lag behind the economic and social,
and to act more as a hindrance than a help.

IV

The social antagonisms and conflicts of eighteenth-century Sweden
were no doubt much more pronounced than those of the great-power
era, but that was not because class differences were more sharply
drawn. It was merely that they could make themselves politically
visible by means which had never existed before. At the same time,
the differences were rendered more complex by the emergence of new
social groups. If we restrict ourselves to the extremes, the class
differences were less marked during the Age of Liberty and the Gustavian period than they had been in the past. The difference between
high and low, between the top of the upper class and the bottom of
the lowest was still glaring—but less glaring than before. The
Reduction and the Great Northern War had destroyed the princely
fortunes of the landowning nobility. The great mass of peasants had

at the same time won greater security, at least in legal terms, which during the first decades after the war was combined with improved material standards. The great increase in population later made the situation more complicated. A gap widened between the 'ordinary' poor and the very poor; the latter, a new landless proletariat, multiplied rapidly. This development was paralleled by growing differences within the 'middle class'—a term which first came into use during the Age of Liberty. The wholesale merchant and manufacturer had nothing in common socially and materially with their 'Estate brothers', the craftman and retailer; nor, for that matter, with the magistrates, who had exercised political influence for so long by virtue of their overrepresentation.

Life was still insecure, but its character had changed since the great-power era. The threat to peasant freedom was definitely averted; but the rapid population growth and the mounting numbers of landless paupers brought new insecurities. In lean years, this social situation wrought considerable hardships on the great mass of people who were forced to work for others, or whose holdings were too small to permit the storage of surpluses from good years—and the eighteenth century certainly had its share of crop failures, which were visited upon the country with the same frequency as the contemporary financial crises. Thus it is no exaggeration to describe 1757–58, 1771–72, 1787–88 and 1799–1800 as years of famine bringing in their train illnesses, epidemics and general enfeeblement, all of which marginally affected the death rate.

Births, bad harvests, disease, severe winters, high mortality. There is no need to invoke the Malthusian doctrine of a population continually held in check by the available food supply (if that were true, Sweden's population would not have continued to increase as fast as it did), to verify their interrelationship. They influenced not only the material conditions of existence, but indeed the whole rhythm and view of life. The propertied and educated sections of the community were emancipating themselves from orthodox doctrines; this freer spirit was manifest, for example, in the abolition of witch trials and in measures undertaken by Gustavus III to outlaw torture and to make prison discipline more humane. Nevertheless, for all the rational enlightenment of the time, there was still plenty of room for the occult and superstition was widespread. Very little is known of the beliefs adhered to among the great mass of peasantry: they left no body of literature behind to tell us. However, there is a great deal of evidence to indicate that the clergy retained their hold on the masses. We can, for instance, find out what the clergy stood for from its

127

resistance to the Gustavian legislation on freedom of worship. For the peasant, nearness to priest and church was an accepted fact of everyday life: there were many children to be baptized, the many dead had to be given a consecrated burial, and the deity was interminably beseeched to bring good weather and crops, and to prevent epidemics. One infant in five never lived to see its first birthday. Averaging out the vital statistics from 1750 to 1780, every woman between the ages of 15 and 40 gave birth during this period to ten children. The actual ratio may even be higher if account is taken of the never-discovered infanticides, especially in the cities to which 'unfortunate' women fled in their desperation. There was surely a high incidence of spontaneous abortions; the number of miscarriages imposed a greater strain on women than the birth rates themselves disclose.

Given these conditions, it is not difficult to imagine the degree of fatalism they must have engendered. Social and political unrest must often have proved an incitement to passion. None the less, the logical reaction for those at the bottom must have been one of profound resignation, preoccupation with the 'ultimate values', which offered excellent soil for the fire-and-brimstone exhortations and revivals in the religious field. It would be audacious to assume that the ideas of the Enlightenment penetrated to great depths in the population at large. Perhaps some of the new social and political theories did get across; if so, they would have been favourably received by the leading creators of public opinion in the peasant community. However, these theories influenced the general outlook on life of only a limited few within the higher and better educated circles. The 'grey masses' remained for a long time in the old faith; or to the extent they became nonconformists, their new religion was often an even more exacting taskmaster.

Life had always been hard and cruel for the landless labourers who were bonded in service to the poorer peasants, craftsmen and merchants. It cannot be argued that their lot was especially bad during the eighteenth century; whatever differences there may have been by comparison with earlier periods, they do not lend themselves to meaningful measurement. On the other hand, it can be asserted that the whole problem was entirely different in scope. According to the classifications then used in the population statistics, the numbers of able-bodied men among the crofters, cottars and paupers increased from 47,000 in 1751 to 104,000 in 1810. If we add to our calculations their relatives, whose numbers increased considerably owing to the high proportion of births to deaths, the lowest agricultural classes multiplied approximately threefold during these sixty years. Even more important, presumably, was that many of the peasants, in consequence of land subdivision and the cultivation of inferior soils, came to merge with the ranks of the really destitute.

During the first decades of the Age of Liberty, the situation was unwittingly worsened by the legislators, who prohibited the formation of crofts and cotes, which in the past had at least made it possible to realize the modest dream of a 'cabbage patch' of one's own. It is impossible to say how important this legislation was in practice. All the same, it emphasized that the politically franchised were the sole arbiters of public interest. While the enfranchised classes held different privileges and widely varying degrees of political influence, they could unite if the issue concerned was thought to promote their common interests, or if special interests could be furthered for one Estate, without infringing on the rights of others. Thus the availability of servants was something on which all four Estates could agree, and the legislation they enacted against crofts and cotes, together with the statutes defining the duties of servants, were all meant to uphold the lord-and-master interest. However, when the peasants were restricted in their right to employ servants—a limitation that applied until Gustavus III's Act of Union and Security in 1789—the Estates parted company, and the wishes of the higher classes, especially the nobility, prevailed.

By the master-and-servant laws of 1723 and 1739 the rights of peasants in this respect were even more sharply circumscribed, in that their able-bodied children at home were included in the number of labourers they were permitted to hire. Over and above the maximum number of employees, including stay-at-home children, the peasant was allowed to have only one son and one daughter in his household.

In other respects, the master-and-servant rules which had evolved in the sixteenth and seventeenth centuries still applied, though in more specific and in far more stringent form. The legislation sought to create a combination of compulsory labour, compulsory military service, poor relief and control over changes in domicile. There was no place in this scheme for idlers. Every rural inhabitant who was not a man of substance had to have a source of livelihood, whether he worked for himself or others. Able-bodied persons who did not take employment within the prescribed period were to be put into a workhouse and earn their living there. The disabled were to be supported by their next of kin or be put in hospital. Children not provided for were to be taken to

E   129

orphanages which in those days were less 'homes' than they were workhouses. Masters were entitled to administer corporal punishment to enforce discipline. Punishment for gross offences, however, came under the jurisdiction of courts. Although this provision nominally assured servants of fair treatment under the law, its operation in practice was more dubious. The courts were usually staffed with judges who tended to side with the master, and the punishments they meted out were severe.

The great-power era had its special safety valve in its need for military troops. Vagrants were promptly turned into soldiers. It is not unlikely that many of the conscripts welcomed the chance to get away from a harsh master or from involuntary unemployment (which was often regarded as self-inflicted by contemporaries). This solution, however, was generally impossible during the Age of Liberty with its fast growing population.

The system began to crack at an early stage too, which made certain legislative reforms inevitable. During the 1740s, the restrictive rules on the formation of crofts and cotes and on land subdivision were relaxed. Instead, these activities began to be deliberately fostered, for example by the granting of tax exemptions for clearings in village forest-land owned in common and for cultivation of fenlands. The peasants were allowed to keep as many able-bodied sons and daughters at home as they liked over and above the fixed number of servants.

If these reforms could be said to vitiate untenable legislation. they did not and could not have solved the core of the problem: the rapid increase of more or less proletarian agricultural classes. The boundary line between them and the lowest rung of the propertied, i.e. those peasants who worked small, niggardly holdings, was also blurred. For the latter group, and indeed for the poorer peasants in general, there was the heavy burden of having to maintain adult children at home, and with new land scarce, they too were pushed towards pauperism. The dream of a 'great' nation, so strongly cherished by politicians of the Age of Liberty, could here find curious expression; for example, marriage was set up as a condition for the parcelling of a homestead, or for getting a croft or cote. As to the real effect that condition had on the incidence of marriages, and hence the birth rate, we can only guess. In so far as it acted as an incentive, this policy helped to worsen the situation. In any event, we are given further proof of how optimistically the policy-makers viewed the population trend, unaware that it was in process of exploding the whole social framework. It is possible to generalize about the

130

contrasts between seventeenth- and eighteenth-century Sweden by say
ing that, for politicians of the great-power era, national glory meant
conquests and military power; whereas to politicians of the Age of
Liberty greatness lay in a growing population which would make the
country 'rich in industries'. There is no cause to feel surprise over
this vision, even less to moralize on it. Whatever its substance, we
are struck by the yawning disparity between the actual conditions of
living for the vast majority of people and the near-incurable san-
guinity of their leaders. Here was a gulf which would reassert itself in
Swedish politics under the new conditions of industrialism in the
latter part of the nineteenth century.

For all their optimism, however, the leaders were not blind to the
difficulties which the development brought in its train. The reformist
policy of the 1740s reflected a resolute attempt to improve conditions
for the broad masses—an attempt whose general social and humanitarian outlook foreshadowed the views so well articulated by Anders
Chydenius two decades later. For the younger Hats who succeeded
Arvid Horn, poverty and hardship were hardly the sort of problems
that could be ignored. Anders Johan von Höpken, Carl Gustav
Tessin, Carl Fredrik Scheffer, Ulric Scheffer, Carl Hårleman, Carl
Ehrensvärd and Jacob Faggot formed a group of eminent Hats upon
whom new humanitarian ideas made a deep impression. They took
charge of the reform work, founded social institutions, and criticized
the harsh provisions of master-and-servant law. The wealth of a
nation was no longer assessed in 'mercantilist' terms, in which it was
equivalent to, and indeed dependent on, the poverty of most of its
members. Instead it was believed that greater, and more widely
distributed wealth, would accrue from population growth and an
active trade and industrial policy, and that agriculture would be more
productive if more persons engaged in it. Faggot went as far as to
suggest that heightened consumption would stimulate production and
thereby enrich the state as well—a far cry from traditional sub-
sistence-wage theories of economic thought. However, the differences
of approach as compared with Nordencrantz in his more liberal
periods, and later with Chydenius, are outstanding. The Hat politicians named above were still ardent mercantilists when it came to
encouraging the non-agricultural branches of the economy, especially
the manufactories. For them, the relaxation of agricultural and
employment regulations went hand in hand with government
subsidies and control of industrial enterprise.

The population grew not because of declining death rates but
because of rising birth rates. Naturally only limited conclusions can

be drawn from the mortality rate of a people. The statistics at any period depend upon the age structure, temporary fluctuations (though often with long-range effects) stemming from epidemics, crop failures and the like, and on the reliability of records. Having made these reservations, we can still gain some idea of Sweden in an 'underdeveloped' phase of her history.

NUMBERS OF BIRTHS AND DEATHS, 1751–1810. Ten-year averages

Year	Average pop. in 1,000's	Live births in 1,000's	Rate per 1,000	Deaths in 1,000's	Rate per 1,000
1751–60	1862	66	36	51	27
1761–70	1982	68	34	55	28
1771–80	2042	67	33	59	29
1781–90	2159	70	32	60	28
1791–00	2283	76	33	58	25
1801–10	2400	74	31	68	28
1960	7480	102	14	75	10

As we have had occasion to observe several times before, the bearing of crop fluctuations on changing birth and death rates is a debatable issue; the use of ten-year averages in the above table has largely evened out the variations. Although we will not enter into the debate here, the most reasonable assumption to make is that a number of factors, such as crops yields, harsh winters and epidemics, interacted with and influenced one another, determining in combination the mortality rate at any one time: no one factor need always have been primarily operative. The search for the 'real cause' may well be chimerical. It is clear at any rate that fluctuations in crop yield were bound to worsen or improve the situation. The fluctuations had an impact first and foremost on employment. In poor crop years, the peasants were forced to discharge some of their help, nor did they use crofters and cottars as casual labour. A 'business cycle' thus spread out over the whole peasant community, naturally wreaking its greatest hardships on those who were worst off even in the good years. That this state of affairs should be combined with constant complaints voiced by both peasants and the higher Estates over the shortage of servants should not lead us astray. They were simply referring to the shortage of cheap servants: no matter how low the wages paid, they were still always too high.

The significance of land subdivision and the formation of crofts and cotes was that large groups came to abandon the old village community: thus these factors may have provided a greater stimulus than the enclosure movement, although that was important too. Many homes were moved out to the open fields or to what had been wastelands. It is impossible to assess the consequences of this migration on the living conditions and attitudes to life of those involved. However, certain reasonable assumptions can be made. Many people must have been pleased to escape the communal compulsions of the old village unit. On the other hand, major disadvantages were no doubt also incurred, and for many these may well have outweighed the advantages.

Village life gave security, with its organized mutual assistance as well as the sense of belonging together. The village was something of a fortress, a place of refuge, particularly during severe winters, when the wolves howled in the fields and woods. The village offered help, solace and cooperation. The loneliness and isolation of remote cottages in newly reclaimed areas must often have been experienced as sinister and menacing, not least by people for whom giants, trolls and evil spirits were living realities.

Isolation was often in itself enough to depress body and soul. Foreign travellers to Sweden at the end of the eighteenth century describe with horror—perhaps exaggerated but essentially plausible— the estrangement, poverty and insanitary conditions (not to say filth) in which people in sparsely populated areas lived. Their wretched dwellings, too poor to be called cottages, had windows that did not open: all ventilation took place through the open chimney. The children were pale and thin, dressed the year round in vile-smelling homespuns. They never washed, never changed clothes before they fell apart, were shy, frightened and intimidated. Just how much better things were in the villages is hard to say. The impressions left by these contemporary accounts from the more fertile and densely settled regions of central Sweden are much brighter, however.

At the same time a rich, sheltered, varying and often culturally advanced life flourished on the manorial and ironworking estates, in the stately town houses, and at the episcopal sees and vicarages. To be sure, the landed aristocracy with its princely retinues had long since disappeared; when Gustavus III visited Övedskloster, the castle built in 1765–76 for the Ramel family, his reaction of surprise, unthinkable for Gustavus Adolphus, Christina or Charles X, was, 'Trop gentil pour un particulier'—much too magnificent for a private subject. Yet pomp, wealth and luxury still existed, though on a somewhat more 'bourgeois' scale, for the new nobility, the higher civil servants, the affluent ironmasters and merchants, an occasional master craftsman, and at the royal court. All this opulence struck many foreigners as unimpressive if not meagre, in which view they were readily seconded by the higher nobles, who never missed the opportunity to bemoan their poverty. But whatever the yardstick, all members of the last-named group looked down from lofty heights on the rest of the population.

One can speak of two different ideals of style governing the way of life for this upper class—ideals which coincided almost exactly with the political cleavage towards mid-century; naturally enough, because this in turn was so much a factor of economic and social conditions. The more 'genteel' of the two was the French style, with a heavy admixture of rococo, represented by such eminent persons in the political and cultural life as Carl Gustav Tessin (1695–1770), Anders Johan von Höpken (1712–89), and later, Gustavus III. It was a way of life marked by luxury, ostentation, sophisticated pleasures, and a diversity of erotic liaisons and escapades; but also a great interest in philosophy, politics, art and culture generally. The aim was to combine the best of the Renaissance and the Enlightenment, two movements which were certainly not mutually exclusive. Perhaps the refinement was more shallow than profound, but its sheer breadth was impressive. Carolean austerity, simplicity and narrowness of intellectual range, still so predominant in the time of Arvid Horn and his somewhat stiff bureaucratic regime, had definitely passed by the 1740s.

Among the more ardent devotees of the French style were the rich merchants, who developed it in their commercial palaces along the Stockholm waterfront and on their rural estates. There were titled families whose financial difficulties broke down their opposition to marriages outside their class, opening the way to marriages with merchant families, so helping to eliminate class differences at the top. Lacking the prefix of a noble title the business magnates could not, it is true, dine at the king's table; but it needed no more than the extension of a moneyed hand towards him or his high officials to gain the door-opening title. The rich merchants were also useful since, by virtue of their travels and business contacts, commodities and capital and furthermore ideas, fashions and new ways of life were filtered through them.

The French style reached its apogee under Gustavus III, the most Gallophile of Sweden's kings. Many historical works, memoirs and contemporary portrayals have described the prevailing sentiments of the time, but their essence has been best captured by the national poet of Sweden, Esaias Tegnér (1782–1846), in these oft-quoted lines:

'There lay a shimmer over Gustav's days,
Fantastic, frivolous, foreign, if you please.
But there was sun therein and howe'er you plain,
Where should we be if they had not been.'

The second way of life was decidedly sterner, simpler and even of Puritanical bent, but whether this was due to economic necessity or free will we leave unsaid. It was what might be described as *petit bourgeois*. That style prevailed among many of the smaller merchants, the craftsmen, even the more affluent ones, the rural gentry who tended their own, not very large estates and stayed away from the big city with its civil servants and royal court. Some within these circles appear to have retained a tradition of Pietist revival brought home by the Carolean soldiers after their release from captivity in Russia, even though something was lost in the translation from heroic spartanism to *petit bourgeois* dutifulness. It was the way of life which was dominant after Gustavus III, in the dreariness and bureaucracy under Reuterholm and Gustavus IV Adolphus, and which later, in the nineteenth-century 'Victorian' period, imparted both strength and weakness to Swedish society. At opportune moments, it could become a false super-patriotism, a smugness cloaked in the mantle of decency and duty. It was a style generally free of the scepticism and the inquiring mind which gave the rococo and the Gustavian period its charm, and at times acuity. On the other hand, it was also free of the opportunism and unabashed corruption which characterized the more 'genteel' style, and which had been so much a part of the Age of Liberty and the Gustavian period. Then civil servants did not take bribes. They accepted 'discretions', a fancy name for the same thing, and politicians of rank right up to the king himself scarcely took the trouble of concealing the subsidies which foreign states advanced for their activities.

When we speak of these two ways of life as the two main currents in eighteenth-century life, our terms of reference are correct in so far as we are referring to the higher classes which so totally dominated the image Sweden presented to the outside world. The way they lived and worked was officially Sweden's. However, the terms are obviously incorrect if they purport to embrace the attitudes and the ordinary course of life of the Swedish people. The cultural, political and ethical theories here involved had great bearing on the masses in the form of legislation and the general social atmosphere or whatever one chooses to call the indefinable spread of a particular mode of living from the top of the social ladder to the community at large. However,

it was not the mode or ideal of the great majority, and it affected
them unconsciously and indirectly rather than directly and consciously. We can form some idea of its quantitative significance by
studying the statistics of the social composition of the Swedish people
in 1760 and 1815.

SOCIAL COMPOSITION OF THE POPULATION IN SWEDEN PROPER, 1760
and 1815

	1760		1815	
	Total	*per cent*	*Total*	*per cent*
Nobility	8,918	0·49	9,681	0·39
Clergy and teachers	14,705	0·80	14,673	0·60
Untitled gentlefolk	26,943	1·47	39,369	1·60
Servants of nobles, clergy and gentlefolk	39,745	2·16	70,309	2·85
Soldiers and ex-soldiers	154,208	8·39	152,442	6·18
Lower officials	26,013	1·41	15,777	0·64
Merchants	10,500	0·57	78,774	0·76
Manufacturers, urban	14,431	0·78	14,632	0·59
Craftsmen, urban	38,786	2·11	62,440	2·53
Shippers and sailors, urban	5,704	0·31	14,348	0·58
Lesser burghers	32,894	1·79	28,142	1·14
Servants of burghers	20,055	1·09	20,476	0·83
Ironworkers, 'metal' workers and miners	58,033	3·16	58,061	2·36
Manufacturers, rural	—	—	17,442	0·71
Craftsmen, rural	39,532	2·16	45,974	1·87
Millers	10,708	0·58	9,569	0·39
Shippers and sailors, rural	6,699	0·36	11,951	0·48
Peasants	888,793	48·37	1,344,163	54·53
Crofters	195,557	10·64	228,260	9·26
Cottars and paupers	236,873	12·89	267,638	10·86
Lapps, settlers, etc.	8,574	0·47	20,975	0·85
Total population	1,837,671	100·00	2,465,066	100·00
Whereof:				
Titled and untitled gentlefolk and their servants	90,311	4·9	134,032	5·4
Townsmen and their servants	122,370	7·2	158,782	6·5
Rural population	1,444,769	79·9	2,004,033	81·3
Other	180,221	8·0	168,219	6·8

Some of the figures in this table merit closer examination. Note
that the two highest franchised groups, the nobility and clergy, show
roughly the same population in 1815 as in 1760, while untitled
gentlefolk have increased by almost 12,500 and the total population

by more than 600,000 or a good 33 per cent. The political divergences described in the preceding section can partly be explained in the light of these figures. To an extent, changed methods of reporting may account for the doubling in size of the upper class servant staffs; but in so far as this increase was real, it tells us that their lords and masters had not, on the whole, suffered economic setbacks.

The more spectacular growth was that of the peasantry, who increased from nearly 890,000 to close on 1,350,000, or by approximately 34 per cent. The crofters, cottars and paupers (considered as a single group), increased from more than 430,000 to nearly 496,000, or by about 15 per cent. This group grew initially during the heavy population increase that took place in the first four decades of the Age of Liberty; the same thing was to happen up to the middle of the nineteenth century after the limits of subdivision had been reached. The numbers of miners and iron metal makers, and of urban manufacturers remained virtually steady. This reflects the fairly constant degree of government control over the iron industry.

Without trying to read too much into these statistics on social composition we can nevertheless observe that they present a picture of a society in which the stagnation of the old ruling groups was paralleled by a vigorous expansion in both the higher and lower social strata of new groups. The picture, in short, portrays nothing less than the disintegration of a rank-ordered society of birth, and points towards the emergence of a varied, freer class society. This type of class society was to be fully developed by the middle of the nineteenth century, after which it rapidly broke down and became a new type of class society; the industrial.

3

DECAY AND REGENERATION

I

IN 1868 the first Riksdag to be founded on a social base other than that of the old Estates concluded its session. The new Organic Law of the Riksdag, passed in 1866, had been followed by elections and a Riksdag session in 1867—and a reform so long discussed and prepared, in response to nearly one hundred years of social pressure, turned out to be what can only be described as politically reactoinary. Only one year after its demise, the outmoded Riksdag of the Four Estates, so incurably conservative in its organization, could go down in history for a liberalism and radicalism for which the new and, in principle, far more 'popular' Riksdag was completely unqualified. In political terms, the radical parliamentary reform undoubtedly signified a big step backwards.

It is not hard to find the cause. The old Riksdag, in particular its leading Estate, the nobility, had sensed the demand for parliamentary reform as a threat to its ancient privileges. Indeed, similar demands were mounting in almost all sectors of national life, and a good deal of the driving force behind them came from the ranks of the nobility itself, many of whose members were among the most perspicacious and radical figures of the time. Because of their position they could easily spread their ideas.

In the Riksdag which followed the 1866 Organic Law, conservative and socially reactionary forces were given completely new scope for their activities. This was especially true at first of the Lower Chamber which was directly elected by the 'people'.

The word 'people' must be put in quotation marks: one reason for the conservatism of the new Riksdag was that the franchise had been restricted to about 25 per cent only of the adult male population. Membership of the Upper Chamber was by indirect election, based on a graduated scale applied at elections to the county and municipal

138

councils; in consequence, the wealthy groups were strongly over-represented in the Upper Chamber, a disporportion that was even more pronounced since affluence was a requirement for inclusion on the electoral rolls. The right to vote in elections to the Lower Chamber was dependent upon possession of an annual income of at least 800 kronor, a high sum in those days, or the ownership of real property valued at not less than 1,000 kronor. Only men could vote and, as already observed, 75 per cent of the male population was debarred from taking part in the first election to the Lower Chamber.

The background to the reform, the disintegration of the foundation on which the old rank-ordered society had rested, has presumably been sufficiently dealt with on the previous pages. Economic and political power had shifted to new groups, in particular to the merchants and the nascent industrialists, and in many cases to commoner civil servants. From that point of view, the reform was a great mistake. As the property qualification for membership of the Riksdag came to operate in practice, it not only gave freer play to 'liberalism' in the economic sense and to those groups which sustained the new industrialization, but it also opened the doors to political advancement for the landowning farmers. This was the great irony. On the eve of a new economic order, when agriculture was beginning to stagnate and its share of the labour force and national income was constantly dwindling, a conservative agrarian class embarked upon a period of greater political influence than it ever enjoyed before.

Another aspect of the new order was the emergence of an industrial working class whose numbers were to shoot upwards, but for which there was no place at the table set by the Act of 1866. If anything the position of this class grew worse. The significance of the reform for these groups was that those who wielded economic power over them were also able to exercise more of the political power. To a very great extent, employers and legislators were one and the same persons, or at least they belonged to the same interest groups.

This was nothing new of course. During the great-power era, and to a lesser extent during the Age of Liberty, the dominant economic and political power had been exercised by the nobility. But the peasantry, which was the group primarily subject to this legislation, had been represented in the Riksdag: a fact that certainly helps to explain why the peasants could not be completely suppressed even before the Reduction, when the nobility was at the height of its power. In spite of the Act of 1866, or rather because of it and the power distribution it reflected, the new working class, then on the threshold of its great expansion, found itself in a position far worse than had ever befallen the peasantry. This class was given no voice in the Riksdag.

Baron Erik Leijonhufvud, put his finger squarely on the problem when the House of Nobility was debating the reform bill:

'Clearly the aim of this proposed constitutional amendment is to put the power into the hands of the middle class . . . Are we to assume that the excluded working class will, in the long run, prefer a system of rule which will be felt all the more oppressive as it will be experienced both in legislation and in the day-to-day relationships between employer and employee?'

In any case, the subsequent course of events demonstrated that the Swedish reform policy had been much more progressive in the twenty years preceding the Act of 1866 than it became afterwards. Free trade had firmly established itself in the economic sphere. In the social sphere, a fairly liberal Poor Relief Law had been passed in 1847. In 1864 the Penal Code was to be revised after twenty years of preparation. The treatment of prisoners had been made more humane. Primary education became compulsory. A new law on religious freedom was enacted in 1860. Women had finally been declared legally capable of managing their own affairs. An Act of 1862 had restored a greater measure of self-government to the local authorities. The right to set up trade was given a broader definition by a reform measure enacted in 1864.

The new Organic Law of the Riksdag was meant to have been the crowning glory of all this work. However, the twenty years which followed its enactment in 1866 proved to be singularly devoid of legislative progress. Thus the Poor Relief reform of 1871 actually turned the clock back, since it deprived the poor of the right, won in 1847, to appeal against decisions of local authorities. Instead of receiving the help as their due, they were thrown back on the mercies of charity. The reformist movement marked time until towards the end of the nineteenth century when it was given new impetus by the neo-liberal criticism of S. A. Hedin, by new economic and social theories, and by the pressures of a growing labour movement. The fight for political equality was destined to be hard and bitter around the turn of the century and in the two decades following.

There are several reasons for what proved to be the rather peculiar character of the 1866 Act. To begin with, the reformists were inspired by an out-dated liberal ethos. Accordingly they feared a more universal democracy with equal suffrage for all; as they saw it, the primacy of reason and liberty would be upheld by restricting the right to vote and by limiting eligibility for public office to the wealthy. To permit the large uneducated masses to decide might imperil both culture and liberty, and that could never be allowed.

Over and above such ideas, which kept closely in line with an important international liberal discussion, there were also real political factors to consider if the Estates Riksdag could be at all persuaded to preside over its own liquidation. Indeed, the royal power imposed a barrier before one could even get so far. Charles XV was as much a conservative as he was an easy-going and popular monarch and he had to be personally assured that abolition of the Estates Riksdag would not unleash Armageddon. Similar sentiments had to be considered in the Riksdag; there the clergy was most apprehensive, with the nobility not far behind. A middle course had to be steered: to gain acceptance, the reform had to be presented as something necessary but not too big or important. Given this prerequisite, as Stig Ekman recently observed in a fully documented study, the reform came close to being no reform at all.

When the Act of 1866 is considered in this light, there is no doubt but that it was a major political achievement for its instigator, the prime minister Louis De Geer (1818–96), to get it passed. As it was, a bicameral system of parliament served in practice to open the doors to a wider democratization, as new power factors asserted themselves and compelled the extension of suffrage and eligibility for candidatures. It can be argued, however, that, had the old Riksdag continued to exist for two or three more decades, the machinery of reform would perhaps have operated at greater speed. The old Riksdag contained more progressive members than the bicameral legislature which replaced it; in any event the constant threat to its existence had provided an incentive for action and reform which the new Riksdag lacked.

The Sweden in which this reform was carried out had definitely abandoned all her military aspiration more than forty years earlier. Gustavus IV Adolphus' war against Russia, resulting in the loss of Finland; Charles XIV John's commitment to the Allied cause against Napoleon; the enforcement of the union with Norway; and the surrender of the last possessions held in Pomerania: these were Sweden's last acts of belligerency and have not been followed by any others. The personal union with Norway, this expansionist move by the first Bernadotte reminiscent of Charles XII and Gustavus IV

Adolphus, was meant to compensate Sweden for the loss of Finland. It was also supposed to re-orientate the country to the west after centuries of facing east across the Baltic. However, it is very much doubted whether the union with Norway furthered these aspirations in the slightest. After all, the westward orientation was anything but new as far as Swedish trade policy was concerned.

Indeed, contrary to the belief of the time, the loss of Finland was nothing that required compensation. Finland had long been an integral part of Sweden, many mutual ties had been formed, and the prospect of Russification was bound to cause anxieties. Sweden was naturally sensitive to 'what was happening to Finland'. If we adopt a narrower definition of Swedish interests, however, the 'loss of Finland' was no loss at all. With regard to possible military expense and potential war risks, it actually represented a positive gain. Also, it was a basic prerequisite for the long period of peace which began when the Convention of Moss was entered into with the Norwegians in August 1814.

For Finland the separation appears to have given rise to certain economic difficulties, some of formidable size. A particularly heavy blow was the withdrawal of Swedish capital, which no longer poured in as before—and which was not replaced by Russian capital. There is no evidence of any such difficulties for Sweden. Commerce went on as before, and insofar as Finnish foreign trade passed Stockholm by, this was no more than a continuance of the trend engendered by the abolition of the Bothian trade compulsion in 1765. Indeed it might even be contended that Sweden benefited economically from the separation. The new investments required to finance the great expansion of Swedish industry not only absorbed all the available domestic capital, but also made it necessary to borrow from the outside. Had Finland remained within the realm, any obligation to continue investing there would have been felt as an embarrassment in the new situation. By around 1800, at any rate, Sweden was definitely 're-orientated' to the west; and by the middle of the nineteenth century, moreover, this change of outlook was to carry her to the point where even external commitments had to give way to the all-absorbing demands of economic transformation on the home front.

The world around Sweden was one simultaneously characterized by restoration, reparation and rapid change. After the French revolution and the Napoleonic wars, with their wholesale reshuffling of the political furniture, the Congress of Vienna duly set out to put the pieces back in their old places again. A period of return to the old, of reaction and conservatism had set in. Naturally the past could not be restored in full: the revolution and Napoleon had altered too much for that, and the forces they had unleashed were importunate in their clamour. Britain was in the middle of her industrial revolution, which would soon have repercussions on the Continent and the United States, and would within the course of a few decades fundamentally change the shape of economic and social conditions—and in so doing reshape the political scene as well.

New ideas, which were basically a reaction against the earlier Enlightenment, spread over Europe: neo-classicism; romanticism; in Sweden a 'Gothicism', which received its particular expression in the Pan-Scandinavian movement (the rigid system of gymnastics devised by Per-Henrik Ling), and in religious revivals influenced by the mytho-Christian theories advanced by Schleiermacher and Chateaubriand. Sentiment was to react against the Enlightenment's exaltation of reason; traditions were to be revived after the great hiatus caused by the social and political upheavals; gay frivolity gave way to profundity, brooding and tears—and a sound mind was considered to be important to a muscular athlete. These patterns of thought were part of the new conservatism, which in France took a purely reactionary turn, representing a retreat to the old Bourbon strongholds. In Sweden, however, the new conservatism maintained those novel ideas implicating the political upheaval of 1809: a polity based on the separation of powers, a system which was both traditional and full of compromises between past extremes, of absolute rule and royal impuissance. It was as if Sweden had returned to the seventeenth-century constitutionalism that existed prior to the reign of Charles XI, but without the aristocratic dominance of that age.

It was over this last point that political party lines diverged, at least up to the Act of 1866. Arrayed against the spirit of conservatism was a liberal school of thought, which sought economic emancipation and political parliamentarism, and opposed royal power, the bureaucracy, and limitations on the freedom of speech; and which from the 1840s up to the Act of 1866, won an increasing number of victories—only to see its greatest triumph, this reform, transformed into a bitter defeat.

The full implications of what had long been taking place abroad, especially in England, could not be grasped in the mid-1860s. To be sure, the break and transition to something new had manifested itself in Sweden, but the change was proceeding at too slow a pace. The liberals, who perceived the ultimate solution of Swedish social problems in the development of modern industries, were right in the long run. However, the domestic scene of the 'forties, 'fifties, and 'sixties, gave them very little visible proof for their contentions. For the time being the conservatives could marshal all the compelling evidence on their side, but they were proved wrong in the end.

Sweden was not the only country to enjoy peace during this period. More than thirty years of respite from war, one of the longest periods of peace on the European continent, elapsed between Waterloo and the Prussian attack on Denmark in 1848. As yet, however, Swedish 'neutrality' in European armed conflicts was anything but a matter to be taken for granted. Thus when the Crimean War broke out in 1854, Oscar I leaned so far towards an alliance with the western powers that Sweden was presumably presented from being involved only by the fairly sudden end of hostilities in 1856. The next opportunity for adventurism occurred under his successor, Charles XV, who in 1863, came close to accepting Danish proposals for a defensive alliance, in the event of another German attack on Schleswig-Holstein. Charles XV was eventually forced to give up his plans by the determined opposition of De Geer and his minister of finance, Johan August Gripenstedt. Monarchical conduct of foreign policy was thwarted—for a time. It was to be resumed with a dangerous vigour in the 'eighties and 'nineties by Oscar II and later by Gustavus V, this time with a strong pro-German bent. However, a death-blow had been inflicted on the pan-Scandinavian movement, which beginning in the 1840s and continuing during the following twenty years had its leading exponents in the universities and the higher military echelons.

In turning first to Britain and then, under Oscar II, to Germany, Sweden was responding to changed conditions in Europe. Towards the end of the century the balance of power shifted both politically and economically. The unification of Germany under Bismarck; his victory over France and Napoleon III in 1871; 'his policy of alliances, first the Three Emperors' League between Germany, Russia and Austria-Hungary, later the Triple Alliance between Germany, Austria-Hungary and Italy; the emergence of Germany as a new colonial and naval power: all these things created a new political power structure. At the same time Germany was rapidly industrializing her economy. Although she had started later than Britain, Germany entered the twentieth century as the strongest and the most modern industrial state in Europe. The high productivity she achieved was in part due to a far-reaching labour discipline and effective restraints on competition.

The delayed industrialization of Sweden, and above all the development of a great consumer goods industry, was greatly influenced by

German theories and techniques. This influence was also strong in other sectors: in politics, in the military establishment, in the views of leading groups on the major social issues, and in the direction taken by the labour movement towards the end of the century. As a generalization, it could be said that the Swedish industrial society received its first important impulses from England. It was that country's rising demand for Swedish wood and iron which set the process in motion. Gradually, however, Germany came to set the pace in regard to trade relations, economic and social policy, science and culture. It was not until after World War I that a westward re-orientation would set in again, and this time it would include the other side of the Atlantic as well.

Actually, however, a peculiar form of Swedish 'Americanization' had been in process for a long time. It has been brilliantly described by Wilhelm Moberg in his classic emigrant epic.[1] Between 1860 and 1910 more than one million Swedes left their homeland, settling mostly in the United States. The New World, with its immensity of arable land, forests and prospects of freedom, offered them escape from poverty and political and spiritual oppression at home. About 55 per cent of the emigrants were men, the majority in their 'best' years. It is estimated that the male exodus accounted for nearly half of the natural increase in the able-bodied population (fifteen to sixty-five years of age) between 1860 and 1870. Between 1870 and 1900 the number of able-bodied male emigrants roughly doubled the number of men who 'emigrated' to the Swedish industrial towns during this period. That people should thus opt for 'Swedish flesh and blood' in America, in preference to 'skin and bones in Sweden', was not surprising. It does nevertheless illuminate Swedish national life and material standards during the latter part of the nineteenth century—the poverty and desperation that was the lot of so many Swedes when the Riksdag Act was passed in 1866. It took at least two more generations before economic development and social reforms could overhaul this country and reshape it into the land of welfare and prosperity.

II

The population of Sweden rose from 2·3–2·4 million in 1800 to 3 million during the 1830s and to 4 million during the 1860s. By

[1] The four novels comprising the Swedish original of Moberg's work have been translated into three English volumes: *The Emigrants*, *Unto a Good Land*, and *The Last Letter Home*.

contrast with the eighteenth century, this tremendous increase did not stem from a higher birth rate but was entirely attributable to declining mortality. The poet Esaias Tegnér, writing of poor relief in 1833, tellingly identified the causes as 'peace, vaccine and potatoes'. He may have exaggerated the importance of peace: not even the bloodletting of the Great Northern War had been on such a scale as to check a persistent trend towards greater numbers. However, there is no faulting Tegnér on the potatoes and the use of smallpox vaccine, which came to Sweden in 1801.

None the less, the price paid for a larger population was a continued lowering of material standards for growing sections of the community, pauperization, and concealed as well as open unemployment.

Out of a total population of nearly 4·2 million in 1870, about 3 million or 72 per cent were engaged in agriculture and related occupations. Of these 3 million, 52 per cent belonged to the peasant class—and many of their number must be described as smallholders who worked farms of extremely low yields. The subdivision of land had reached the stage where it could not practically be carried any further. Its results were twofold: a very large number of farms that were far too small to provide a means of livelihood; and only meagre crofts or no land at all for an ever growing segment of the agrarian population. As of 1870 a full 16 per cent of this population consisted of crofters, 18 per cent of cottars and paupers, and nearly 14 per cent of servants. The swift rate at which the countryside was pauperized is revealed by statistics from around 1800. At that time 60 per cent of the agrarian population still consisted of freeholders, 14 per cent of crofters, and 10 per cent of cottars and paupers. At the beginning of Gustavus' III reign, 66 per cent had been freeholders, 11 per cent crofters, 6 per cent cottars and paupers. Thus almost two-thirds of the increase since 1800 occurred in the lower agricultural classes. Whereas the total agrarian population grew by 1·3 million from 1800 to 1870, the numbers of true farmers increased by only 400,000, which left about 900,000 in a subservient position. During the last ten years of this period alone, 122,500 persons emigrated, and of these about 90,000 came directly from the farms. By far the greatest growth of the lower classes, however, had occurred since the 1830s. Until then all groups had increased at approximately equal rates. This means that the trend towards pauperization had gained momentum towards 1870 when the real big problems began to pile up. The public debate on this issue, which due to growing poor relief caused no little anxiety, also became particularly lively as from the 1830s.

In spite of the miserable conditions which admittedly existed, it would be inaccurate to restrict our palette even in this period to the dreary colours of poverty. The real situation was far more complex, as has been shown conclusively by Arthur Montgomery in his fundamental work on the rise of industrialism in Sweden, and by Gustaf Utterström in his detailed dissertation on agricultural labourers from the Age of Liberty to the middle of the nineteenth century.

The fact that Sweden's population could increase on this scale in the first place, proves that the Malthusian ceiling of food supply had not been reached. Actually, the production of foodstuffs rose in some quarters, though this was achieved by sacrificing the quality of meat and butter. A decisive role seems to have been played by the victorious progress of the potato during the century's first two or three decades. In spite of the population increase, the former heavy surplus of grain imports could be terminated in 1820 or thereabouts, and before long a considerable surplus appeared on the export side. However, this should not be interpreted to mean that the country had suddenly come into abundance. The export surplus is probably explicable with reference to two circumstances. The one points to the uneven distribution of ownership and income which prevailed in agriculture: food surpluses accumulated on the large estates and on farms in the more fertile areas; these were earmarked for exportation, which yielded higher profits than sales to deficit areas—in spite of their obvious need for more food. The deficit areas had to make do with the potato and the traditional cultivation of root crops to meet their requirements—which provides the second explanation of why it was possible to combine a population increase with an export surplus of grain products.

The pauperization of large and growing groups was paralleled not only by the retention of good material standards for propertied members of the agrarian population, but also by enormous improvements for those who were already well off. The buying of former crown land continued, and farmers with resources could consolidate their holdings and become large-scale proprietors in return for very modest outlays. This propertied class was also well served by the population increase. It became easier and cheaper to hire labour, and thereby run farms more efficiently. Further, improvements in farming methods mostly benefited the larger and better managed farms: the enclosure movement, which created large compact acreages; the digging of drainage ditches; and the shift to rotating crops in place of the system where half or one-third of the fields were left fallow

147

every year. The use of rotating crops brought with it a greater emphasis on fodder cultivation, which on the richer and more rationally managed farms generated a renaissance in animal husbandry, and in turn led to higher standards of quality. Oats, a food suitable both for man and beast, quickly gained ground at the expense of cereals and became the grain which accounted for the bulk of the export surplus.

The picture was changing in another way too. In many areas the enclosure of the fields had put an end to the old villages and their communal way of life. This need not have been a direct and necessary consequence of enclosure. The villages could have been retained with provision made to reapportion the fields into large unbroken holdings, as happened to some extent in Dalarna, though the enclosure movement there was far less extensive than in Skåne and the central Swedish provinces. A solution along those lines would have conferred considerable advantages. It would have preserved the old social mould even after its former economic basis had been substantially diminished. Easier arrangements could have been made for co-operative efforts and division of labour: some observers, in assessing the effects of the enclosure movement, have gone so far as to contend that if the village community had remained intact until agriculture was mechanized, its mechanization would have been speeded by the common purchase and use of expensive equipment. In any event, the facilities which would eventually be needed for water supply, sewage, electricity and telephone communications would have been much easier and cheaper to obtain if enclosures had been carried out without disrupting the villages.

There were reasons for the break-up of the villages, however. The main cause was transport conditions. Cultivators wanted to be close to field and meadow, to be 'on location', as it were. Had the villages stayed intact, the journey to and from work would have sapped too much strength—especially in regard to the transport of the finished products to barns, haylofts, and silos. The organization of the work, with the women working part-time in field and meadow and the rest of the time in barn and kitchen, also made short journeys a basic essential for rational operation.

The result was the transformation not only of ownership patterns and social grouping, but also of the physical appearance of the Swedish countryside. By the middle of the nineteenth century agricultural regions had taken on what was to be their typical appearance, so different from that which had existed for centuries. Now there were large compact farms with houses, stables, barns and provision-sheds spread out over the different tenant holdings and forming solitary family units, separated from each other by fields, meadows and wooded pastures.

It would have been possible to speculate at length on the psychological changes, on the transformation in attitudes and communication, to which this new sociology of agriculture should have given rise. Unfortunately, we do not know very much about this, except that attitudes to life must have largely readapted themselves to the new pattern of settlement and the cessation of old village regulations. We might surmise that greater scope was afforded for individualism; that a spirit of personal self-sufficiency had found a more favourable environment; that people became less social when they no longer lived in a collective—and that in this way, too, the old agrarian culture was replaced by a new. But how is this change to be measured, and what values should be assigned to the advantages of greater individualism when weighed against the social bonds of the village community?

Another result which cannot be measured, but which we may nevertheless assume to have occurred, was that the enclosure movement and the disruption of villages aggravated class differences within the agrarian population, both in real and psychological terms. The disparities increased in proportion to the extent to which consolidated holdings could be rationalized. All evidence suggests that the benefits of rationalization were progressive, even making allowance for certain initial advantages, in that they were proportionally higher on larger than small holdings. This is all the more likely considering that labour was cheap and in abundant supply; hence the marginal income would rise in relation to the marginal cost of new labour. It would be reasonable to believe that the theory of surplus value found its practical application on the larger farms in the more fertile districts. Since large areas of new land with lower yields and more expensive production were put under the plough at the same time, Ricardo's theory of rent operated, with heavy profits for the large, fertile and most efficient farms as a result. Inevitably, the peasant class began to split into the affluent, the less affluent, the tolerably well-off, and the poor. In the meantime, at the bottom of the scale, the really underprivileged swelled in numbers: the crofters, cottars, paupers and itinerant labourers, often under-employed if employed at all.

As yet the richer agricultural districts lay in central Sweden, mainly grouped along the axis formed by the Göta Canal. These areas, covering about 25 per cent of Sweden's land surface, contained about

60 per cent of the total population. Here, too, lay the three largest cities: Stockholm, Göteborg and Norrköping. Only one-tenth of the population could be classified as urban. However, the three cities named accounted for no less than 40 per cent of this urban population.

To what extent the special sidelines of agriculture, in particular *sloyd* or homecrafts, managed to compensate for under-employment and improve the lot of those who were forced to buy the necessities of life we do not know. In any case, a parallel development of *sloyd* for private consumption and for sale seems to have taken place during the first half of the nineteenth century. Naturally, there was an internal competition between the two kinds of production. Insofar as production for home use increased—that is, as the domestic system or self-sufficient economy grew in scope—correspondingly less was made for the market. In the main, however, this effect was presumably 'hidden', since the total market for both branches of *sloyd* expanded so vigorously. It expanded because of the rapid increase in population, but also because of the growing class differences. If large groups of the poor and the only moderately well-off continued with their *sloyd* and even enlarged it, then there was no lack of more affluent people who could afford to buy more handicrafted products. An indication of this fragmented market situation is the solicitude shown by the authorities for *sloyd* of higher quality. Further, it was almost in the nature of things to increase specialization and to produce and sell in a more organized fashion. A growing proportion of the *sloyd* intended for sale was drawn into the *förlag* system of credit advances, which quickly transformed the self-employed craftsmen into hired workers. This trend was accelerated by recurring periods of economic depression, as in the 1830s, 1850s and the mid-1860s.

The most important *sloyd* in terms of production volume, the textile *sloyd*, underwent another important change, which in turn hastened the trends towards the credit advance system, centralization, and factory production. In 1793 an American, Eli Whitney, had constructed his cotton gin, which together with the machines invented earlier in England by Hargreaves, Arkwright, Crompton and Cartwright for spinning and weaving, were shortly to revolutionize textile manufacturing. The initial impact of Whitney's invention on Swedish *sloyd* was a greatly increased supply of cotton at rapidly falling prices. Within the space of a few decades, the new gin had 'industrialized' the cultivation of cotton in the southern United States. The fruits of rising production were literally flung on the European market.

150

Cotton did not oust the old material, flax; but it offered flax keen competition, especially in the Sjuhärads area of western Sweden, which was favourably located for importation and established increasingly strong ties with the leading merchants in Göteborg, who functioned as importers, financiers and marketers. As textile *sloyd* thus became more industrialized, it also became more sensitive to the general economic cycle, especially to fluctuations in world cotton prices. The quantities of cotton imported and fabricated could also be greatly affected by an event like the American Civil War. From 1851 to 1855, nearly 4,800 tons of cotton were imported; from 1856 to 1860 more than 6,200 tons; but from 1861 to 1865 only 3,000 tons. Roughly the same curve was described by the imports of different cotton yarns.

Next to textiles, the most important branches were woodwork and metalwork. The greater part of this production was probably intended for home use. In both branches however, there had existed a long tradition of producing for the market; articles of wood in particular seem to have found ready outlets close to home. In Småland province, wooden *sloyd* developed from about 1850 into a more extensive woodworking craft and thence into small-scale industry. The woodworking here and in other places gradually put increasing emphasis on furniture. However, it was not until Sweden started urbanizing in earnest that this industry made rapid advances.

An important centre of both woodworking and metalworking was Dalarna, especially the northern parts of the province. The explanation here lies partly in the ready availability of raw materials, and partly in overpopulation and poverty which made pursuits other than agriculture and livestock-raising a stark necessity. In wood, the Dalecarlians turned their hand to trays, bowls, spoons, ladles, toys, cabinets, chests, and handlooms, not to mention the well-known Mora clocks; in metal, products of forged iron became a provincial speciality. Tanning of leather was an important supplementary trade, especially at Malung, which thereby established its name in Swedish 'industry'.

The sale of homecrafted products seems for a long time to have been chiefly handled by the producers themselves and their families. Upper Dalarna became the centre of an itinerant trade which extended to the southern reaches of Sweden and even penetrated as far as Denmark, Germany, Norway, Finland and Russia. To all appearances, the most extensive travellers were the women (*hørkullor*) who sold delicately crafted ornaments of human hair. Transportation was not much of a problem for them: they could easily obtain new

151

raw material en route and work while they travelled. The tanners of Malung also wandered far and wide; it was their practice to work for a customer, who would supply them with food, drink and lodging—and of course the raw material—until they had finished their work for him. Otherwise the transport problems were often nearly insoluble, and certainly made it necessary to limit journeys involving heavy goods. One solution, though it could not be applied everywhere, was to adopt the classical technique of the Västgöta pedlars, which was to combine hawking with horse-trading. Another was the credit advance (*förlag*) system and the sale of products through merchants.

New conditions were to be created for the itinerant craftsmen by improved transport on water, made possible by canal building and steam vessels, and by the construction of railways. It soon transpired, however, that these new prospects were much too good. The result was that with the possibility of mass transports, the development of mass-production proved advantageous. The shift to factory methods drove most of the home craftsmen out of business. Those left survived largely as picturesque adjuncts to the tourist trade—a quaint backwater secluded from the mainstream of production.

Roughly the same fate befell another form of *sloyd* in a nearby province: shoemaking in Närke. This was a homecraft of fairly recent origin. During the 1840s several young men in Kumla had taken to making shoes for stock instead of to order. Making shoes in quantity soon gained widespread adoption, and the old home shoemakers were turned into subcontractors often with a specialized production. The leather dealers of Örebro undertook to be suppliers of working capital, and before long they by-passed the wholesale producers and ordered directly from the home craftsmen. In this case, however, the systems of selling and advancing credit did not merge. Instead, a new occupational group, the shoe wholesalers, stepped in between to play the role of middlemen. The field lay increasingly open for capital investment on a larger scale and for the transition from *sloyd*, handicraft and *förlag* credit advances towards a modern factory system.

Similar tendencies manifested themselves at the same time in the marginal domains between *sloyd*, handicrafts and manufactures which the production of food, beverages and tobacco represented. The making of paper can be included within this group in the change-over from *sloyd* and handicraft to industry. Industrialization was particularly swift in distilling and brewing. A separate, 'artificial' market was created for aquavit with the disappearance of household distilling during the 1850s; from 1861 to 1865 the Swedish distilleries

152

seem to have produced at levels which exceeded the value of timber exports. By then the breweries had been operating on an industrial scale for about twenty years; the impetus towards new production methods and business organization had come from Germany, with part of the skill supplied by immigrants and the rest by what now would be termed as industrial espionage and patent infringement.

The boundary line between rural handicrafts and *sloyd* produced for the market had always been blurred, and became increasingly difficult to demarcate as *sloyd* became more specialized. Certainly many of the home craftsmen and pedlars, as in upper Dalarna, also farmed small plots of land and kept some livestock. It became fairly common, however, to organize a division of labour within the family so as to let certain members devote all their energies to *sloyd*; or, as often was the case, whole villages would develop specialities of their own. In addition, many of the rural craftsmen earned a subsidiary livelihood from the tilled patches and an occasional cow or goat. After the restrictions on the right to set up trade were eased in 1846, and again in 1864, the attempts by the government to regulate these conditions came to an end—at all events it no longer made sense in real-economic terms, that is in regard to products made, methods of production, selling, financing, and social conditions, to speak of *sloyd* and rural handicrafts as separate branches of economic activity from the middle of the nineteenth century and onwards.

As for the urban handicrafts, circumstances were somewhat different. Here, too, the decrees broadening the right to set up trade served to dissolve the old guild rules and their special privileges. However, because of tenacious traditions and the requirement of vocational skills, these occupations did not change very fast or to any great extent. Industrialization did more than the relaxation of government regulations to offer the handicrafts competition of a kind that compelled them to react if they were not to go under. The responses they made varied from one craft to another. Some of the leading master craftsmen accepted the challenge forthwith, installed the new machines in their workshops, and passed over into 'light industry'—a category that is also admittedly capable of elastic definition. Other craftsmen discontinued production altogether or relegated it to secondary importance, establishing themselves instead as repair and servicing enterprises, often with the resale of industrially produced goods included in the business. A third group specialized in fancier production, tending more and more towards quality craftsmanship. As long as industrial production fell short of desired quality, precision and aesthetic standards, this quality craftsmanship could control a considerable market and create a tradition—and the traditional attitude of customers as to the qualitative superiority of the handmade product—which built up a strong position for the future, a position which persisted long after industrial fabrication had greatly improved its standards.

These different changes combined to give the handicrafts broader scope. According to Tom Söderberg, who has described the handicrafts of nineteenth-century Sweden, they employed between 62,000 and 65,000 persons in 1855 (counting the master craftsmen and adult employees). The figure soared to 93,000 twenty-five years later, an increase of roughly 50 per cent. This trend, of course, reflects the parallel increase in population and the growing needs it generated. However, since urbanization was delayed until the approach of the 1880s, this explanation is incomplete. To all appearances, the decisive incentive came from industrialization itself, which, though feared and damned by so many artisans, and in spite of the hardships it undoubtedly inflicted in individual cases, proved in the end to be a general benefactor. Thanks to the increased total flow of goods and the specialization of labour, there was more work to do, not less. It imparted a new kind of purchasing power, even though it often necessitated a difficult adjustment to the new conditions and tasks. Small-scale enterprise and its typically traditional exponent, the handicrafts, could thus embark on renewed expansion under the cloak of industrialism and new methods of mass production.

Around 1870, however, industrialization had not progressed beyond very modest beginnings. It was not until towards the turn of the century that the rather meaningless term 'Industrial Revolution', could be said to apply to Swedish conditions. On the other hand, the incitements towards a new era were clear. They came chiefly from the outside, and their first important manifestations were in the timber sector.

That the precedents for Sweden's industrialization should so largely have been set abroad is not at all strange. Inherent in the concept of industrialism is the tendency towards a progressive specialization. That can be achieved internally, so to speak, and indeed, to a certain extent, it was; but specialization would have been rather narrowly confined if it had developed in national isolation. Sweden was too small, with too few people distributed over too large an area, to carry out a profitable, extensive specialization; in many cases, specialization requires large-scale operation and mass production to be economically worthwhile, and mass production in turn requires large markets. A small country must therefore specialize in relation to other countries if the potential benefits are to be fully realized. Thus small countries usually carry on more foreign trade per capita than larger countries: and if a small country has, like Sweden, an economy based on a handful of important natural resources, the need for specialization in relation to the outside world is even more acute.

The first important impulse towards industrialization was given the timber sector at the beginning of the 1850s and demonstrates the significance of external demand. Out in Europe, and in Britain particularly, industrial expansion had reached the point where investment in plant and equipment had become very important. At the same time the larger numbers of people and their growing mobility generated an enormous demand for new construction. All this burgeoning activity put a premium on iron and wood, and for wood in particular the deforested countries of Europe had to rely heavily on imports.

In 1842 Britain had abolished her preferential tariffs, which had favoured the timber products coming from Canada, and in 1849 the remaining British restrictions on trade were lifted. A huge market was thus laid open. In 1842 Sweden repealed the restrictions which had formerly subjected sawing to strict licencing. This virtually did away with the official controls of the timber trade, whose original justification had been to assure the iron industry of adequate fuel supplies; on paper, however, the last vestige of control, defining the right to establish new sawmills, remained until 1863.

At the same time, it transpired that Norway could no longer hold her own on the world market. To begin with, the Norwegian forests had been badly depleted, while the forests of Norrland had just begun to be exploited in earnest. Secondly, the costs of transportation had fallen, and it had been in the low freight charges that Norway had had her previous advantage; it had been for that reason too, that the forests of Värmland had held a strong competitive advantage over those in the north. A gratuitous advantage was conferred on Sweden by the delay in Finland's development of the timber industry, which no doubt stemmed from the longer persistence of government controls in that country. Of equal importance if not greater, however, was Finland's lack of capital, since that from Sweden stopped coming in after the Russian annexation.

The changes in transportation costs were due to technological advance, more specifically the use of steam power. This innovation had a two-fold impact on the Swedish timber trade: first, goods could be carried over the seas by steamship; and second, steam power was harnessed by the sawmills themselves for their own production. In 1850 Sweden had acquired the largest steamship fleet of any country in continental Europe. It totalled 67 vessels with a combined capacity of 3,000 horsepower. Twenty years later the fleet numbered 368 vessels, totalling 11,601 horsepower. Sixty-one of them plied foreign-trade routes exclusively. The first steam sawmills were also built around 1850. Pride of place is usually accorded Wifstavarf, which was erected from 1850 to 1852; but the distinction goes more properly to Tunadal, outside Sundsvall, which was founded in 1849.

Apart from increased production rates, the steam sawmills had another advantage over the water-driven mills in that they did not have to be sited near inland falls. Instead they could be located along the coasts, which offered much better facilities for transport, collection and stowage. Once a good system of floatways had developed, logs could be conveniently transported to the coast at low costs. The logs from different forests could then be assembled at the floatway mouths, where ships could also pull in to receive the finished product.

However, it took decades to build the steam sawmills and a proper system of floatways. The water-driven mills were not driven out of business with the arrival of the steam plants. At the same time as more than 100 steam sawmills were built between 1850 and 1870, the water-driven mills were greatly improved technically, especially with the introduction of hydraulic turbines.

These changes in transportation and production techniques made possible a tremendously increased output, which matched a steadily rising demand, albeit one highly sensitive to market fluctuations:

EXPORTS OF SAWN AND PLANED TIMBER, 1846–1870

Annually	Cubic metres
1845–50	393,300
1851–55	667,200
1856–60	800,200
1861–65	1,125,100
1866–70	1,781,800

Even during the period from 1850 to 1870, this development of the timber industry bore the stamp which is emotionally linked with the labels 'Industrial Revolution' and 'private capitalism', and to a greater degree than was the case for any other Swedish industry. A gradual and hence better 'balanced' expansion from small-scale to large-scale enterprise was far more characteristic of other important

156

branches of industrial production. By the standards of that day, the building of sawmills and floatways devoured extremely large amounts of capital. A particular uniformity of effort was required throughout the whole chain of production, which gave a special impetus towards integration from the very beginning. The industry took on at an early stage the character of a large-scale enterprise operated by large companies. The timber industry had few ties with the past. It was developed in Norrland, a region without traditions of such work. Many of the workers came from other parts of the country, and were often totally ignorant of their new trade. They were thrown together in small sawmill communities along the coast, where their housing conditions usually were wretched. At the same time profits in the millions accrued to the owners, who lived lives of luxury, not to mention vulgar extravagance.

In addition to all this 'capitalist' organization, there was the sensitivity to business cycles, typical of an export industry. The continuous price fluctuations in wood products gave the whole timber industry a speculative taint. Falling prices and market potentials hit the labour force in the form of depressed wages and unemployment. The 1870s, which opened with a tremendous boom, ended with a disastrous fall in prices on the British market. In 1879 Sweden experienced her first big strike. The fact that it took place in Sundsvall, the 'timber capital' of northern Sweden, was no coincidence. Those crisis years of the 1870s were the worst ever experienced by the timber industry. In a statistical review of the Swedish economy and its development from 1870 to 1915, the Board of Commerce has this to say: 'A time of trial which on the one hand incurred heavy losses, but on the other hand consolidated the position of this industry and swept away the noxious weeds left from its rapid development phase.'

Here, however, we are on the verge of running ahead of our story. We must return to the middle of the nineteenth century for a description of the other important export industry, iron-working, on the eve of the real industrial breakthrough.

At the beginning of the nineteenth century, the changed situation with regard to the iron industry resulted from its relation to the world market and its English industry especially. This change, which was an extension of the difficulties encountered in the eighteenth century, and led to the imposition of government controls on production, was most unfortunate for Sweden. The increased difficulties stemmed from metallurgical advances in England. During the 1780s the English had progressed so far in their development of fossil fuel that it could be used not only to make cast iron (coal had in fact been used for this purpose since the beginning of the eighteenth century), but also for the production of malleable iron. This process, known as puddling, had been perfected to the point where malleable iron could satisfy quality standards by the second decade of the nineteenth century, and the future for Swedish iron exports was seriously menaced. The consequences were first felt towards 1820, when the unusually high demand for iron generated by the war dropped to more normal levels. The competitive strength which Sweden long had enjoyed in quality iron was now lost—although, as we have just seen this was soon to benefit the Swedish timber industry.

Improved technique came to the rescue of ironworking, enabling Swedish charcoal-smelted iron to outstrip coal-smelted iron in quality. The lack of domestic coal resources made every other expedient economically unfeasible. Further, the adoption of this course lay ready to hand for Swedish ironworking, which had based most of its former repute on high-quality output. Thus the eighteenth century controls on production had a lingering beneficial impact even after they had been relaxed, although they were not completely abolished until 1859. The controls had helped the industry to accustom itself to the demand for quality.

For the time being, however, the changes effected did not proceed beyond the adoption of the Lancashire method in the 1830s, which was adapted to Swedish requirements, that is to charcoal operation. Like its predecessors, described in an earlier chapter, the Lancashire method involved decarburization in an open hearth furnace, and as such could be described as an improvement on the Walloon forge. It also employed two hearths, rather than the one hearth associated with the German forge. The Lancashire process consumed less fuel and imparted a more uniform quality to the iron.

The really far-reaching changes in the field of decarburization did not come until the 1850s and 1860s, when the 'ingot-iron' process was introduced. Iron and above all steel could now be produced in the desired quality, by relatively simple means and in far greater quantities. There were two different methods, the older called Bessemer, the other Siemens-Martin or, simply, Martin. The Bessemer method was adopted by G. F. Göransson at Sandviken in 1858, and the Martin method exactly ten years later. Both of them, however, had to wait nearly two decades before coming into more widespread use. The Bessemer method has two advantages: it consumes little fuel—the impurities are blown out by air forced through the molten metal, where the heat is maintained by the combustion of silicon and carbon in the pig iron; and the decarburization process is rapid. In the Martin process, already decarburized iron in the form of scrap or the like is added to the molten iron in a reverberatory furnace, which reduces the pig's carbon content. Since this process is slower than the Bessemer, the combustion of silicon and carbon in the pig iron does not suffice to maintain the right temperature. Accordingly, the Martin process requires far more fuel, which in Sweden meant that its wider adoption also necessitated the importation of coal.

For the most part, however, these developments were to have their chief impact on Swedish ironworking after 1870, the year which marks a rough boundary line in this section of our narrative.

By the mid-nineteenth century it was evident that something was beginning to happen in other branches of the Swedish economy, related to ironworking but more concerned with the domestic market. A number of industries based on metal working, and upon Swedish iron and steel in particular, had come into being. At least twenty engineering plants were engaged in making products as diverse as steam engines, turbines, rolling mills, threshers, bridges, and machine tools; they also functioned as servicing and repair shops. Most of these metalworking establishments had to contend with great difficulties, and it was not until after they were reorganized into joint-stock companies and received infusions of external capital, often supplied by the large merchant houses of the day, that they achieved greater stability. Before mid-century, according to Torsten Gårdlund, 'in point of fact, none of the larger engineering enterprises in our country was economically viable'. Many of them survived, though with the passage of time often in the form of new financial and productive units: the Motala plant, which in 1850 was the country's largest engineering establishment with a labour force of 450 men; Bergsund and Bolinder in Stockholm; Jonsered, Keiller, Lindholmen, and Eriksberg in Göteborg; Kockums in Malmö; Nyqvist and Holm at Trollhättan; and Munktell at Eskilstuna, all of which employed about 100 persons each. But in the engineering industry too, the most important things were to happen in a later period. From certain points of view, its subsequent growth was all the more remarkable: the result was a heyday for Swedish applied science which presumably few at the end of the 1860s would have envisioned even in their wildest dreams.

One area which was to have decisive importance for further industrialization, and which did more than any other, at least indirectly, to alter the national scene, was communications. Very little had happened in this area since the basic framework of the Swedish road system was built in the great-power era. During the first half of the nineteenth century, however, one improvement followed hard on the heels of the other. First came the Göta Canal, a vast construction project that was finally finished in 1832, three years after the death of its chief engineer, Baltzar von Platen. Then came the advent of what was for Sweden a not inconsiderable steamship fleet (the size of which in 1850 and 1870 has already been given). Although comparisons of numbers and tonnage between sailing and steam vessels have little meaning owing to their great dissimilarities, we can form some idea by adding that 2,744 sailing vessels were registered in 1850 as against 67 steamships; while the figures for 1870 were 3,008 and 368, respectively. The net tonnage in 1870 totalled 319,247 tons for the sailing ships, and 27,616 tons for the steamers. Even if we triple the steam tonnage, which is supposed to achieve rough comparability with the carrying capacity of sailing vessels, it does not come to more than 82,848 tons, that is about a quarter of the sailing tonnage.

In the matter of speed, no average rates can be given. When the winds were favourable, the very large sailing ships could actually outstrip the steamers. As a general rule, however, with virtually no exceptions as far as Swedish conditions were concerned, the laurels went to steam in the speed race. Above all, of course, the steamships enjoyed an inherent advantage in their steadier motion. It was easy for Sweden to exploit the steam engine for shipping at an early stage, owing to the relatively calm waters which prevailed for both inland and Baltic traffic. The earlier paddle-wheelers were best suited for such waters; the world's first steamer, Robert Fulton's 'Clermont', first plied the Hudson River in the United States in 1807, while Sweden's first workable model, constructed by Samuel Owen did her test run on Lake Mälaren in 1818. With John Ericsson's invention of the marine screw propeller in 1836, new vistas were opened for the potentials of steam propulsion: dependence on weather, wind and water conditions diminished; surer progress could be made across water, and speeds accelerated.

Of greater importance than the advances in shipping, however, were the new developments in communications over land, considered both in their own right and in terms of their impact on the economy. The principal change came with the railways. Their initial construction dates from the 1850s, though the real upsurge did not occur until two decades later. The figures opposite, giving the length of rail in kilometres, tell the story.

The man who devised the Swedish railways system was Nils

160

Ericson. His fundamental idea was to have the state build and operate a trunk network, with private enterprise left to fill in the branches. By this means the state would have a predominant influence over the whole network. The private lines which fed into the trunk would be unable to conduct a policy deviating from that approved by the trunk owner. This guiding principle was put into practice, as the little table above indicates. During the course of the 1870s the privately owned railways attained twice the length of the state-owned. They were to retain this commanding lead until the great nationalization of railways set in during the 1930s. At no time, however, did the private lines dominate Swedish railway traffic. Considered in this light, their ultimate nationalization was motivated less by economic reasons, than by the desire to improve the efficiency of management. Throughout their existence the private railways generally operated to supplement, not compete with, the state trunk network.

Year	State-owned	Privately-owned	Total
1860	303	224	527
1870	1118	609	1727
1880	1956	3920	5876

The construction of railways under state and—to some degree—under private auspices did not abide by the basic rule which came to apply to other forms of industrialization, namely to gear the level of operations to current demand. This guiding principle, regarded as so 'right' and 'natural' during the generally liberal period in which industrialization took place, as well as in the period that followed, also meant that the early obsolescence of investments and activities had to be accepted in a never-ending short-term cycle.

In the field of railways construction a general consideration was certainly paid to national requirements: after all the need for new communications was unlimited. Where the Swedish railways flouted 'economic law', however, was that they did not extend line by line in response to the most pressing need at any given time. Indeed, they did not even obey the geometric law of a straight line as the shortest distance between two points, even when the points happened to be two towns in need of a connecting link. The main routes of the state system were mapped out at the very beginning. When Nils Ericson committed his designs to paper, he deliberately subordinated links between established economic centres, preferring instead to draw the tracks through areas where industry was poorly developed, or even where there existed no settlement at all. The theory was that this laid

F
161

the foundation for a flourishing economy in new regions. Cultural and military considerations were also taken into account. Although the result did not quite live up to expectation, there is no gainsaying that this approach to railway construction, beginning in the 1850s and pursued during a period of ardent liberalism, proved to be an example of forethought in government economic planning which has never been surpassed in Sweden, or for that matter, in many other countries.

This exercise in economic planning had other aspects. Before Ericson arrived on the scene, all plans for the building of railways had proceded from the theory that their basic function was as a complement to other means of communication. They were supposed to connect the different lake systems, which had served as the backbone of internal communications since time immemorial and had been given their most recent flowering in the Göta Canal construction. Ericson won over the 1853–54 Riksdag to his plan: the railways were to form a separate framework for transportation within the country. Given the basic design which he imparted to the railways system, he probably did more than any other one to create the basic 'infrastructure' for the environment in which Swedish industry developed.

The first piece of legislation affecting joint-stock companies was a crown ordinance, passed in 1848. However, it does not appear to have acquired any importance for about a quarter of a century. Insofar as such companies were formed at all before the 1880s, ownership of the shares seems to have been limited chiefly to the founders and a few persons closely associated with them. The formation of joint-stock companies or corporations did not become more general until the 1880s. As late as World War I, however, many of them continued to operate as family businesses. Neither did the banks around 1850, or even at the beginning of the first major industrial expansion, play a more decisive role in financing; and this in spite of the fact that 1856 was the founding year of Stockholm's Enskilda Bank, which under André Oscar Wallenberg (1816–86) was to do more than any other institution in paving the way for a modern banking system.

Nevertheless, even if development prior to 1870 was relatively modest in scope, all these new activities—sawmilling, engineering, the production of consumer goods—required capital on a scale which up to then had applied only to the iron industry and perhaps the manufactories. Where, then, did the money come from?

In most sectors a major role was played by the merchants, both those who represented the old and large trading houses in Stockholm and Göteborg, and those who operated in smaller towns, often in the northern provinces. Considering the importance which external demand and contacts with foreign markets had for the emergence of the timber industry in Norrland (as it had earlier for the industry in Värmland), it was scarcely remarkable that the merchants often came to occupy a key position both as financiers and as company founders. They knew the markets best, had the money or at least the connections for obtaining credit, and not a few of them were of enterprising, dynamic bent. Like their forerunners, they were fond of combining their commercial activities with other lines of business, with a special preference for ironworking. This tendency was to benefit many industries and companies in the new era.

A hotly debated question, which probably will never be clarified wholly, is the extent to which the infusions of new capital into different industries were of domestic or foreign origin. The most penetrating study to date is that by Torsten Gårdlund on Swedish industrial financing during the breakthrough period from 1830 to 1913. Gärdlund assumes that Sweden, in comparison with other countries, had an unusually great need of capital for her industrialization. Given the size of the country, huge investments were particularly necessary for communications. The two natural resources on which the whole industrialization process was founded, iron ore and forests, required heavy investment for their exploitation. Industrial distribution also took on a special pattern in Sweden with plants scattered over many small communities rather than concentrated in a few large industrial towns, as in England; this meant that costs incurred for such requirements as water supplies, sewerage, schools and hospitals were extra-high. It could not be otherwise when, to quote Gårdlund, 'urban development was run on the lines of small enterprises, as it were'.

Foreign capital was crucial as far as communications were concerned. Much of the state's railway-building programme was financed by money borrowed abroad, especially in France and Britain. The state and various institutions receiving state support also contracted sizable foreign loans for housing construction. Similarly, Söderlund has shown that merchants were largely instrumental in obtaining foreign capital, mainly British and French, to help build up the timber industry.

Other industries, however, were chiefly financed by domestic capital according to Gårdlund's findings. Over and above the leading merchants (though in regard to them it is very difficult to draw a boundary line between what they advanced from their own savings and what they borrowed abroad), most of the investment capital was forthcoming from high-ranking public officials and from wealthy men in the professions. In addition, and this undoubtedly was often the most important, many of the new companies started on a very modest scale and expanded in response to rising demand and when profits were large enough to permit re-investment. Literature abounds in stories of how the early captains of industry lived exceptionally frugally in order to plough back more profits into their enterprises Just how far such stories correspond with the facts we leave unsaid; the important thing is that considerable profits could be earned and that demand was mounting rapidly. In such a situation, many an entrepreneur could afford to take a chance on the future; even if he lacked his own resources, he could expand with the help of extremely short-term credits, and the money could be counted on to come in fast enough to keep the business solvent.

There was another and very important reason for the apparently high degree of self-financing. Many of the newly started enterprises enjoyed virtual monopolies for a long time. The new products they made were exclusive to them, at least within a very large geographic area. As long as transportation costs were so high, it was not difficult to maintain a regional monopoly. Where they had to make room for others was in regard to the old products they made with new methods. Even so, these methods—involving a greater measure of mass production—yielded comfortable profit margins, since prices could be set in relation to the old prices fetched by the products of *sloyd* and handicraft. Whatever aspect this nascent industrial enterprise is viewed from, it was as remote from the notion of free, open competition as anything that could be imagined. No entrepreneur ever surrendered to any free play of supply and demand, which was the cherished dream of Adam Smith. Instead, each entrepreneur exercised a relatively complete control over his market. Profits could thus be kept high, and in the shelter of accelerated investments and rapidly rising values it became possible for the new class of entrepreneurs to amass huge fortunes. This provided a fertile soil for the theory that the majority of people are exploited to make a minority rich.

Because Sweden's industrialization did not advance in earnest until around 1880, the problems of financing were as yet of limited scope. By then, too, other vital changes had taken place. The building of railways had been accelerated, and, through the medium of state loans, incomes were generated for other sectors of the economy, since large-scale investment not only absorbs capital but also

164

produces returns that can go into new capital formation. The banking system had begun to attain a remarkable development and stability. France had appeared on the scene as a significant exporter of capital. Migration from farm to factory was gaining momentum. The future was taking a shape which could not have been reasonably imagined even as late as the 1860s.

III

Earlier in this account we had occasion to discuss whatever paradoxical significance poverty may have had for the creation of wealth: specifically for the advent of new and often prosperous trades, such as *sloyd* and light industry in the provinces of Västergötland, Småland, Dalarna and Ångermanland. As was noted at the same time, it took more than poverty to achieve the good results; nevertheless, poverty did count in calling attention to the inability of the old forms of trade to provide an adequate livelihood and emphasizing the need for something new to take their place. Necessity stepped in as the mother of intention. While this argument should not be pressed too far, it undoubtedly has some merit.

In regard to the industrial breakthrough or indeed earlier, when the first modest glimpses of such a breakthrough began to be discernible in the later 1860s poverty may be said to have played a role in the general scheme of things. The new situation did not so much involve the ability of large groups to fend for themselves in finding employment and income, as it did the ability of a relatively small number of entrepreneurs to obtain cheap and readily available labour for their activities. Had Sweden in 1850 been an agrarian nation consisting exclusively of prosperous, landed peasants, as those who nostalgically yearn for the 'good, old days' often seem to imagine, industrialization would certainly have been impeded and delayed. There would have been little or no incentive to leave a farm which offered independence and a decent income for an insecure, often hard and ill-paid job in the new factories. Nor did this happen: the people who moved to the industrial towns were not the freeholders, but the agrarian proleteriat—the poor, the underprivileged, the underemployed. For them the choice was entering the factories, emigrating to America, or staying on the land to continue a hopeless existence of destitution and famine.

Naturally this does not mean that the proletarianization of agriculture was the initial or only prerequisite for the development of an industrial economy. It was merely that the two phenomena coincided favourably. Industrialization came with its offer of new jobs to constantly growing hordes of applicants at a time when the pressure of population would otherwise have been overwhelming. In the absence of an alternative, large groups of the population would within a few generations, have sunk into a life of undernourishment, underemployment and total resignation: a pattern so familiar to us today from many of the underdeveloped, 'overpopulated' countries.

Either that would have happened or political and social revolutions would have become inevitable. Instead, the gates of factories could be opened to masses who were shut off from the land. The chance of a new start in life was offered by the iron, timber and engineering industries, or by the activity in the construction of railways and houses.

The start was slow, however. In 1870 more than 70 per cent of the total population was still engaged in agriculture and its subsidiaries, while only 20 per cent were in industry, handicrafts and trade. As late as 1890 the agricultural sector employed over 60 per cent of the total population, which by then had risen to 4·8 million, an increase of 600,000 since 1870. To some extent attempts were made by political means to prevent the redistribution of population. The local authorities, fearing that the newcomers might become public charges, did their utmost to enforce the old statutes on domicile. It is an open question as to whether this really was a deterrent to migration from the farms to the new industrial communities. Presumably the barriers did not operate very effectively. Yet the matter is worth mentioning, if only because it reveals the ambivalence of attitude towards the new which prevailed in many places.

The ambivalence was far from being peculiar to Sweden. Except for certain distinctly Swedish features, it was a faithful replica of what was happening in all countries on the dawn of their industrialization. Many feared the unknown and refused to see the potential for increased production and better living conditions. Among the conservative, the former 'mercantilist' rapture over 'industry' had given way to distrust and aversion. Political and economic conservatism joined forces in an effort to safeguard the old, or at least to prevent it from changing too rapidly.

Given the social substructure of political power, this was not strange. The men who led and made decisions still came from the civil service and the landowning class. In social terms the emergent group of new entrepreneurs consisted largely of upstarts and outsiders, who were supported in their new economic theories by an

166

intelligentsia, also a dubious group (in the eyes of the magnates)—and the members of the intelligentsia, whatever their background, were always an embarassment to the prosperous farmers who had been elevated to power by the Riksdag Act of 1866. Although their Ruralist party came to include several prominent 'urban liberals', it was permeated with petty haggling nad bickering which contrasted sharply with the sweeping changes that the innovators wished to institute in the country at large.

The revolutionaries of 1809 had long identified themselves with the conservative cause. To have risen up in revolt once in their lives sufficed for them; it was now their duty, they felt, to protect the results. One of the most influential of them was Hans Järta (1774–1847), 'father' of the new constitution; he had been one of the most radical Riksdagsmen at Norrköping in 1800, where he renounced his noble title. This conservatism received ideological nourishment in the philosophy of Christopher Boström (1797–1866), a devoted advocate of corporate representation. This school of thought was influential as long as Charles XIV John lived: a self-willed but brilliant monarch who became increasingly conservative with the years; as the former Marshal Bernadotte, he too was the son of a revolution, and moreover, one that wrought far greater effects than did the revolt of 1809.

On the other hand, because it was typified by the monarchy, aristocracy and leading civil servants, it would be wrong to regard this conservatism utterly reactionary. Neither was it consistently upheld everywhere. In the first place it was concerned with the maintenance of the constitution of 1809, and as such was more political than economic and social. The fiercest conflicts concerned the purely political situation. They were about the constitution, the demand for a reform of the franchise, and differing interpretations of the constitution, such as the definition of the personal power of the king. There can be no doubt however, that Swedish society was suffused with conservatism for a long time. In addition to its political dominance it held sway in literature and culture, highlighted by some of the most prominent poets and historians of the time. Romanticism, Gothicism and conservatism were here combined—and all were reflected in the attitude of, for example, Tegnér in 1842, when he opposed the passing of a bill to make primary education compulsory and thus end illiteracy within a few decades. The conservatives argued that a people who could read might end up as dangerous revolutionaries.

A deeply rotted patriarchical outlook was another reason why the conservatives viewed emergent industrialization with misgivings. They feared that life in the new factories would aggravate spiritual poverty and destroy the popular *mores*, about which there had been romantic notions for generations. As they saw it, the new order of things would encourage crime and social unrest.

Subsequent socialist criticism had much in common with these conservative strictures against industrialism. Roughly speaking, this attitude had two bases: the lessons learned from research, especially from Britain, and an exaggeratedly optimistic view of existing agrarian society and its ability to cope with the problems posed by a steadily growing population. Life in the 'country' no doubt had its charms for the landowners and the well-situated farmers. They were in a position to realize the dream of the independent, honourable man of property, the very pillar of society in Sweden as the yeoman was held to be in England. But the poor, the crofters, cottars, farmhands and seasonal labourers did not fit into this picture—and they comprised about half the agricultural population.

Parallel with the political conflict, a profound spiritual change was taking place among growing numbers. It was a change which would help to dissolve the old order, yet at the same time stiffen its resistance and will to fight. Revivalist movements of different kinds had begun to disintegrate the country's religious unity. The Pietists and the Moravians, known from the Age of Liberty, had exerted no more than local influence. A much greater impact was made by the new movements, which emanated both from within the established Lutheran Church and from outside: Schartauanism in western Sweden, Laestadianism in Lapland, Baptism and Methodism. Although they were to burst into full bloom during the century's last three decades, by 1860 the foundations had been laid. Each movement acquired its distinctive social character. Generally speaking, a clear boundary line separated the revival movements of the poor from those of the lower middle classes. Their sociological backgrounds had certain aspects in common, however. With the disruption of old village life, the established Church lost much of its influence over people. It no longer either literally or figuratively stood in the middle of the village. Dissenting views, long persecuted by the clergy as heretical, could now make headway more easily. No doubt the general discontent caused by the poverty and sense of 'alienation' experienced by so many was an important factor too. Social protests intermingled with religious protest against a Church that was so subservient to the will of the mighty and privileged.

Thus religious protest readily assumed a political tinge. If a man could read his Bible, believe in *his* God, and serve him as his own conscience, and not authority, dictated, might he not also hold a contrary opinion on mundane matters and dare to express it? If bishops and priests were no longer held in respect, then what respect should be owed to the agents of secular power, the local authorities and crown bailiffs, and all other authority, who in times of religious persecution let the State Church lead them by the nose? Did not God's will count for more than a royal power and a government which, far from protecting freedom of conscience, sought to subjugate it? If the message of the spirit conflicted with the temporal power, should not the former always take precedence?

These were the new tendencies; at least the description fits the Baptist movement. Its first congregation was formed in Sweden in 1848. Before long the movement acquired not only a religious but also a politically radical character. The Baptist newspaper, *Wecko-Posten*, was an early promoter of universal suffrage, and several of the movement's leading men figured in the formulation of liberal views and policy towards the end of the century. Gradually, however, the movement shed its radicalism and grew fearful of socialism in view of the 'anti-religious' bias adopted by the early labour movements (so also did its more extreme religious offshoot, Pentecostalism, which at first, held aloof from mundane affairs, and later championed the pronounced conservatism of the 'common people', regardless of its members' party-political affiliations).

The temperance movement which emerged in the 1830s exhibited similar trends. It might be something of an exaggeration to say that the Swedes at that time were a besotted people. Nevertheless drunkenness was widespread: aquavit, the national alcoholic beverage, gave the poor man strength and solace to endure a wretched existence. To an extent that can scarcely be grasped today the consumption of spirits was then a formidable problem of public health. Seen from that angle, the temperance movement came to play a great social and political role. Like the various nonconformist movements, and often in actual combination with them, the temperance movement developed into a training ground for democracy. It schooled many of its members for subsequent tasks in trade unions, political organizations, and government on the local and county level. It stood in the vanguard of the adult education movement.

A reciprocal process was no doubt at work too. Anyone who elected to join the nonconformist and temperance movements in their early stages had to have plenty of personal courage, idealism and fighting spirit to propagate their cause. For this reason the movements recruited people of a special calibre, especially for the leading posts,

F*   169

who had achieved greater emancipation from their environment and who were skilled in the arts of agitation and strife. The new faith reinforced these qualities, by making it necessary to keep them in a constant state of preparedness, as it were. In an unmistakable sense, too, these movements had the characteristics of 'popular movements'. Their teachings reached broad sections of the community, the lower middle classes and the really poor, first in the countryside, and later in the factories. As the century neared its end, the labour movement certainly had cause to remember its revivalist and temperance forebears with gratitude. They would be justified in travestying Tegnér's line about Gustavus' III days: 'Where should we be if they had not been?'

By dint of their activities, the popular movements created a balance in the quest for education and culture which became increasingly widespread towards the 1860s. The better-off farmers were among those who took the lead in sending their children to gymnasia and universities. Now and then, a 'farmer student' of humbler origin might follow in the footsteps of his more affluent brethren. Further, vocational training in agriculture and its techniques was beginning to assume great importance. The county agricultural societies had long sponsored educational programmes; in the 1830s the first agricultural institutes were founded; the famous schools at Ultuna and Alnarp were founded in 1848 and 1862, respectively. That peculiarly Scandinavian institution, the 'peoples' high school' started its first Swedish establishments in 1868, with most of the pupils recruited from the ranks of more prosperous farmers. New schools were built to cater for the engineering trades: the Falun Schools of Mining in 1822, the Stockholm Institute of Technology in 1826, the Stockholm College of Forestry in 1826, the Chalmers Institute of Technology at Göteborg in 1828, and the School of Mining at Filipstad in 1830.

Economically and socially, the nascent popular movements were far from homogenous; nor on the whole were they the harbingers of the future. Those which chiefly appealed to the lower middle class— to the groups of craftsmen, small industrialists and tradesmen— inevitably came to reflect the largely conservative opinions of their recruits. Fear of the new industrialism was often pronounced within these groups, and they were strong in their support of old restrictive legislation—although opinions diverged on this point. On the whole, the politically conservative civil servants, the aristocracy, and the political leaders close to the royal throne and in the Council were much more liberal in economic matters. Although inclined to distrust industrialism as a social and political danger, they were in principle committed to a freer economic order and opposed controls which favoured group and guild interests on the production side. The civil servants and aristocrats constituted large consumer groups, and as such traditionally opposed the old burgher class.

As far as reforms 'for the people' and general tolerance were concerned, this mixture of political conservatism, economic liberalism and, to some extent social radicalism flourished under Oscar I, who reigned from 1844 to 1859. He maintained sedulous vigilance over the preservation of royal power and Estate privileges. Nevertheless, he put his seal of approval on measures such as the freedom of trade and on a number of other 'liberal' reforms, as mentioned in the first section of this chapter. This whole pattern of action vividly recalls the ideas of eighteenth century philosophy on the enlightened despot, and his role as the guardian of liberty.

However, as we have had occasion to emphasize repeatedly in the foregoing, the Riksdag Act of 1866 altered the picture. Peasant conservatism now became a power factor—and while this conservatism was less productive of grand political theories, less intellectual and ambivalent, it was all the more solid where interests were concerned. It might be described as a dour, pig-headed preoccupation with the retention of the status quo, and a concentration on such political matters as the abolition of land taxes (using the national defence issue as a bargaining weapon), the protection of agricultural interests against foreign competition, and the protection of the electoral laws which had put these interest groups into power.

The 1866 franchise reform had certainly assured the urban professions a significant overrepresentation as long as industry was poorly developed and the workers did not have the vote. Even so, agricultural interests predominated. In a work published in 1966, *Society and Riksdag (Samhälle och Riksdag)*, commemorating the 100th anniversary of the parliamentary reform, Lars Sköld and Arne Halvarson present some interesting data on the social composition of the Riksdag. It will suffice here to select the statistics concerning the occupational distribution and educational levels of the Riksdagsmen who comprised the first post-reform session.

Out of the 190 members of the Lower Chamber in 1867, 135 or more than 70 per cent lived in the countryside, while 55 or less than 30 per cent lived in towns. Concerning their occupations, 99 were landowners or proprietor farmers, 48 were high-ranking civil servants, and 31 were affiliated with industry and trade. Educational attainments were high. No less than 73 of the 190 members had completed upper secondary school (gymnasia), and of these 61 had continued to obtain university degrees.

In the long run, of course, the overrepresentation of urban occupations, due to the restrictions on income and property which were in effect, could not but have significance. The liberal opposition, and above all the franchise movement, was thereby given a political foundation for its work which it would have lacked otherwise. Nevertheless, the conservative dominance of the countryside was crushing—and above all socially distorted in relation to the 'people' it represented, since the poor or less-well-off constituted 75 per cent of the agrarian population and lacked both the vote and Riksdag spokesmen.

As was pointed out earlier, the composition of the new Riksdag turned into a poorer instrument for political liberalization than the diet of Estates which it replaced. By virtue of the economic and social changes over the past two centuries or so, the Estates had become fragmented and heterogeneous; it was not uncommon for one Estate to harbour a number of highly divergent interests. The new Riksdag was more homogeneous, representing to a far greater degree the social and economic interests of a limited upper class.

It is impossible to determine just how far this conservative attitude, of which one index was the resignation of Louis De Geer in 1870, delayed the social transformation that was under way; as far as industrialization was concerned however, one may safely hazard the generalization that it largely lacked importance.

The processes which already had been set in motion were to gather such momentum that political obstacles could scarcely have stopped them. On the other hand, it is clear enough that conservatism mattered a great deal in the field of social legislation: its impact was negative. Even here, however, one should not entertain exaggerated hopes as to what might otherwise have been possible. There was a lack of economic resources for more sweeping reforms as long as industrialization made so little headway. Besides, the social pressures that persisted within the framework of an order still dominated by the agrarian way of life could not be reduced other than by industrialization. To all intents and purposes, the political scene during the first twenty years after the parliamentary reform manifested a general paralysis. Apart from certain measures concerning the responsibilities of local authorities for fire-fighting, health and building services, nothing constructive was accomplished. The reactionary poor-relief legislation of 1873, a manifestation of the municipal parsimoniousness which found so many able supporters in the new

Riksdag became in time a special monument marking this dreary epoch.

How could this inertia persist in the midst of so much misery? The main reason is to be found in the declining pressure of population owing to the emigration, the growth of new industries, and the continued extention of communications.

A series of poor harvests in the late 1860s, the result of an unusual succession of severe winters and dry summers, turned 1869 into a year of stark hunger in certain parts of the country, especially in Norrland, Småland, Värmland and Blekinge. The death rate rose to 22 per thousand, the highest ever recorded in Sweden. This situation caused the heaviest wave of emigration yet. From 1868 to 1870, inclusive, 80,000 Swedes resettled in the United States, more than had arrived during the whole period from 1851 to 1867. The American Civil War was over and a generous piece of legislation, the Homestead Act of 1862, had opened up new westward land to anyone who was willing to cultivate it; each settler was offered 160 acres. Swedish settlements in the northern states of the Middle West developed and young men schooled in the ways of Swedish forestry flocked to the contracting and building trades in the new, fast-growing American cities.

Conditions in Sweden improved in the 1870s. Harvests were back to satisfactory levels, and continued railway-building and industrialization could absorb some of the new manpower that entered the labour market. Emigration continued and, taking the decade as a whole, exceeded that of the 1860s, though it fell far below the 1867 to 1871 level. A total of approximately 150,000 persons left Sweden during this decade.

With the 1880s another depression set in. The chronic difficulties of agriculture were compounded by a twofold crisis. Production of grains increased at a slower rate, and the compensation sought through imports from Russia and the United States depressed prices, giving rise to grave marketing problems for Swedish farmers. The new means of transportation—railways in the United States and Russia, steamships on the high seas, and the operation of a now respectably-sized domestic railway network—made it possible to move enormous quantities of grain at low freight costs. This agricultural crisis gave renewed impetus to emigration, which attained a volume never seen before or since: about 400,000 persons left the country, comprising over 8 per cent of the population as against between 3 and 4 per cent in the 1870s and 5 per cent in the 1890s. The number of Swedish-born Americans, estimated at 200,000 in

1880, reached nearly 490,000 in 1890. During the 1880s the Swedes who had resettled abroad added more to their numbers than those who remained in Sweden: the increases were about 280,000 and 220,000 respectively.

The crisis in agriculture also manifested itself at the economic and political level. Beginning in the 1840s the gradually relaxed official restrictions on industry and commerce also came to include Swedish external trade—in response to strong foreign pressure. The definite step towards complete liberalization had been taken in 1865. By virtue of a commercial treaty with France, Sweden had become affiliated to the *perpetuum mobile* of free trade which the Cobden treaty of 1860 between Britain and France signified. Included in this treaty was a provision that is generally called the 'most-favoured-nation' clause. Thus if Britain and France were to conclude a similar agreement with any other country, that country would come into enjoyment of the same concessions granted to one another by the original signatories. Conversely, both Britain and France were to obtain the same privileges which either of them might extend by agreement to other countries, and such countries in turn would be similarly bound in relation to one another.

It was this system which began to be subject to debate when Sweden suffered her agricultural crisis in the 1880s. However, the clamour for tariffs did not emanate solely from the powerful political strongholds of the farm producers. Protection was also demanded by strong industrial interests, not least the new industries which were producing for the home market. This reconsideration of the tariff policy was by no means peculiar to Sweden. Virtually the whole of Western Europe had experienced the parallel development of, on the one hand the advantages to be gained from an abundant supply of cheaper food and, on the other, the difficulties which American and Russian grain surpluses had inflicted on domestic agriculture. In the industrially more advanced countries, such as Britain and Belgium, where the initial position in regard to occupational distribution was different, the consequences of this development were an accelerated rural depopulation process, followed by a time of rising unemployment, which in turn gradually diminished as industry was able to absorb more labour. Denmark took the calculated risk of shifting rapidly from field crops to livestock-raising, which permitted a greater export of meat and dairy produce to meet rising demand abroad. The course chosen by Austria-Hungary and Germany, already embarked upon in the 1870s, was to rely on protectionism as a cure, preferably in the form of 'reciprocal' protective tariffs for both agriculture and industry. This policy was chiefly based on the new theories propounded by Friedrich List in his *Nationales System der Politischen Oekonomie* of 1840, with their blend of romanticism, national mysticism, belief in an élite, and demands for government protection of business. In economic terms, his theories represented a kind of 'neo-mercantilism' which, ironically, considering the role which agricultural tariffs acquired as an opening wedge for the new system, were confined in List's grand design solely to industry.

In Sweden, however, the forces favouring free trade and protectionism were so evenly matched for a long time that the latter did not win the day until 1888, and then only through a sheer political accident. The story of how it happened has become celebrated. In the general election of 1888, a majority was returned for the free traders, but it was found that one of the elected was disqualified as he owed 11 kronor and 58 öre in taxes. The whole free-trade ticket was declared invalid and 22 free-traders had to give up their seats to 22 protectionists. That tore down the remaining barriers to a new policy, and Sweden thereby turned her back on three decades of free trade. Four years after the introduction of grain tariffs, the industries received their 'payment' in the form of industrial tariffs. However, these could not be put in force until 1895, since Sweden still was tied to the 'Cobden family' on the strength of her treaty with France thirty years earlier.

The close voting both at the polls and in the Riksdag demonstrated that not even the franchised farmers were of one mind about the new policy. The ideas of free trade had coursed too deeply in the veins of many Ruralist voters and leaders to be relinquished even in the face of an agricultural crisis. Naturally this division in Ruralist ranks was not due to differences in ideology alone. Imports of grain and falling prices did not hurt all farmers alike; different impacts were felt according to the degree of grain cultivation. As I pointed out earlier, a shift from the exclusive cultivation of grain to fodder crops and animal husbandry had taken place. This trend was accentuated in the 1870s and 1880s by the introduction of industrial methods in agriculture, through the use of machinery provided by a vigorously expanding engineering industry. Nor did the protective tariffs affect this development. The tariffs enabled Sweden to maintain a larger share of bread-grain production than Denmark, but in general the same agricultural development was taking place in the two countries. It was fairly obvious that the farmers who already had altered their production basis before the settlement of the tariff conflict, often sided with the free traders. At the same time, it appears that the reason for the relative success of the free traders at the polls as late as 1888 was that the agricultural crisis had robbed many of the previously franchised of the vote. Losses in income placed many of the farmers below the income and property qualification minimum, and naturally enough, those most seriously affected constituted the overwhelming majority of supporters for protectionism.

This also reinforced opposition to the prevailing political system. The Ruralist party did manage to close its ranks again in 1895, but the reunion proved to be more an organizational move than a true marriage of ideas. New groups had emerged. A party system along foreign lines, with a left-to-right spectrum of social democracy, liberalism and conservatism, was taking shape, and as from 1913 a separate party for agrarian interests began to develop. The old alignments of town and industry versus country and agriculture were no longer recognizable. The focus of power had begun to shift in response to a new social change, more profound and far-reaching than that which had slowly but remorselessly shattered the old rank-ordered society. The modern Sweden had begun to emerge, even if her shape was rather indistinct as yet.

IV

When Tegnér, in 1833, identified the potato as one of the causes of the population increase, this master of imagery was not merely indulging his fancy for figurative expression. The potato was the most important article of the Swedish diet at the time and was to remain so for many decades to come. In the many contemporary accounts of life led on small farms, crofts, and cotes, and in the barracks occupied by field labourers, the potato is mentioned as the staple food. A dish of red whortleberries would augment and embellish the everyday diet, with a herring added now and then when times were better, while beef or pork were reserved for more ceremonious occasions. The poorer people's diet naturally varied from one part of the country to another. In the large grain-producing districts, moreover, the less-well-off could afford to be a little choosier than their counterparts in the deficit areas. On the other hand, and this was especially true in Norrland, hunting and fishing could occasionally augment even the poorest diets.

Since the variations tended to be so great—between different parts of Sweden, between years of good and bad harvest, and between different employers or landlords—it is very hard to generalize. For the most part, however, it can be said that the agrarian lower classes fared better the more wealthy their masters were. To work as a crofter, cottar or hired labourer on a manor or estate, was usually more advantageous than to take orders from a farmer, and in the latter case it was better to serve a large proprietor than a small-holder. The treatment of labour, at least from the purely material aspect, was ultimately determined by the existing economic resources. Then, too, traditions made a difference: the larger the farms, and the better the economic status of their owners, the greater was the likeli-hood that a sense of social responsibility and solidarity towards subordinates would be acknowledged.

A series of articles on Swedish manorial estates, published by the Stockholm newspaper, *Svenska Dagbladet*, in the summer of 1966, has described conditions at the juncture of the nineteenth and twentieth centuries. By then various changes had occurred, and some of them were tremendous changes. None the less, they were not so extensive as to have altered the essential pattern of life as lived on the estates, farms and crofts. The stories may have been touched up in the telling, since they relate mostly to the idyllic memories of child-hood retained by elderly ladies of the manor. Even so, several specific details seem worth noting, considering how firmly rooted the tradi-tions were once upon a time.

Lady Ingeborg Björnstierna, daughter of the liberal politician, Baron Gösta Tamm (1866–1931), reminisced as follows about Malstanäs, a manorial estate in Södermanland province:

'All the people employed on the estate worked as cottars. This meant that besides receiving an insignificant wage in money, they were entitled to certain quantities of wheat, rye, bran and groats. Also included were one firlot of herring per year and four litres of milk a day—the milk ration was increased as families grew large. Household fuel requirements were also part of the payment in kind. In addition paraffin and ground for the cultivation of potatoes were included.

'The crofters, of course, had their own holdings and their cows, but both cottars and crofters kept pigs and chickens. Besides this, many crofters grew flax, which their wives spun and sold to the estate. In those days people usually had many children and lived in terribly crowded conditions. That may have been a bigger problem than keeping the larder stocked with food. I especially remember a crofter's wife whom I admired very much. She had a dozen children, all of them brought up to be sturdy people. This family, like the others, lived in one room and kitchen, plus a room in the attic. The children lay in rows on the floor and in the pull-out sofa, while the baby slept in a basket-bed suspended from the ceiling.

[Continued Lady Björnstierna]: 'If an estate was any good at all, the older people never had to end up in the 'poor-house', which was their worst dread. The pensioners, as we would call them today, were put on exemption, which meant that they lived in small cottages on half-pay. The old women received coffee, sugar and candles. When a lot of baking was done in the big kitchen, free loaves would be distributed. In the autumn hunting season, venison would be handed out to the households in proportion to their size. It was also customary practice for the manor to buy everything put up for sale by the employees whether it was needed or not.'

This tale breathes an unmistakable air of paternalism, which in the present instance appears to have worked mostly for the good. The big worry in early nineteenth-century debate on population and poor-relief issues was that this paternal system stood on its last legs: the agricultural poor had been left increasingly to fend for themselves; the landed man of property no longer felt the same solicitude for 'his people'. Those apprehensions were undoubtedly justified. As the lower classes grew in numbers, more and more individuals came to lose the protection which long had been one of the benefits provided by the legislation on servitude and legal residence. This protection continued on manorial estates, and by an occasional large-scale farmer. However, it must be pointed out that these were the exceptions, and that the overwhelming majority were left entirely to the mercies of weather and harvests.

It may be assumed that the old, the ill and the orphaned usually received protection and help when they served under estates and manors. A worse fate constantly threatened the others. They could be forced to 'do the rounds' or to do 'billeting by rotation'. This was a kind of legalized beggary augmented by such odd jobs for unskilled labour as were available. The 'billeters' wandered from farm to farm in that part of a parish which constituted a *rote*, or ward, for the purposes of administering the Poor Law, and where they might be permitted to do some work to earn their meals. Either that, or the commune could auction them to the bidder who demanded the lowest public remuneration for taking care of them. It is not difficult to imagine the conditions of life for these 'lodgers', since they had often to earn their keep under a mean master. The system has been portrayed by a number of writers, among them Harry Martinson in his

Nässlorna Blomma (Flowering Nettles); the boy Martin, the author's
alter ego, is auctioned off for a maintenance sum of five kronor a
month. Rotation-billeting and auctioning were not abolished until
the Poor Law was amended in 1918.

The other measures taken by the authorities to deal with the hardships were sporadic, contradictory, and in some respects more likely
to exacerbate than alleviate. Inadequate resources led to conflicting
demands. The amended Poor Law Acts of 1847 and 1853 laid down
that communal assistance was a right, and the Crown heard appeals
against the decisions of the local authorities. This right was taken
away in 1871. Ambivalence at the top was never more clearly manifest: the authorities wanted to encourage migration to the new
industrial areas, as well as from the deficit to surplus areas within
agriculture itself; but at the same time their enforcement of the Poor
Law, with its insistence on domiciliary rights, prevented people from
migrating and made many communes disinclined to accept newcomers. Some of the public workhouses wanted their inmates to earn
their living by doing a good day's work, but at the same time refused
to pay them current wages, arguing that it would have removed the
incentive to look for 'proper' work. At the same time the manufacturers, who had to bid competitively for their labour, could not be
expected to take kindly to the low wages which the workhouses were
paying.

When Lady Björnstierna said, in the interview quoted above, that
housing was often a more troublesome problem than the stock of
food in the larder, her observation was certainly correct, and this was
true not only for the period she recalled but also earlier. The crofts
and cotes were small, as a rule poorly insulated against damp and cold,
badly ventilated, and wretchedly heated. Many of the cotes (*back-
stugor*) fully lived up to their name; the word *backe* means hillside, and
the dwellings were built with the front parts consisting of roofs and
walls as in ordinary houses, while the backs burrowed into the hill.

The distance to water was often great, and access to a well was far
from universal. Lakes, rivers and brooks were also used for drinking
water. Wood was often in scanty supply, and for many families the
main part of the essential fuel requirements had to be satisfied
through the collection of cones and twigs. When winters were severe,
the only way to keep warm in many cases was to stay in bed under
piles of rags or, for the more fortunate, under skin rugs. In such dire
extremes overcrowding could actually be a blessing: the members of
a large family were able to stay alive by huddling together and warm-
ing each other.

Under such conditions it is not to be wondered at that epidemics spread easily. The greatest scourge of all, tuberculosis, regularly carried off large numbers. Its death toll was highest in the cities, especially in the two 'metropoles' Stockholm and Göteborg. There the conditions of housing and sanitation among the poor were, if possible, even worse.

Although the population statistics for Stockholm show virtual stagnation up to the 1850s, this does not mean that births and deaths balanced each other, in contrast with the rest of the country as a whole, where birth rates far outstripped mortality. The annual number of deaths in the capital greatly exceeded the number of people who were born there. Only a constant influx from the outside kept Stockholm from dwindling slowly but surely into insignificance. It is estimated that about 15,000 persons came to settle in Stockholm each decade between 1800 and 1870. Yet the city's population, 76,000 in 1800, had risen to only 93,000 in 1850 and 136,000 in 1870. The reason for this long stagnation becomes obvious when the following vital statistics are studied. (*Figures are given in rates per thousand.*)

Year	Born in wedlock	Born out of wedlock	Deaths	Difference
1801–10	20·0	12·9	49·6	−16·7
1821–30	20·5	12·5	44·4	−11·4
1841–50	18·0	14·6	38·2	− 5·6
1861–70	20·8	13·8	32·2	+ 2·4

These death rates stand out in an appalling light when compared with those for the whole of Sweden. The national rates for the decades shown were 28·2, 23·6 and 20·2 respectively. Between 1851 and 1855, when mortality in Stockholm reached an acme of 45 per thousand, the corresponding rates in other towns were: Göteborg, 36; Norrköping, 33; Malmö, 27; and Gävle and Karlskrona, 37 per thousand.

A distinct improvement set in during the later 1860s, a decade which nevertheless ended with sharply increased nation-wide mortality owing to the poor harvest of 1869. The explanation is easy to find, and sheds some light on the state of affairs which prevailed earlier. In 1864 something had finally been done about the old problem of water supply and sewage. Before that a handful of wells and landing piers along Lake Mälaren had served to keep the whole city supplied with water. One can readily imagine what this water was like in an age without piped sewerage, when garbage was dumped into the streets and carried off into the lake by rainfall, in so far as the contents of latrine boxes and other refuse were not emptied directly into the water. Stockholm was a city of filth and stench; as far as its inhabitants were concerned, talk of clean sweet country air had real meaning.

The central parts of town, comprising the site of the original settlement Gamla Stan (the Old Town) and its immediate environs, could manage tolerably well. As a city built up on both sides of a ridge, the worst filth could easily wash off and flow down to Mälaren or to Saltsjön, the innermost reach of the Baltic. Incidentally, this was the classic pattern adopted by the cities all over Europe which had managed to survive their medieval origins. They survived because the ridges or hills, selected at first for strategic reasons, saved them from a sanitary nightmare.

Matters were worse in Stockholm's outlying districts. These, too, could count on a degree of natural sanitation, by virtue of undulating topography, but their streets were less steep than in the Old Town. Sanitation in these districts was handicapped by the wretched housing, coupled with widespread economic and social misery. Except for an elegant town house here and there, the outlying quarters housed the city's poor. A miserable wooden shed of one or two rooms often housed ten or twelve people. At fairly frequent intervals large areas of such ramshackle housing burnt to the ground, and efforts would be made to build better on the old sites and improve the townscape at the same time. But that did not necessarily reduce the overcrowding; the new buildings, mostly of stone, had rents too high for the displaced poor. The new tenants were, instead, the well-to-do, who in the course of time were joined by the better-paid workers. The only recourse for the poor was to crowd even more densely in the ramshackle buildings that remained.

Statistics give evidence of frightful slum conditions in Stockholm in former times. First of all it should be noted that the capital had a very favourable age composition thanks to a steady influx of numbers. Most of the newcomers were young people. When one considers that mortality was nevertheless between 75 and 80 per cent higher than the national average, the city's 'risks' stand out as truly formidable. Above all, tuberculosis exacted a much higher toll of the young and middle-aged in Stockholm than elsewhere in Sweden. The number of deaths from tuberculosis per 1,000 inhabitants were:

Year	Stockholm	Nation-wide
1771–80	7·44	2·08
1801–10	8·72	2·51
1821–30	9·31	2·77

Stockholm also held a unique position in regard to infant mortality. Here again the outlying areas set the dismal records. Whereas more than one child in three died before its first birthday in the city as a whole, the rates in the central area ranged from 20 to 30 per cent, but in the outlying districts exceeded 40 per cent. One reason for this difference can be traced to the high frequency of unmarried mothers. About half their children died before the age of one, a rate that no doubt was socially determined. Virtually all the children born out of wedlock belonged to the poorest groups. Although premarital liaisons were far from unusual among the burghers, farmers and the upper strata, these groups were generally able to save 'the family honour'—and the child—by putting the earliest possible legitimacy on fruitful connections.

Sweden reaped immense social advantages from having been spared the shape which cities acquired in Britain, Belgium and Germany because of the industrial location policy decreed by iron and coal. The wider dispersion of factory enterprise in Sweden made possible the more organic and harmonious growth of small industrial communities. This is not to suggest that they developed into idyllic places. The sawmill districts, the new metalworking towns, the old iron-mill towns which continued to attract newcomers because they were more compact, were more concerned with rapid and easy labour recruitment than with sanitary planning and decent housing. The new working-class quarters usually consisted of a conglomeration of barracks and rows of shanties with small apartments, with a poor water supply, worse sewage facilities, and generally overcrowded conditions. In her book *Sø bodde vi* (That is how we lived), Rut Liedgren describes the conditions at Sandviken, where the steel mill was founded in 1863. In the beginning the workers had to find accommodation on nearby farms or build their own huts. Some fifty small earth-covered log cabins were the homes of as many families. When house-building eventually got under way, the typical project called for a one-storey house of eight rooms, divided into four flats, and with two rooms in the attic. Alternatively the houses consisted of two storeys, with eight rooms on each and as many flats to each floor. The standard accommodation came to consist of one room and kitchen per flat. Since the mill expanded faster than the new dwellings became available, this pattern was abandoned, and instead two or even three families would be housed in each flat. It is relevant to add that the mill's owner and managing director Göran Fredrik Göransson (1819–1900), was one of the industrialists who devoted care and attention to the question of worker housing and invested unusually large sums towards its solution.

The situation was certainly not improved by the fact that many of the new worker families came from the poorest of the lower rural classes, unable to impose demands, without assets, and without rights. At the same time many of the new employers were merchants who tended to look on their new ventures chiefly as a way of making fast profit. Others were small entrepreneurs of mechanical aptitude and inventive bent, who had worked their way up; parsimonious and hard-hearted, they had little sympathy for the humanitarian and social obligations that the old landowner class undoubtedly felt, whatever their other failings may have been.

Then, too, there was probably very little sense of solidarity among the workers themselves in the beginning, thrust as they all were into a new environment. They came from different regions, spoke different dialects, represented different traditions. They were shy and suspicious, or adopted a bullying attitude, frequently drunk, and often involved in fights and brawls with each other.

As already indicated, it became characteristic of the new industrial communities that the working class and employer class lived in different districts. The working-class district was further divided into areas reserved for permanent labour and those for casual labour, which included a heavy component of women. The casuals lived outside the 'city limits', and comprised a kind of regular reserve. In the new sawmill towns which sprang up along the coast, the casuals consisted mainly of seamen, who were looked down on by the other working-class categories. This contempt turned into a feeling of hostility in regard to the 'trash-timber' girls, so called because they loaded ballast or wood into barge-holds. They were held in such low esteem because they freely mixed with the seamen. For them the only accommodation was in barracks on the outskirts, located as far as possible from the homes of respectable full-time workers.

If the gospel of solidarity and the message of human dignity and human rights were to have any influence in these places, they would certainly have to be preached with force. The task of conversion was initially undertaken by the revivalists, though often without success in these rough-and-tumble environments. The temperance movement also lent a helping hand. With the passage of time, the trade union movement and socialism took over, and to some extent joined forces in trying to indoctrinate the new captains of industry with a 'social liberalism'. That, however, takes us to a period of forty or fifty years after the parliamentary reform—to a Sweden that had altered considerably since 1866.

4

AT THE HALFWAY MARK

I

THE year 1908 was a hard one. The international crisis of 1907 had quickly spread to Sweden. Business was slumping, factories stood still or worked at half steam, unemployment was extensive. Bitterness and unrest were aggravated by political conflicts, in particular the fight for universal suffrage.

A high degree of economic, social and political awareness had been aroused in the working man, and this awareness spelled action: the Social Democratic party had been formed in 1889; the trade union movement had closed ranks with the founding of *Landsorganisationen* (the Swedish Confederation of Trade Unions) in 1898, which was to provide the movement with a unified leadership as from 1909. To counter this movement, the employers had joined forces in 1902 to form the *Svenska Arbetsgivareföreningen* (the Swedish Employers' Confederation). The 'organizing' of society, which culminated after World War II, had begun.

A law granting universal male suffrage in elections to the Lower Chamber had been approved in 1907, and held in abeyance by constitutional prescription until the 1909 Riksdag finally adopted it. At the same time the procedure for local elections was reformed, but not to the same democratic extent. According to a scale of plural vote determined by income, one local elector could cast as many as forty votes; this, in combination with the rule of double proportionality holding for elections to the Upper Chamber, ensured the continued preponderance of the wealthy in this body. Once again (shades of the Act of 1866!) the reforms involved were *ex post facto* acknowledgements of social and economic changes that had already occurred. They conserved the old instead of opening gates to the new that was on its way.

Developments had moved apace since the late 1860s, and accelerated

185

still further in the years immediately before and after the turn of the century. In the field of foreign affairs there was one change worthy of special note: in 1905 Sweden dissolved her personal union with Norway, relinquishing this last remnant of what had once been a Swedish great-power dream. Gone was the 'compensation' for the loss of the Finnish tributary state.

In 1870 more than 70 per cent of the population still earned their living from agriculture and its subsidiaries. This proportion had fallen to 50 per cent shortly after the beginning of the twentieth century. By 1910 the occupational distribution presented a somewhat different picture: 32 per cent of the people lived off industry, 13 per cent off trade and commerce, and 6 per cent were in public service and the professions. In that year the total population had risen to 5·5 million from 4·2 million in 1870, and 3·9 million in 1860. In fifty years there had thus been an increase of more than 1·5 million or nearly 40 per cent. The changes can be illustrated in another way. In 1860 the agrarian population slightly exceeded 2·8 million, and 1910 it fell just short of 2·8 million. The entire population increase had either become engaged in urban occupations or left the country. Meanwhile the agricultural community had marked time, and as from the new century it slowly but surely began to dwindle even in absolute numbers.

In 1870, the urban population did not exceed 13 per cent of the total. Only one city had more than 100,000 inhabitants: Stockholm, with 136,000. Göteborg had a population of 56,000, Malmö 26,000 and Norrköping 24,000. Karlskrona held fifth place with 17,000.

The urban share reached 25 per cent in 1910, when 13 towns had more than 20,000 inhabitants. Stockholm had 342,000, Göteborg 167,000 and Malmö 83,000. Örebro, Borås, Eskilstuna and Lund now numbered more than 20,000 people. Västerås came close with a figure of over 19,000.

If we use the word 'urban' in its broad sense to mean any built-up area where non-farming occupations are pursued—its percentage of the total population was about 15 in 1870 and 40 in 1910.

Other changes had occurred. Although the high proportion of births to deaths remained constant (or fell only negligibly), this was due not to any stable birth rate, but rather to a marked decline in both nativity and mortality. The mortality rate, which towards the end of the eighteenth century lay at 27 per thousand and continued at higher than 20 until the 1860s, fell as from the 1880s to 16 and after the turn of the century to below 15 per thousand.

The probable life expectancy at birth—or the time taken to reduce an age group by half—was 55 years in the 1860s and 67 years in the first decade of the twentieth century. The average life expectancy at birth—that is, the average number of years of life remaining for persons of a given age group, was 43 years for men and 46 for women in the 1860s, and 55 years for men and 57 years for women from 1901 to 1910.

Industrial development during the latter half of the nineteenth century and the first decade of the twentieth varied from industry to industry. The 1870s saw the initial breakthrough, and progress continued gradual until a significant upsurge during the 1890s.

It was during the 1870s and 1880s that the principal earners of export revenue, ironworking and timber, definitely switched over to an industrial economy. At the same time the network of communications continued to expand rapidly. The railways added more than 6,000 kilometres to their length; over two-thirds of this distance was laid during the 1870s, the largest Swedish increase ever in a single decade. A similarly vigorous expansion was shown by the steamship fleet: in 1890 there were 1,016 steamers of 141,267 tons net weight and a rated output of 37,843 horsepower.

The engineering industry (defined as the manufacture of metal products, machinery and transport equipment) kept pace with communications, ironworking and the forest-based industries in this development. However, engineering was not to achieve its real breakthrough until the 1890s.

That decade also saw the virtually complete change-over to industrial processing of the consumer goods production. Not until then did the rural exodus become extensive enough to destroy the old self-supply economy and to make the great majority of the population dependent on specialized firms for the everyday necessities of life. The previously described protectionist policy, enforced by successive stages in 1888 and 1892, is especially relevant in this connection. Because of the protection afforded by the tariffs, a consumer goods industry based on the home market was enabled to grow faster and to attain greater scope than would otherwise have been the case. The second industrial breakthrough differed from its predecessor in that the course it took was partly guided by official policy towards a more diversified industrial production and a more widely ramified structure.

In addition to an increased demand and the protective tariffs policy came improved technical resources. For the most part, demand and technology followed similar lines of development; this was natural enough, since each conditioned the other. Their interaction conferred on Swedish industries what has become their typical hallmark: a constant shift towards a higher degree of processing in their products. The beginning was made in the export sector with the output of products having a relatively low processing component: bar iron, battens, planks and round timber. The major period of construction in the industrial development of Britain and the Continent had created a demand for these products. Initially, this demand could be satisfied with the rather awkward machines that did not have to meet exacting standards of precision. Soon, however, more highly export goods were required: finished articles of ferrous and nonferrous metal, finer grades of battens and boards, furniture and paper. Because of new inventions and the successive improvement of earlier production methods, more ingenious machines were available to meet this demand. Thus when industrialization reached the point where a large-scale demand for consumer goods could be sustained, a technology was at hand which made it possible to start a diversified production of these goods. However, many years were to elapse before the machines became more reliable precision instruments than the human hand. For a long time to come only the handicrafts could produce goods of first-rate quality, and some of them are still doing so today. During this period the process of invention increasingly became a deliberate act of applied science. Here, too, one is reinforced in the belief that the primary cause of industrial advance (if the effort of identifying the different 'causes' is worth making at all) was economic, not technical. After the more 'playful' experiments of the first period, the increasing sophistication of technology was chiefly the result of deliberate scientific research. The aim of this research was determined by the demand for new products, or by the expectations of entrepreneurs and inventors that such a demand could be created. When inventors now went to work, they set industrial utility as the main target for their creations. A number of Swedish inventions thus came to lay the foundations for large new enterprises. Among the firms that typically owe their origins to 'genius' are Asea, Separator, Atlas Copco, SKF, AGA, and Volvo.

The developments which gave the Swedish economy its structural pattern just before the outbreak of World War I are worth noting. The trade statistics give fair evidence of what was happening in the exporting industries. Throughout this period the forest-based industries maintained the lead they had gained around 1900, in spite of a slight decline towards the end. A sharply rising curve was shown by the products of the paper industry, as well as by minerals and mineral products. Processed and unprocessed metals varied but their relative importance remained unchanged in long-range terms. After the decline in the 1880s and 1890s, their share of exports recovered at the beginning of the twentieth century.

During this period, from 1870 to 1914, the total value of Swedish exports rose from about 200 million kronor to about 720 million. Allowing roughly 25 per cent for depreciated money, this increase is equivalent to a tripling of the export volume.

At the same time as Swedish industries were exporting more, they were also improving the quality of their products. Within the forestry sector, the emergence of a large pulp and paper industry was most significant. Producers changed their basic raw material from rags to wood. The first innovation was to use mechanical pulp, which was gradually replaced by chemical pulp or cellulose. These methods had begun to gain ground in the 1870s and 1880s. In the mid-1890s, the manufacture of pulp began to make tremendous advances as a result of the adoption of the sulphite-cooking process. There followed dizzying rates of expansion in output and exports, as the following table makes clear.

MANUFACTURE AND EXPORTS OF PAPER PULP, 1876–1915

Period	Annual output in tons	Annual exports in tons	Export per cent of output
1876–80	11,700	7,300	62
1891–95	153,500	89,900	59
1901–05	430,400	290,600	67
1911–15	1,124,300	813,500	72

Chemical pulp first began to exceed mechanical pulp in volume towards the end of the 1890s. In 1908 it attained a level of 537,000 tons as against 214,000 tons for mechanical pulp; in 1914 the figures were 865,900 and 270,000 tons respectively.

This upsurge in the pulp industry involved a significant alteration in the proportional distribution of the uses to which the forests were put. The demand for timber as such began to decline in the 1890s, at the same time as the pulp and paper industries needed appreciably more wood. Even within the timber industry proper there was a definite trend towards finer and more highly processed products.

The woodworking industries had experienced their first breakthrough in the 1870s, when they concentrated on building cottages and private homes, together with such accessories as doors and window-frames. A new upswing set in towards the end of the 1880s for the joinery workshops, especially those in Småland province.

They had a most varied production including chairs, tables, broom handles, bobbins and barrels. Factory-made furniture began to capture the market in the 1890s when not only the joinery shops, but also the woodworker artisans turned their hands to it. However, the skills of handicraft were still relied upon to supply the fancier articles. Most of the buyers of factory-made furniture were to be found among the working class and the lower middle class.

The technical revolution in ironworking was described in the previous chapter. A completely different pattern of manufacture had developed from the adoption of the new ingot-iron processes. As the use of the basic process became more widespread, the industry's geographic distribution was altered. It began with the exploitation of the Grängesberg fields, followed by the phosphoric ore fields in Norrbotten province. Mining operations, once confined almost exclusively to the Bergslagen region of central Sweden, were now concentrated in the far north. It will be recalled that a similar south-to-north transplantation had taken place several decades earlier in the timber industry.

The changes in manufacture had to do with degrees of processing. They followed two different lines, one concentrating on the exportation of pig iron and ore, the other on increased production and exportation of steel and hardware.

Sweden had the basic ingot-iron process to thank for her exports of crude ore. It was extensively used in the German iron industry, which as a result began to buy Swedish ore of a high phosphorous content. The mining and export of iron also rose rapidly: 930 thousand tons were mined in 1886–90, 2·3 million tons in 1896–1900 and 4·6 million tons in 1906–10. Exports of pig iron also increased— rather a new development, since in the past most of the pig had remained in Sweden to go into bar iron or (though to a far lesser extent) steel. In 1886–90 59,000 tons were exported, in 1896–1900 83,000 tons and in 1906–10 118,000 tons.

The ingot-iron process, however, did more than generate a German demand for Swedish iron ore. It also put greater emphasis on the domestic manufacture of steel. This in turn enhanced the importance of steel, either as it was or in further processed form, in the exportation of ferrous products.

These developments were important for the engineering industry too. Of course the metalworking plants did not discontinue their earlier functions as repair and servicing agencies of the iron industry and communications after 1870. But from then on, and especially from the 1890s, engineering stands out as a fully-fledged industry in

190

its own right, and an ever-increasing share of its output came to be earmarked for foreign buyers. It is estimated that between 30 and 40 per cent of the engineering output in 1913 was exported, a figure that should suffice to show how greatly the metalworking plants had changed in character. As before, the range of production still included power-transmission devices, steam engines, farm machinery, locomotives and wagons; but the jack-of-all-trades orientation which had marked the initial period of industrialization disappeared towards the end of the century in favour of fairly extensive specialization. If a buyer back in the 1860s and 1870s could count on one and the same firm to supply him with virtually anything from nails to steam engines, he now had to turn to specialized firms. This division of labour, which conferred qualitative and economic benefits, was made possible because demand in other industrial sectors had increased so sharply. The earlier system of working to custom orders, which meant that a little of everything had to be made to keep the business running, could now give way to producing for stock in large series. An inevitable corollary of this development was standardization, which seems to have received a special boost in the 1890s with the advent of the internal combustion engine.

Electrotechnology first developed as an important section of the engineering industry in the 1890s. Its two main branches were from the start telephones and heavy electrical equipment. The internationally known telecommunications firm, L. M. Ericsson, had started to make telephones in 1876, and a public service company, Stockholms Allmänna Telefon Aktiebolag, was founded in 1883 to build and operate telephone lines. In that same year, the first manufacturer of electrical machinery, Elektriska Aktiebolaget (later Asea), was established at Arboga. The plant was moved in 1891 to Västerås, which ever since has been the electrical capital of Sweden. Not only was electrotechnology of conclusive importance for industrial development in general, but it also brought about tremendous changes in working conditions and everyday life. The transmission of electricity over long distances eliminated the need for locating industrial plants close to their sources of energy; greater attention could now be paid to other factors. The new source of energy and light also made possible continuous factory operation, permitting a greater utilization of invested capital. It also led to increased demands for night work and shift work. Further, electricity spurred the trend towards precision and standardization of manufacture, and thus foreshadowed a coming age of mass production by industrial giants.

It was in the 1890s, too, that a great era in shipbuilding started.

The growth of consumer-goods production took place in two branches: clothing and textiles; and food, beverages and tobacco. Both had begun to switch over to factory methods during the pre-industrial era up to 1870. The textile industry, after a setback in the 1860s caused by the cotton shortage in consequence of the American Civil War, continued to progress rapidly during the 1870s and 1880s. During the 1870s some 40 factories with a combined labour force of 6,000 persons, constituted the cotton industry. About 20 of these factories were spinneries, while the rest were weaving mills or combinations of the two. Of the 6,000 workers about 4,000 were employed in the spinneries, Some twenty years later there were 54 factories, divided equally between spinning and weaving. The labour force now approached 9,000, of which nearly 5,000 were employed in the spinning mills. In 1913 there were 31 spinneries and 48 weaving mills and combined factories employing more than 13,000 workers, of whom 5,500 worked in the spinneries.

An almost identical pattern of development took place in the fabrication of wool, though on a higher level, as it were. The number of factories, both spinneries and weaving mills, just about tripled those of the cotton industry for each of the years cited above. At the same time, wool production tended to require a smaller labour force than cotton. Output quantities were also lower. In 1913 the cotton mills produced 20 million kilograms of yarn and 13 million kilograms of woven fabrics, while the woollen mills yielded only 12 million kilograms of yarn and 9 million kilograms of cloth. The main reason why the woollen mills turned out so much less with roughly the same number of workers overall was their relatively low efficiency; note that the total labour force was spread out over three times as many production units as in the cotton industry. This difference of structure was no doubt in part due to the fact that the cotton mills could obtain large quantities of more uniform raw material. In the case of wool, a higher proportion of which had to be obtained on the home market, the deliveries were much smaller, and their quality was uneven.

As from the 1880s, the manufacture of knitwear exhibited a development similar to that of cotton and wool, while the fabrication of silk dwindled to vanishing point.

In the matter of garments or ready-made clothing, Sweden did not have an industry worth mention until the turn of the century. As late as the beginning of World War I, the factories still employed fewer workers than the home tailors who operated under the old credit-advance system. In 1914 the garment industry consisted of about

140 plants with a combined output value of about 30 million kronor and employing some 3,000 workers.

The industrial statistics for 1871–75 disclose the presence of but one shoe factory. It was situated at Vänersborg. Four factories turn up in the data for 1886–90, with a combined labour force of 243 persons. Then came the period of great expansion, and we see no less than 50 factories reported for 1901–05, employing 3,800 workers and turning out goods to the value of 15 million kronor. A frenzy of factory construction set in after 1897, in consequence of the rise in tariffs on imported shoes that same year.

In the production of beverages and tobacco, developments continued along the lines already marked out before 1870. Moreover, the making of tobacco had advanced beyond the handicraft stage, as evidenced by the unchanged number of enterprises (indeed they even diminished at times) in combination with rising outputs and labour force. In 1871–75 there were 103 factories employing 3,400 workers and producing 4·6 million kilograms of tobacco; in 1913, 68 factories, 4,700 workers and 8·5 million kilograms. The number of factories had fallen by 33 per cent, the number of workers increased by 38 per cent, and the output by nearly 85 per cent.

By 1890 the distilling industry had undergone an extensive concentration which brought down the number of production units to 172, having been 600 in the 1860s. This downward trend continued at a negligible rate thereafter, while both the labour force and the volume of output was stable up to 1913. It thus appears that the *per capita* consumption of aquavit must have fallen considerably. That the temperance movement had enjoyed considerable success can be gauged from the stagnation of the distilling industry in a country with a growing population. Aquavit was largely made from potatoes, but some varieties were extracted from grain. Beginning in 1909, use was made of a new ingredient, wood spirits, the waste effluent of sulphite cellulose production. Ten years later, the Royal Board of Trade gave vent to glowing hopes in these words from its annual report: 'This manufacture, which began in 1909 and as from 1910–11 has been conducted at three large sulphite mills, has since expanded vigorously and promises to develop handsomely.'

The brewing industry also developed the familiar characteristics of a large-scale enterprise. In the statistical period from 1876 to 1880, 112 breweries were in operation, manned by 1,600 workers and producing potables to a total of 480,000 hectolitres. The corresponding figures for 1912 were 649 breweries, 5,700 workers and 2·6 million hectolitres.

G

Of the food processing industries developed significantly from the 1890s onwards, the most important were flour-milling, baking, margarine and the sugar industries. Up to 1900 Sweden had some 1,500 flour mills, which employed 4,500 workers and attained an output value in excess of 100 million kronor. There were roughly 70 large bakeries and biscuit factories, manned by 2,000 workers and turning out products worth 16 million kronor. In addition, a great deal of baking was still being carried on as a craft: the figures for 1900 show 2,500 master bakers and 4,300 helpers thus employed; by 1915 their numbers had risen to 3,300 and 5,300, respectively. The industrial bakeries then numbered 148, including the biscuit factories; together they had 3,500 workers and an output value of nearly 40 million kronor.

The first Swedish margarine factory was built in 1881 at Hälsingborg. During the 1890s the number increased to 7, with a total labour force of 236 persons and a production of 6 million kilograms. By 1910 the margarine industry consisted of 10 plants, employed 585 workers, and turned out products totalling 23 million kilograms.

The sugar industry emerged in the 1890s using domestic sugar supplies. At the turn of the century there were some 20 plants employing 5,600 workers. Only 4 plants are reported in operation twenty-five years earlier, and nothing is known about the size of their labour force. Production at the turn of the century totalled around 100 million kilograms. Fifteen years earlier only about one-tenth as much sugar was processed. By 1900 Sweden had achieved virtual self-sufficiency in sugar. Torsten Gårdlund writes: 'As the century neared its end, the sugar boxes had been unlocked in Swedish homes. Once a luxury, sugar had in the course of a few decades become an item of everyday fare.' The annual *per capita* consumption rose from 7 kilograms in the 1870s to 27 kilograms in 1913. Anyone who visits today's 'country auctions' can still bid for sugar boxes. Well into the twentieth century, the market offered spice cabinets with tiny drawers for sugar, a silent testimonial to the strict economy that had to be observed for a precious commodity, as compared with the more commodious space reserved in these cabinets for an article like salt.

A very important side of industrialization during its great period of expansion has yet to be mentioned: the rationalization of agriculture. One of the by-products obtained in the basic ingot-iron process was Thomas meal, a phosphate which could be used as an artificial fertilizer. However, that was hardly the sole gift of industry to agriculture. Ploughs, harrows and clod-crushers from the engineering industry, and later threshers, tractors, electric power plants and dairy machinery made farming easier and more efficient. Vigorously expanding communications also played a part in these improvements, though the real transformation here came with the more extensive use of motor vehicles in the 1920s. Agriculture made its own contributions too: a regular sequence of crop rotation was adopted, so that large fields no longer had to lie fallow every year; more and more farmers engaged in foddercrop cultivation; ditching and drainage enlarged the arable and improved its average quality. There was an increase in the numbers of livestock carried, and it continued even after the protective tariff of 1888 went into force. The tariffs did not provide complete protection against imports. Up to the outbreak of World War I, Sweden still imported 30 per cent of her cereal requirements. The output of animal husbandry also rose at a faster rate than the population, thereby contributing significantly to a general improvement of the Swedish diet. Grades and yields of livestock were improved by more regular supplies of better fodder. A rising output, in spite of unchanged population figures, demonstrates agricultural rationalization. No doubt the results would have been even more impressive if another agricultural policy, like that in Denmark, had operated, but that is another matter.

Since Sweden consistently imported more than she exported from the middle of the nineteenth century until shortly after the turn of the new century, she was an importer of capital. Her industrial expansion was partly financed by capital from abroad. By and large, it appears that the system of division of labour which applied to financing during the first phase of railway construction was in use in various spheres throughout this period. The central government, local authorities and mortgage institutions set up for house-building financed their investments by foreign borrowings. Industry looked first of all to the domestic capital market for its needs. It is estimated that, in 1913, the central government, local authorities and mortgage institutions owed about 900 million kronor to foreign lenders. Sweden's aggregate net debt to foreign countries at this time was probably in the neighbourhood of 1,000 million kronor. In other words, the three borrower categories named owed about 90 per cent of the total, while only 10 per cent fell on industrial and other private firms. France had been the biggest lender from the later 1870s; it is estimated that 600 millions of the 900-million debt had been contracted with the French.

Actually, Sweden was not the only country regarded by the French as a good investment. Throughout this period, France held a position of power as exporter to the international capital market. One explanation was the high incidence of savings in that country, especially among the rural population. This was combined with a system of deposit banks which made it possible to deploy the savings. At the same time a population without initiative and a slow rate of industrial development in France diminished the attractiveness of domestic investment. As a rule, the official discount rate was the lowest in Europe. Money found its way across the frontiers and France found herself in the position, not unusual for rentier countries, of financing the industrial expansion of others at good rates of interest and neglecting her own.

For Sweden the situation was the other way round: she was investing feverishly, domestic savings were inadequate, and her capital market had not developed beyond a rudimentary stage. In such a situation, the willingness of France to advance loans came in handy. Most of the loans were in the form of bonds, which usually were floated by the commercial banks founded in the decades after 1850, though it was not until towards the end of the century that one could speak of commercial banking in its modern sense. In due course these banks also acquired greater importance for industrial financing, in the form of direct advances as well as bonds.

It is impossible to pinpoint the exact time when the banks regularly supplied industry with most of its capital. In any event, other sources were more important during the period of the 1870s, among them the merchant houses, different private bankers and tradesmen, and not least, the investments and ploughed-back profits of industry itself. Gradually, too, the market for shares grew as a source of money. With so many new firms apparently destined for the empyrean blue, the interest in 'getting in on it' could sometimes assume frenzied proportions. Too much should not be read into this development, however: the overwhelming number of shareholders came from fairly limited circles who had plenty of money to start with and were willing to take speculative risks with it; further, it was only seldom that the later diffusion of share ownership reached the point where the secure voting majority of a tiny group of shareholder-owners was ever seriously threatened.

A few statistics selected from 1913 will show the spread of the limited liability company or corporation. In that year 9,266 establishments were reported for the industrial sector, with a combined force of more than 360,000 workers. Of these establishments 40 per cent were owned by corporations, and 40 per cent by 'single proprietors'. The corporation-owned units employed 76 per cent of this labour force, or about 275,000 workers. The findings of another study show that, in the same year, 492 large-scale manufacturing and shipping enterprises had equity capital totalling 13,000 million kronor, and liabilities of 378 millions for bonds and 330 millions owed to banks. Several years earlier, in 1908, the total amount of capital paid in to all corporations had slightly exceeded 2,000 million kronor.

In 1900 the commercial banks owned total assets worth more than 1,300 million kronor; their assets exceeded 2,800 millions in 1913. Their equity capital including reserves amounted to 650 million kronor, and deposits totalled 1,700 millions. All these holdings represented a volume of business that had more than doubled since the turn of the century, and increased six or sevenfold since 1880.

A significant change took place just before 1900. The private banks had been empowered to print paper money ever since the 1830s. Their total note issue, amounting to 30 million kronor in 1860, 50 millions in 1880 and 82 millions in 1900, had consistently outstripped that of the *Riksbank* and in the late 1870s was actually twice as large. Then in 1877 the exclusive right to issue paper money was vested in the *Riksbank* (all the notes from private banks had been redeemed by 1907), which at the same time discontinued the commercial business it had conducted earlier in accepting interest-bearing deposits. It now assumed the role of a true central bank, whose future dealings with the general public would be mediated almost exclusively by the 'ordinary' banks. Henceforth its main task was to guide the domestic capital market by fixing the terms of private-bank borrowing and rediscounting with the central bank so as to achieve harmony with the international currency obligations. There was no more kicking over the traces now that the value of money had to be safeguarded. With the currency reform of 1843 Sweden had returned to a silver standard. Thanks to a combination of fortuitous circumstances, the gold standard could be adopted in 1873, transforming the basis of Sweden's monetary system with a minimum of agony. The obligation to preserve the gold parity of Swedish currency made it necessary for the *Riksbank* to keep lending within narrow limits. If one so chooses, this could be called an active and independent central-bank policy, in that both the Cabinet and Riksdag had to keep their hands off and adapt their financial allocations to its requirements. Actually, of course, it was a highly passive policy, tied as it was to the 'idiotic confines' imposed by the gold standard. When strains of a more serious kind occurred, as in the crisis of 1879, 1893

197

and 1907–08, the adjustments were harder to make than they would have been if an active policy had functioned. It was even less possible to cushion the shock for private enterprise, which was left no alternative but to follow a slumping business cycle right to the bitter end. Eventually the strain became so intolerable that the gold standard was abandoned; and when it was resumed in the 1920s it was at the price of a harsh deflationary policy.

Why did it take so long for a modern banking system geared to the financing of industry to reach Sweden? The best answer is that for many years such a system was not really necessary. The first banks were not founded in the cities, or indeed in any of the industrial and financial centres. They were provincial, often conducting a limited local business, and usually catered for agriculture rather than industry. In financial and industrial centres, true banking services were rendered instead by firms of merchants and financiers. A change did come, however, and it was undoubtedly stimulated by the repeal in 1864 of the old legal ceiling on interest, which had compelled the banks to pay such low rates on their deposits that companies and individuals both preferred to place their money in a 'freer' market. A further deterrent had been the peculiar rules under which banks allowed money to be withdrawn from deposit accounts. Stockholms Enskilda Bank, under the leadership of A. O. Wallenberg, worked indefatigably to develop a deposit business that could be specifically deployed for the benefit of industry. The other banks, among them the Skandinaviska Kreditaktiebolaget (later Skandinaviska Banken) and an offshoot of Stockholms Enskilda Bank, Stockholms Handelsbank (now Svenska Handelsbanken), founded in 1871, followed in Wallenberg's footsteps. The different provincial banks increased their activities in the field of industrial lending. Towards the end of the century, the business of lending money to industrial firms on the strength of their shares became most important. Out of the total bank advances outstanding in 1913, 36 per cent was lent against securities in shares.

The main developments may be gathered from selected statistics. In 1860 there had existed 12 banks housed in 27 offices. By 1880 the number had risen to 44 banks with 205 offices, and in 1913 to 75 banks with 630 offices. Between 1877 and 1896 outstanding claims of commercial banks rose from 450 to 900 million kronor, averaging out at an increase of 20 million kronor per year. Advances then rose at an annual rate of 100 million kronor up to 1913, when they began to approach the 3,000-million mark.

Large sums of capital were also accumulated in savings banks and, as the century neared its end, in insurance companies. At the close of 1913 there were 440 savings banks with total deposits of 953 million kronor, mostly invested in building credits and bonds.

Where did the money come from that commercial banks, savings banks and insurance companies used to help finance a quickly expanding economy? What was the market for deposits, for the savings which in the final instance were responsible for the investment strength required for expansion?

As a first and more general answer to these questions, the new industries financed themselves to a great extent by virtue of the higher national income they created—once the wheels had been set in motion, chiefly with the help of foreign borrowing for railway and housing construction. These large investments accounted for an income accumulation and to a great extent for direct demand—which made it possible for many firms to get started and grow. Profits were ploughed back into these enterprises on a considerable scale, but they also generated demand and income in new sectors of the economy, with new investments, profit plough-backs and further diffusion of income as the results. The country was gradually becoming wealthier, and by contrast with the old wealth, of which so much had been tied up in manors and estates, the new wealth took shapes that permitted its continuous redeployment to new purposes. At the same time, the huge reservoir of manpower that was provided by the increase in population, and the 'concealed' unemployment within agriculture, made it possible to let increased consumption proceed at a slower rate than economic growth. In other words, a relatively large share of the higher national income could be retained for reinvestment. Over and above the facilities provided by increased saving, credit could not be expanded on any appreciable scale owing to the rigidities imposed by the gold standard, and that made it necessary to borrow from abroad. The economy grew without inflation or even price rises worth mentioning. Consumer prices rose by an estimated 25 per cent in the whole period from 1860 to 1914. Considering the constant improvement of product quality throughout these 55 years, it can be argued that prices did not rise at all. In the meantime the national income appears to have increased fourfold in fixed prices, or tripled in per capita terms. The incomes of industrial workers increased approximately 2·75 times, and of farm labourers about twice. Thus the *share* of these groups in the total income declined during the period, while the *share* of other groups increased in corresponding measure. The distribution of incomes

199

became more fragmented. It was these groups benefiting most from this development who were mainly responsible for the increase in savings—and for the accumulation of fortunes.

In using the words 'responsible for' we are not suggesting that the savings represented the fruits of travail and frugality. There was nothing here of puritan self-denial. The large savings were the results of huge profits and earnings carved out in the expectation of even bigger profits, and which it seemed advantageous to plough back in business or invest in bonds, bank accounts and insurance policies.

Considered as an individual feat, the act of saving was thus passive and easy to perform rather than the reverse. This point needs to be emphasized because of the stereotype, still widespread in literature on the subject, that the capital for growth was arduously accumulated by people who led Spartan lives. It is the old story of 'many a mickle makes a muckle', which in this case is supposed to have been incarnated in a thrifty, hardworking middle class.

No matter where we turn, we find a capital market restricted to the few. The earlier phases of industrialization were built up by a handful of entrepreneurs, much fewer in number than the new enterprises which came into being. To quote Erik Dahmén in his study of Swedish industry: 'The same twenty or so names keep cropping up in at least a hundred of the firms that sprang up during the initial decades of Swedish industrialism.' As Torsten Gårdlund has demonstrated, the corporation as a form of business organization was long preferred, not so much to bring in new capital from the 'outside', as in order to have a shield of anonymity and limited liability to hide behind. In addition, a mere sprinkling of shareholders held safe majorities in the largest companies. Even though many small savers opened accounts with the new commercial banks, these institutions long continued to depend primarily on the large depositors: companies, company owners, and a small group of 'private capitalists' from the older upper class. When, in due course, Stockholms Enskilda Bank became the bank of industry above all others, it managed and actually owned 'its' industries, which were responsible for a large part of the bank's deposits as well as its advances. The funds to finance new enterprises, or to develop and transform old ones, came from the profits and money deposited by their siblings in the bank's industrial empire.

The economic strength in this system of uneven income distribution was that savings issued forth in large quantities by means which the consumer goods hunger among the majority of the population would have made impossible had incomes been distributed more evenly.

Its weakness was that it probably yielded more violent and speculative fluctuations in savings than would have resulted from the money dutifully set aside by the working and middle classes for that 'rainy day'. The structure of savings at that time must be explained in large part by the sensitivity to liquidity fluctuations which characterized both the national and international financial community during the period of industrial build-up. In the final analysis, all the major crises were crises of liquidity.

The ability to help towards capital formation by active saving was unevenly spread; most of the people helped, but involuntarily so, by having to restrain their consumption. A look at the distribution of property and income discloses inequalities above a broad but very low base level. The best statistics here have been compiled by S. Flodström in a survey of Sweden's national wealth in 1908. His total estimate comes to 14,000 million kronor, of which 11,600 million kronor was in private hands. Fortunes of 30,000 kronor and higher were held by not quite 40,000 persons, or 1·5 per cent of the two million holders. This 1·5 per cent, however, accounted for 55 per cent of the total wealth. In the class of 300,000 kronor per fortune or higher, there were 2,620 holders with combined assets of 29,000 millions or an average of 1·1 million kronor each. In other words, 25 per cent of the country's private property was in the hands of one-thousandth of the property owners. The full tabulation is shown below:

Property worth	Number of holdings	Per cent of holdings	Money value in millions	Per cent of money value
000– 9,999	1,942,500	93·5	3,370	30
10,000– 99,999	122,700	6·0	3,736	32
100,000–299,999	8,180	0·4	1,582	13
300,000 and higher	2,620	0·1	2,909	25
Totals	2,076,000	100	11,597	100

The situation is further illustrated by the figures for wages paid. Wages must not be confused with *incomes*, which of course included dividends and interest accruing to the unevenly distributed fortunes. Further, I have deducted from these wages the sums paid to farm labourers; only a part of their pay was received in cash, often not even the biggest part, and any comparisons which include them will therefore be misleading.

Of the wages paid to industrial workers, artisans, privately employed office personnel, company directors, and employees in government service—totalling 485 million kronor to 435,000 wage-earners—the 3,000 company directors took 30 millions; that is, 0·6 per cent of the wage or salary earners received nearly 6 per cent of the whole. The average salary for a company director was 10,000 kronor. Together, the 2,000 higher-ranking employees of the central government earned 15 millions, averaging 7,500 kronor per person. 250,000 male workers in industry and crafts earned 300 millions or 1,250 kronor per person, while the 50,000 female workers earned 20 millions or 400 kronor each. The average salary of a lower-ranking employee in central or local government came to 4,000 kronor; of an office clerk in private employment, 1,500 kronor. This means that the average company director earned (and bear in mind that we are talking about wages and salaries only), 33 per cent more than the average higher-ranking employee of central government, 160 per cent more than the 'ordinary' employee of central or local government, and 700 per cent more than—or eight times as much as—the industrial workers. To which we can add that there was no progressive taxation of any kind; the surtax was not introduced until 1909. Nor was there any levelling-out in the form of transfer payments dictated by social policy. The first very modest step in this direction was taken with the introduction of the old-age pensions scheme of 1913. Indeed, transfer payments did not assume any appreciable scope before the scheme was reformed in 1936, and in any event gained no real importance until the later 1940s.

The uneven distribution of property and incomes, with its corollary of slowly improved standards of living for the mass of people, was an important factor behind the rapid rate of investment. More than that, it had significant repercussions on the social and political arena. One of the effects, galvanized by two years of slumping business, was the general strike of 1909. Although the strike turned into a political and organizational fiasco it revealed that the industrial society had attained a certain maturity: the strike served notice that a new class society had been created and a new power factor was on the march.

II

The industrial society was unlike the old agrarian society in almost every respect. It was a fluid, protean society, with constant fluctuation in what comprised the paramount trades and occupations; in technology; and in geographic distribution of incomes, material standards and positions of power. To be sure, there had been major changes in the pre-industrial society: the crumbling distinctions of rank, the emergence of underprivileged classes in agriculture, the adoption of new production methods. But these changes had proceeded slowly, and the basic structure of the society had stayed virtually the same from decade to decade, indeed from century to century. The agrarian society of early nineteenth century Sweden was vastly different from its predecessor in the great-power era. Yet the two had more in common with each other than, say, the Sweden of 1868 had with that of 1908.

Industrialization had provided more people with work and livelihood than agriculture could offer to those who still lived on the land. It had also wrought great changes in the lives of the remaining agricultural population. Those who had left had come from the lower classes: the crofters, cottars and paupers. Many crofts and cottages stood empty and deserted. Small apple orchards were left to grow wild. The evidence is still visible here and there in areas of former poverty: the remains of a house foundation; a grassed-over cellar in the earth; a few uncared-for apple trees; fences built of rocks hewn or picked from a field to make it tillable; land once enclosed again transformed into a meadow or a clearing in the wood. The owners may have departed towards the end of the nineteenth century, or perhaps during the first years of the twentieth, either for America or for jobs in a Swedish factory. Thus did industrialization relieve the countryside of its worst poverty, though the move undoubtedly must have been a hard and bitter experience for many. The lower agricultural classes became the industrial working classes.

The gradual rural exodus was accompanied by major changes in the composition of the agricultural population. Its component of free-holding farmers continued to grow slowly from about 230,000 in 1870 to 270,000 in 1910. The old division between landowners and cultivators faded as more and more tenants had their obligations reduced to the mere payment of rent. By means of a new law on leases and other limited interests relating to real property, passed in 1907, the once-vague relationships between tenants and owners were regularized; at one stroke of the pen, tenants were relieved of insecurity regarding their legal rights. Towards the end of the century, in the midst of the general rural exodus, efforts were again made to bring new land under cultivation. As from 1904 this movement received a measure of state support with the establishment of an own-home building-loan fund, whereby farmer sons, workers and others of modest means could borrow money to start their own farms. This was a romantic but misguided attempt to provide the lower agricultural classes with an alternative to seeking work in the factories. Some success was achieved in starting new farms under state loans, especially in the far northern counties, and to a lesser degree on the former estates of central Sweden, which had been divided up.

This was no solution for the great mass of rural poor. For them, however, the new factory gates stood open—and the way through them was also an escape from poverty into another condition which, though at first seemed to offer scant improvement, was in fact destined to do so, and at an accelerated pace. This point should not be forgotten when the new industrial society is held up for examination: for all their bad sides, the factories did provide work and a means of livelihood; for all the deferred rises in the incomes of the great majority, the new techniques did set the stage for a slow but sure increase in material standards. The worst evils and difficulties— inordinately long hours of work, and the sweated labour of women and children—vanished or were mitigated before long by laws and collective agreements.

The industrial society was built in a mixed climate of extreme optimism and extreme pessimism: quite natural perhaps, considering the scope and violence of the changes involved. The conservative fears and alarms which the new aroused, when everything was at its newest, in the middle of the nineteenth century, have been dealt with in the previous section. Some of these apprehensions persisted and may even have been further nourished as industrialization proceeded and its undeniably dark sides came into view. At the same time, however, conservative ideas in the economic sphere were being ousted by more liberal theories. The menaces of industrialism were banished by its attractions; pessimism gave way to faith in development, speculative zeal and optimism. The conservatives joined forces with the 'true' liberals in demanding liberty to pursue trades and in the trust they placed in the blessings that would flow from free enterprise. To a great extent this faith in the future coloured political policy, embraced as it was by the most powerful groups with a handful of leading politicians, industrialists and capitalists at their head.

Nevertheless, all this euphoria could not hide the pessimism that was felt about social conditions: the concern and solicitude for the poor, oppressed and rootless in the new industrial working class. It was a pessimism and anxiety which in many cases was combined with demands for protective laws and social reforms.

Pessimism, or perhaps rather a feeling of dull despair, also descended upon large groups of the new working class. It was true that the switch to industry had been a deliverance for tens of thousands; and as real wages rose, the factory hands came into enjoyment of material standards far higher than those they left behind, and not a few even surpassed the standards achieved by many proprietor and tenant farmers. But often the change was involuntary, necessitated by hardship and starvation. More often than not the new job was harder, dirtier, more disciplined and subordinated. In relation to certain criteria, the housing conditions were actually worse, and socially more wretched in the new huddle of ramshackle barracks in working class districts. Above all, the feeling of proletarianization, of grey, poor hopelessness, became more obtrusive and humiliating in this different setting. It was as if the newcomer had encountered a mass edition of his own misery.

New doctrines, preached from England by Karl Marx and Friedrich Engels, and introduced into Sweden by way of Germany, were also making themselves felt. They spoke of exploitation and impoverishment, of the social evils and brutality of capitalism, but also of the pride in work, human dignity, equality and fraternity that would come when capitalism attained full maturity and the revolution was carried out. Influenced by these teachings, but always with more immediate, practical reform in mind, the trade union movement launched its programmes of organization, negotiations and education. However, the prospect that several decades were likely to pass before anything valuable was accomplished long imbued the movement with pessimism. When the Social Democratic party was founded in 1889, its leaders spoke with zeal and confidence of the end of exploitation and impoverishment, believing that large-scale proletarianization would continue after the Marxist model. These were concepts borrowed from Britain and Germany where conditions were in some ways much more difficult (although even in those countries such concepts were not really applicable).

In Sweden, however, the prospects for large numbers of people remained theoretical: notions of a constantly bleaker future struck a broad responsive chord, and found expression in political slogans. The different economic crises were interpreted, in conformity with the abortive predictions and ingenious explanations of Karl Marx, as signs of capitalism's inherent contradictions and inevitable suicide. Disaffection was fermented, and bitterness ran deep.

Nevertheless, pragmatism and demands for feasible reforms slowly gained the upper hand. These were the axiomatic considerations for the trade union movement. From the start, unions sought to effect improvements by negotiation. These considerations also became absolutely essential for the rising Social Democratic party. A party has to engage in practical politics, try to gain influence, bring about change; to await passively the maturity of capitalism and its result, the great revolution, proved impossible. In the less glamourous world of everyday politics, they would have to lower their sights onto minor reforms and gradual improvements. At the same time, the conception of reality itself began to change, in response to revisionism in Germany and new statistical data on industrial production and its distribution in Sweden.

In due course, after the Social Democrats had accepted universal suffrage and parliamentary government as the institutional framework for their political exertions, they consciously or unconsciously came to adhere to a more optimistic view of the future. No longer were impoverishment, crises, mass poverty and major social and economic discrepancies regarded as inevitable. They were not ordained by any 'natural' order of things. Society could be reformed and improved even if progress was slow and piece-meal. There may have been some connection between the brighter outlook and the appearance of at least one opening for social reform. The programme of social welfare, presented in 1881 by Bismarck, and largely carried out in the ensuing decade, had already begun to set a pattern for Sweden. To be sure, this 'lecture-room socialism' was a poor instrument for the redistribution of incomes, material standards and social status; and Swedish workers, or in any event their representatives in the trade unions and the new labour parties, had good reason to suspect that the German government was rendering favours of grace but little substance. Even so, this programme did acknowledge that a state was beholden to its citizens in matters other than to act as their 'night watchmen'. It paved the way for the conviction that the security of the individual was a legitimate concern of politics. The tariff controversies of the 1870s and 1880s in various countries may have played a role here. After several decades of fairly complete liberalism, the widespread adoption of protective tariffs threw open the doors to government intervention in broad sectors of national life, setting the stage (though on a modest scale as yet) for 'economic planning'. The 1880s had also witnessed Sweden's debut in the field of major social reforms. In 1884, S. A. Hedin had submitted a parliamentary bill which qualifies as a Swedish Magna Carta of social rights; he called for an official commission of inquiry to study and propose measures to guard against occupational hazards, to set up a system of workmen's compensation, and to provide workers with old-age insurance.

In addition, the fight waged by the young labour movement for its existence no doubt served to instil faith in the future and in the feasibility of reforms. The setbacks encountered were many and harsh, but the small triumphs won reinforced courage and confidence. They proved that society could be changed within the limits of the existing order. Of considerable importance in this respect were the struggles waged by workers to gain the right to combine. In the face of the 'threat' posed by the formation of *Landsorganisationen* (LO) in 1898, many employers were prompted to take up arms against trade unionism. Workers who had joined a union were told to get out of it or lose their jobs. The unorganized were granted higher wages than their militant fellow workers, or were promised other benefits. Union leaders were evicted from their homes; some were arrested or exposed to other harassments by organs of government. Management launched its biggest counterattack in the sawmill industry with the so-called Sundsvall lockout of 1899. A long and bitter conflict developed which extended into the new century. At the same time, however, it brought to light the great sympathies which the most widely different sections of the community felt for the young trade union movement.

In the lectures on social policy published by Gustaf Cassel in 1902, the movement was praised as a fitting instrument for working-class education and as a means towards a fairer distribution of incomes. This attitude was widely current among that day's social scientists in both Britain and Germany. Prominent intellectuals organized collections to help strengthen the strike funds of union workers. Bitterness towards employers and government officials could be substantially mitigated by the knowledge that not a few of the 'higher-ups' were pro-labour.

None the less, there is no getting away from the continuous and basic undertone of bitterness and pessimism. The higher standard of living was there for anyone who could read statistics. Yet it was still possible for the results of many years of work to be wiped out, given one or two more mouths to feed, illness in the family, or a few weeks of unemployment. Political and unionist agitation, which fought for reforms and improvements, simultaneously increased awareness of how serious this situation was. To instil such awareness—the self-same class consciousness preached by Marx—was in the end, of course, one of the principal aims of this agitation. We may feel sure that a sense of impotence, mistrust and hopelessness must often have overpowered many leaders of the young labour movement. The great political successes did not start until the suffrage reform of 1909, while the organization of workers progressed very slowly. In 1902 only 66,000 members were enrolled in all the unions, equivalent to about 25 per cent of the workers employed in industry. By 1909 the figure had risen to 231,000 or about two-thirds of the industrial labour force. But in that year came the general strike, which proved how difficult it was to keep the ranks closed when adversity set in. The general-strike weapon turned out to be double-edged. It became clearer than ever that the arduous road of parliamentary reform would have to be travelled in order to reach political objects. The failure of the general strike meant the victory of reformism and 'revisionism' within the trade union movement and the Social Democratic party.

Industrialism had emancipated the individual from the old patriarchal ties, which often had been harsh and humiliating. Many of the new captains of industry admittedly tried—for good and ill, like the patricians who preceded them—to apply the same rules of hierarchy. The 'old spirit' seems to have survived with particular tenacity in the ironworks. Their executives were wont to behave with dictatorial airs (arrogance and impudence being thrown in for good measure), but some of them could also be solicitous and helpful. Gårdlund relates a telling example. Shortly before 1900, the workers at a brewery, Hornsberg, had been summoned by the managing director; after leaving his room, they noted with delighted surprise that they had been treated with a courtesy and openhandedness as if they were human beings of nearly the same worth as the director himself.

It is impossible to determine to what extent organized labour and social democracy effected the gradual improvement and humanization in dealings between the different classes of society. Certainly, these movements were of special importance in the following two ways.

With help from the Liberal party, Hjalmar Branting took his seat in the 1897 Riksdag as the first Social Democratic member. This gave the labour movement a social and political influence of almost priceless value. It had gained a forum from which it could be heard, a means for controlling the activities of government and administration, and also social status. These advantages were strengthened by the fact that the Social Democrat happened to be Hjalmar Branting and no other. For on the movement was cast some of the light emanating from his personality which was such that even the most conceited and hierarchically minded would think twice before putting on airs. In 1911, when the first election was held after the franchise reform of 1909, the Social Democrats won 64 seats in the Lower Chamber.

Within the trade union movement, the attempt to acquire education and discipline was of great importance. To a great extent this work tied in with that which the nonconformist and temperance movements had been carrying on for several decades. Education and discipline were vital prerequisites at a time when the attainment of power depended so greatly on the degree of solidarity and cohesion that could be achieved. This also induced political and social respect. Eventually, too, the chief opponents of trade unionism were compelled to recognize the movement's important moral role as a popular educator. Even those for whom the very word 'socialism' was anathema could find solace in the visible evidence of the parliamentary orderliness, moderation, good sense, and indeed bureaucratism shown by the trade unionists as a result of their training.

In any case, anyone who had a good ear for the Swedish language could rest assured after reading the minutes of meetings held by the LO Secretariats. Potential assassins and revolutionaries were hardly likely to employ such carefully phrased officialese.

Once employers realized that lockouts, dismissals and threats of reprisals were unavailing against the trade unions, they started banding together in unions of their own, which as from 1902 were merged in a central organization, *Svenska Arbetsgivareföreningen* (SAF, the Swedish Employers' Confederation). The idea behind SAF was to stiffen employer resistance to pay demands. If the employers stood united, the trade unions could not pick them off one by one in pressing their claims. While this objective of closed management ranks was attained, the very formation of SAF served to improve the social and political status of labour. It was now recognized as an equal partner. No longer could employers refuse to negotiate. If an employer did refuse, he could be turned over to the mercies of his own association. The organized employers became increasingly concerned to sit at the conference table with strong union officials who were empowered to enter into agreements and stand by them, and who had the authority to maintain order and discipline among the workers. By the same token, the unions much referred to deal with employer associations of proven ability to keep their members in line. The disposition of SAF to view unionism as a 'non-political' and 'non-ideological' movement was also important. Since it was in business to negotiate, SAF had to regard the adversary as a fully legal bargaining organization.

It was to a great extent by bolstering one another in this fashion that both labour and management gained in political power and social esteem. In Social Democratic eyes, perhaps, the process of elevating the unions to full-fledged status within the labour market and the 'system' may have proceeded too well and a little too fast. It was feared that the political interests of labour would flag, that it would start to desert the socialist ranks, that it would make too much show of neutrality. These apprehensions were important in 1898, when the Social Democrats under Branting supported Fredrik Sterky as a candidate for the chairmanship of LO, formed in the same year. Sterky, a well-to-do brewer who had devoted himself to union and political work, could be relied on to uphold the banners of party and socialism in the new labour organization.

Naturally the speed and scope of the trend towards equality of rights and social status hinted at here must not be overestimated. Nor is there cause to hold exaggerated notions about the depth to which increased self-respect and morale penetrated among the great majority of workers. The other side of the story needs qualification too: the early resistance of employers to unions and their persecution was neither organized nor widespread. It was possible to build up myths around the few conflicts that did occur, because they were abnormal and hence sensational. The dramas enacted were exceptions. They were important exceptions, since they forced developments and created traditions: but they must not mislead us into believing that they were of a universal trend; or even that they were common, everyday occurrences.

III

Hours of work had been shortened in consequence of different collective agreements. By the time the new century was a few years old, they averaged at ten hours a day for adult male workers; an eight-hour day was observed for especially heavy or hazardous occupations such as mining. Compulsory schooling had put a definite end to the worst evils of child labour. Here labour and management accomplished much more by voluntary agreement than legislators by fiat: according to the statutes still in force, dating from 1881, children between the ages of 12 and 14 were not to work more than six hours a day, and between the ages of 14 and 18 not more than ten hours. The regulation of hourly rates, overtime pay and piece rates was agreed and carried out or at least forseeable in all major industries. The old practice of varying pay by seasons was abolished. Shift work was regulated. Arbitrariness had been replaced by contracts, order and fixed rules, the observance of which was enforced by both the organized employers and workmen. Industrialization had become institutionalized.

All this had vital repercussions on daily life. A modest minimum of security and protection under law was created. The great majority had achieved a material standard several notches above the bare minimum for existence. Expansion of the home-market industry from the later 1880s and onwards had shifted the emphasis of investment from communications and heavy industry to the consumption sector, and this was now paying dividends in the form of more consumer goods to meet the needs of the great majority. By comparison with the course taken by later industrialization in the communist countries, the focus on military investments and fabrication had been modest. Militarism and the burdens of defence were admittedly discussed, and gave rise to increasingly fierce controversies as the clouds of war began to gather over Europe. However, in relation to national income the amounts involved were extremely small, and as such cannot have had more than a negligible effect on the overall picture of rising wages and consumption.

The chief scourges were economic crises and unemployment, and poverty was most pronounced in regard to housing. Owing to the rapid growth of industrial communities and the very slow turnover of capital invested in buildings, the housing problem was twofold: dwellings could not be built fast enough to accommodate the influx, while much of the existing housing rapidly grew out-dated and became dilapidated. Social scientists like Cassel, Steffen and the young Bagge constantly drew attention to housing as the most serious and urgent social problem. It was to remain that way for decades.

A population 50 per cent larger than in the later 1860s enjoyed a standard of living that was at least 100 per cent higher. Much had become easier. However, a great deal had also become more difficult.

Machines had replaced the human hand for many and heavy, dirty sequences of production. Here electricity, especially, had proved to be the liberating force. Just before the outbreak of World War I, the internal combustion engine was also harnessed in the service of industry. The machines had, however, produced new dirt, a harsher discipline, a lack of freedom, and alienation; to balance the different effects, one against another is not easy.

'Of course it was easy, but all the same an agony which is beyond comprehension,' [wrote Ragnar Casparsson of his first boyhood job in a sheet metal mill. He continues]: 'The sheet edges were sharp as

211

razor blades, and they dropped fast. I had to borrow a pair of leather gloves, because it was impossible to grasp the metal with one's bare hands. I cut myself nearly up to the armpits and my newly ironed blouse was soon hanging in shreds. Worst of all, the flywheel for the shears whirred unprotected in the metal hole at a height of three feet. If I forgot myself and lifted my head, I'd bump into the wide belt which connected with a shafting under the roof and moved the shears. Hot vapours from the milling work formed a mist beneath the ceiling, where soot from ages past lay in heaps on iron frames and beams. The smoke of coal burning in the welding furnace smelled like coke fumes and made me dizzy. I'd have to go out and vomit. The old-timers told me that all beginners had the same trouble. But you get used to it, they said consolingly.'

Loneliness and solitude had been replaced by dense housing and social proximity—but often the results had also been crowding, over-population, even big-city slums. Both gains and losses had been made, but they were not all measurable. Perhaps it can be summed up as follows: if the old life before industrialization was nothing to pine for, there was much in the new to get away from.

The Marxists have discussed the problem of alienation: the sense of estrangement experienced by the masses from the production they worked with; their reduction to the role of cogs in a vast machinery, over which they had no say. A ready comparison was available in Sweden: the peasant and artisan were their own bosses; their work was meaningful to them as individuals; they were the masters of the tools they used.

The comparison was not perfect, however. Consider the lot of so many people before the industrial breakthrough: they were neither their own bosses nor masters over their tools, but others' man-servants and maidservants, journeymen and apprentices, crofters and field labourers, and their life was generally miserable and oppressed. Nevertheless, there is no doubt that industrialization altered the relations of workers to their masters and their tasks, so as to engender a sense of alienation. The old masters—landowner, peasant pro-prietor and artisan, stood there as concrete manifestations, and there was no unknown or secretive power exercising ultimate control. But behind the foremen, engineers and executives in the new factories, there loomed the 'company' and 'company bosses': they represented something anonymous and institutional, hence inhuman, strange and often menacing. It was on this level, beyond the ordinary worker's reach, that big business was transacted, new industrial combinations formed, new enterprises hatched, and old ones put out of commission or merged with others. There, in the board room, decisions were reached on employment levels and redundancies, the final word was said on wages and other working conditions; and there entrepreneurship was played as a game not only with money in the millions—but also with machines and human beings. It was a game that no outsider was allowed to watch. The mushrooming bank palaces could well stand as a symbol of the strange and secretive: the grated windows, the enormous street doors, and the exclusiveness of board rooms and executive offices, whose sombre magnificence the uninitiated could imagine through hearsay only.The organs of central authority, the police and courts, were widely regarded as lackeys of the rich and mighty—a feeling reinforced by mounted police charges into the ranks of demonstrators and by a number of judicial verdicts which, though upholding the letter of the law, were considered to violate its spirit. Alienation from work was conjoined with alienation from society.

Attention has been drawn in the foregoing to the great educational role played by the temperance, nonconformist and trade-union movements. But it was long before their efforts were rewarded by any far-reaching results. Many of those who clamoured most loudly for their own rights and the restoration of lost human dignity were zealous in trampling others under foot. Intimidation was still widespread in industry. The young workers were bullied, forced to wait on their elders, beaten and plagued. At many places it was not unusual to subject newcomers to some sort of brutal initiation rites which often contained ignominious undertones of sexual sadism. It was bad enough that the work should be so heavy, demanding, and unhygienic and require two performances in shift. The system was hardly improved by this rough 'education' delivered by fellow workers.

Conditions in the home, with its overcrowding and relative poverty were far from ideal, either. Here, too, brutality persisted in the upbringing of children. Corporal punishment was the accepted thing in all classes of society. However, it could take especially offensive forms in the poor working class homes, where feelings of insecurity, oppression and inferiority were often strong and demanded their 'safety valves'. Many stories of that day tell of how wives and children were regularly beaten in the aftermath of weekend drinking parties. How widespread these practices were is of course impossible to say.

Much of the old rank-ordered society still remained in this era, which perhaps more properly should be called semi-industrialized

Sweden. The traditions of officialdom and of the higher ranking clergy still had influence, and pride of birth had not ceased to assert itself. A count was assuredly a count, a governor or director-general was a 'superior'. The new upper class of bank directors, industrialists and wholesale merchants did the best they could to imitate the 'true' upper class in their habits, good and bad, but a certain aloofness was nevertheless maintained between the two groups. The greater prestige still attached to the high-ranking civil servant and the count, even though their purses were usually leaner. If the director of a large bank happened to have once held an assistant judgeship, he much preferred to be addressed by the title of 'Judge'. If the director of an iron mill held a baronetcy, woe to the man who simply called him 'Director'.[1]

In 1905, when Alfred Peterson (1860–1920) became the 'first farmer to sit at the King's council-table' (he was a landowner, of course) by virtue of the portfolio given to him in Christian Lundeberg's Cabinet, there were many who believed that the end of the world was nigh. For most of the upper classes, the workers were a large, grey mass. They were upright citizens, to be sure, but inclined to be lazy and unfortunately the victims of wicked socialists and unionist agitators. Not infrequently the workers were regarded as people of another sort, if not of a different race. The word 'worker' designated not only an occupational position, but also a social, moral and even intellectual classification. That being the case, it also came to designate a political attitude. The process of social circulation set in motion by industrialization had to only a negligible extent elevated factory hands to leading positions in government or business. If any kind of upward advance occurred at all outside the circles of nobility and public functionaries, it was limited to the 'climbers' of a limited middle class.

The eleven members who made up Arvid Lindman's ministry in 1908 included six noblemen. Of the eight who headed the government departments, four came from the nobility, and thirteen of the twenty-three county governors had similar origins. Noblemen constituted 35 per cent of the commissioned officers in the armed forces. Out of what might be called the upper bureaucracy, comprising the eminent politicians and civil servants holding directorial rank, about 90 per cent were the sons of big businessmen, university graduates and, as has been shown, included a large component of nobility. Within the upper managerial ranks of industry, only a very few stemmed from

[1] *Translator's note:* Occupational titles, it may be mentioned, are extremely widely used in Sweden, sometimes even to the point where direct address is put in the third person, with the use of a title instead of a pronoun.

the homes of small farmers, workers, or from the lower middle class. Most of the 'big' names emanated from a much 'higher' background. Some were nobles, more came from the upper civil-service stratum or from families of wholesalers and manufacturers. The social background of academically qualified people was likewise limited. Of the number who passed the university entrance examination in 1910 (1,285 men and 164 women), 36 per cent were the children of big businessmen and professional men, 27 per cent came from the homes of civil servants, and 21 per cent from the families of small businessmen. Only 8 per cent had farmers as their fathers, and only 7 per cent were the sons and daughters of labourers.

An unmistakable air of the *nouveau riche* with all its well-known accompaniments of ostentation and Philistinism, pervaded certain groups of the middle class: those who had 'worked their way up' through business deals, speculations, and unearned increments. It was the period of the 'wholesalers', a somewhat indefinable social group, ranking somewhere below the captains of industry. Uneducated, swaggering and grand of manner, they were likely to lose their fortunes as quickly as they made them, due to their penchant for extravagance. They built villas and summer cottages with turrets and pinnacles that suggested miniature fortresses. Their boastfulness with wooden castles, yachts and servants, filled the 'really superior' people with contempt, the poor with jealousy and hatred, and inspired Strindberg, Hjalmar Bergman and other writers to pen their portraits with superb irony. The wholesalers hounded their sons into pursuing studies for which they were not always fitted, all for the glory of achieving the *studentexamen* (university entrance examination), which would definitely set the seal on the family's superior position in society. Countless scenes of weeping children, embarrassed tutors and irate fathers were enacted in these families. The 'wholesalers' (and many of them, incidentally, were in fact wholesalers) admittedly had moved upwards in the economic sphere, and it will be conceded that they often tried to affix social status to their accomplishments by putting their sons through university and by generally comporting themselves so as to gain official honours. The figure created by Hjalmar Bergman, Markurell in Wadköping (a thinly disguised Örebro), was a good representative of this group, at least as manifested in a small town full of civil service traditions, rank consciousness and pretentions to learning.

A certain lowering of class barriers had begun to operate in the political and organizational arenas. To some extent the Social Democratic Riksdagsmen represented an upper class sprung from the broad mass of people, a new stratum of leaders in the community. Not all of them, however, were proletarian in their origins. On the contrary, several of the leaders came from the upper bourgoisie, and were themselves university graduates and civil servants. A larger proportion of the trade-union officials had started out as factory hands, but a long time was to elapse before they achieved the social status of, say, a professor or a department head in a government agency. The social circulation which in due course was brought about by means of the labour movement's political power was in some individual cases spectacular and significant as evidenced by the title which Waldemar Swahn gave his biography of Per Albin Hansson: *The Messenger Boy Who Became Prime Minister*. This, however, applied only to a relatively small stratum, and it is safe to generalize that the labour movement as an instrument of social circulation came to benefit the middle class and civil service groups more than the working class.

The changes in class composition reflected in the Riksdag were also moderate, and smaller than the shifts within the different categories which were consequences of urbanization and the gradual transfer of property from rural economies to the urban. Thus in 1906, 35 per cent of the Lower Chamber members lived in cities and towns as compared with 29 per cent in 1867. In 1909, 27 per cent of the Upper Chamber members lived in Stockholm, whereas 16 per cent had done so in 1867. High-ranking civil servants held 44 seats in the Lower Chamber in 1906 as against 48 in 1867 and 44 in 1876. The larger entrepreneurs held 23 seats in 1906 as against 22 immediately following the parliamentary reform of 1866. Working men were completely absent before 1906, when they held five seats. After the franchise of 1912, the Riksdag had 19 working men, all of them Social Democrats. Workers accordingly held less than 30 per cent of the 64 Social Democratic seats in the Lower Chamber, whereas five Social Democrats belonged to the higher ranks of the civil service, eight to the lower ranks (including officials of local government), and 19 were in the professions. Of these 19, seven were journalists, nine were trade union officials, and three were party functionaries. Inasmuch as the majority of these 19 stemmed from a working-class environment—but not all—it can be roughly estimated that about half of the Social Democratic Riksdagsmen, who emerged after the party's parliamentary breakthrough in 1911 merited the designation of working men or ex-working men. In short, not even the rise of the labour movement had as yet been able to bring about any greater degree of 'political' social mobility.

Power in society was in the process of shifting its centre of gravity towards new groups and new ideas. A displacement of ideas within the 'old' groups—seen from both the political and social points of view—was also on its way. The party system had acquired clear and socially more distinct outlines. The different parties in the Riksdag had developed into national parties, with organizations and support from permanent cadres among the electorate. The Social Democrats had constituted a national party from the start, that is, before they were even represented in the Riksdag. Liberal groups had found their national organization in the *Frisinnade Landsföreningen*, founded in 1902; two years earlier, these groups had joined forces in a parliamentary coalition, *Liberala samlingspartiet*. In 1904 the different conservative groups in the Riksdag, building on the remains of a fragmented *Lantmannapartiet*, had acquired a joint electioneering organization in *Allmänna valmansförbundet*. The respective groupings of conservatism, liberalism and socialism had been established, with an admittedly far from 'pure' social composition, yet with clear social stratifications. The new Conservative banner gathered the civil servants, land owners and large farmers (including other categories of agriculturalists before separate agrarian parties were formed), and groups within industry and commerce, where the party penetrated fairly deeply into the ranks of small businessmen; on the other hand, far from all the big businessmen could be drawn into the Conservative fold. The Liberal party gathered groups of wider social disparity under its wing. During the first decades of their existence the Liberals could come forward as an ideological party with historical roots in urban radicalism, temperance and religious dissent, and—as the business of government took an increasingly democratic turn—with parliamentarism and universal suffrage as the most important rallying planks in its platform. Its members included a number of the most eminent people in the business community, due in great measure to that combination of economic liberalism and zeal for social reforms which came to imbue the party; certain radical groups among the professional worker sand other intellectuals; and, lastly, large groups within the 'petite bourgeoisie': small businessmen, farmers with relatively small holdings and of nonconformist persuasions, and some lower civil servants and workers. The Social Democratic party was most consciously bound to its social origins as a labour party, and the workers came to comprise the largest proportion of its electorate. However, the party also appealed to lower civil servants, some farmers, and certain groups of small businessmen.

The essential social composition of each party was clear, but as

217

the margins between them were blurred, marginal issues were as influential and politically important as the main ones.

This situation contributed to a measure of cooperation across party lines, to a quest for balance and compromise in major areas, which was to be characteristic of Swedish party politics through the years, and cut straight through the hard and bitter struggles that cropped up from time to time. As already noted, Branting received support from Liberal votes when first elected to the Riksdag. His party's increasingly marked orientation towards parliamentarism and franchise reform around the turn of the century fashioned strong links with the Liberal party, making it possible to forge a Liberal-Social Democratic 'front' on a number of important issues. At the same time, the two parties were separated by certain irreconcilable differences of principle and ideology: the Liberals rejected every extra-parliamentary attempt to bring pressure to bear on the Government, such as the general strike of 1909; for them there was no storming of the barricades in revolutionary fervour. The Liberals were also opposed to nationalization schemes and more cautious in the matter of social reforms. When the suffrage finally became universal after World War I, these differences could no longer be ignored. The Social Democrats and Liberals increasingly went their separate ways, and new alignments in Swedish politics emerged in the 1930s.

The monarchy still remained an important power factor, or perhaps it would be more accurate to identify this factor with the Conservative big businessmen, public officials and politicians who sought to protect their ideas and interests behind the cloak of royal power. Gustav V did not recognize parliamentarism as an obligatory principle, even though in practice he was forced to pay great deference to it. He looked on the Cabinet ministers as 'his' advisers, whom he could freely choose as he saw fit. When crises of state erupted, he jealously safeguarded his right to take personal command and appear before the people as a creator of public opinion. This policy was most ostentatiously demonstrated in what is known as the courtyard crisis of 1914, when the king spoke to an assembled group of protesting farmers; the Liberal Government resigned, and the Hammarskjöld-Wallenberg Government took office. The crisis had primarily originated over the issue of national defence, and the resulting antagonisms cut deeply. For years an increasingly bitter campaign had been waged against the Liberal leader, Karl Staaff (1860–1915). He was accused of high treason, of having accepted Russian bribes, of trying to restore the polity of the Age of Liberty, and of behaving like another Carl Fredrik Pechlin (1720–96), the Swedish 'arch-traitor' in the eighteenth century.

An unease and rancour peeped out here from beneath the balancing and compromising—a sense of deadly conflict between Conservative groups and the more radical Liberals, which throughout the period from about 1900 to 1914 gave the Social Democrats and trade unionists a partially protective umbrella for carrying on with their work. The conflict was not exclusively limited to these new groups versus the 'community'. From time to time an equally bare-knuckled conflict was waged between the established members of this same community. This circumstance helped ease the process of adjustment for the Social Democrats, and strengthened their inclination to align themselves with parliamentarianism and to achieve their goals by reforms. They did not have to confront a united non-socialist bloc, but one that was highly fragmented. Accordingly, they were given a latitude for political manœuvre that would otherwise have been hard to attain.

This balancing situation made itself perceptible not least during the general strike of 1909. As we noted earlier, it proved a fiasco for labour, though perhaps only in the short run. The strike had its background in the international economic crisis of 1907. The whole atmosphere was infected by earlier strikes and lockouts, in particular the Amalthea incident of 1908, when a bomb outrage was committed against English strikebreakers at Malmö. Reductions in wages were demanded and put into effect by some employers. In August 1909, SAF (the Swedish Employers' Confederation) imposed a lockout to end the recalcitrance of labour. LO (the Swedish Confederation of Trade Unions) responded by calling a general strike. On the whole it was well-organized and ran an orderly course; but its main purpose, to demonstrate the community's total dependence on industrial workers, failed, and the strike petered out. Thanks to the franchise reform in the same year, the way was paved for labour's political influence. However, the strike had been aimed not only against SAF, but also against the state, and hence more or less explicitly against the community and the public power as a 'civil' organ. It had thereby acquired a strong political undertone, accentuated by a walkout of typographers, which silenced most of the newspapers and made a free debate impossible. Karl Staaff, in a celebrated speech delivered at Eskilstuna in November 1909, repudiated these 'anarchistic' methods and excoriated the Social Democrats and trade unionists both for their tendency to resort to extra-parliamentary weapons and for their close alliance. According to Staaff, the labour movement had thereby turned itself into a state within the state, and as such had placed itself politically and morally outside the community. When, then, should the general strike be resorted to as an exclusively political weapon, as a method of revolution?

Two weeks later at the same place, Branting delivered his answer. Extra-parliamentary methods might be necessary, he said, as long as the community was not fully democratic, as long as Conservatives and Liberals identified only themselves with the community and shut out the workers. The workers could not feel solidarity with the community as long as they did not have a part in it. They were instead being impelled by a strong and justifiable class solidarity.

Both speeches, however, contained qualifying and conciliatory formulations, with hints of cooperation and mutual adjustment. The combatants were brandishing their swords from opposite sides of a bridge. Nevertheless, it was clear that not even the inflamed passions provoked by the general strike could induce them to demolish the bridge. Fundamentally, Branting said, the strike was a unionist and not a political conflict, since it was concerned with collective labour agreements. He acknowledged the dubiety of a paralysed press and public debate caused by the typographers with their walkout. However, even these workers, he went on, must have the right to strike.

Whatever the extent of purely reactionary tendencies in the labour movement, and these had primarily been manifested by the 'young socialists', the general strike itself made it clear to the better informed and more far-seeing that revolution was not the path to tread. The labour movement had become a power factor. However, its power was not great enough to permit a taking-over of government reins by means of revolt and revolution. The movement did not have the cohesion needed to survive ordeals; its power of endurance were poor, its numbers too small. Even if labour had wanted a revolution, it certainly lacked the capability. With the franchise reform of 1909, the longer but safer way to power was opened from within; or if not that, at least the means for exerting vital influence on the transformation of society. The choice of this path also accorded best with the increasing emphasis on democracy and parliamentarism as principles of government.

In the midst of these heated struggles, significant reforms were achieved, and with a large measure of unity as time went on. In 1906 public machinery was set up for mediating in labour-management disputes, signifying the state's official recognition of the trade union movement as an institution. A law on forest purchases, passed in 1909, protected farms against the encroachments of timber companies.

After a lengthy inquiry, an old-age pension scheme was adopted in 1913. Statutes relating to industrial safety were successively enlarged in scope. Schemes of insurance against sickness and unemployment were studied, and in 1909 a bill was passed on voluntary sickness benefit societies; in 1911 a bill was proposed for maternity insurance. In the following year, the sickness benefit societies were enabled to add a maternity allowance financed from public funds. Indeed, there was intense activity in the field of social welfare, the like of which was not to be seen again until the 1930s and 1940s. The government committees appointed to investigate and draft social legislation included several Social Democrats; Branting himself was a member of most of them.

As we have had occasion to observe earlier, the importance of this reform work should not be overestimated in regard to its influence on income distribution, or the creation of social security in general. All the same, a minimum of security was established. Even more important, probably, was an awareness that the first steps had been taken away from 'lecture-room socialism', that the possibility existed for the erection of a measure of social democracy. This awareness may lie behind the tendency towards balance and compromise which began to be typical of the new class society.

The quest for balance and compromise was to be subjected to severe strains during World War I and under the Hammarskjöld regime. However, a liberal-socialist election victory in 1917 resulted in the formation of a Liberal and Social Democrat coalition government which saw the enactment of universal suffrage for women, and the abolition of plural votes in local elections in 1918—this being of great importance as the Upper Chamber was elected by local 'parliaments': all this served to strengthen the position of democracy and parliamentarianism. These advances did not occur without difficulties and internal conflicts. In 1917 a young-socialist wing broke with the Social Democrats and formed a Left-wing Socialist group, which in turn gave birth to a faction that formed the Swedish Communist party in 1921. Some of the leading Social Democrats in the Riksdag voiced more or less concealed threats of dire consequences in the event of thwarted reforms. Perhaps the threats were seriously meant, perhaps they were chiefly tactical, as an extra means of exerting pressure. None the less, in a world of revolutions and upheavals, Swedish political democracy could be established in parliamentary order—and all major sections of the community were to give it their complete support.

In the process, the doors were thrown open to a new complex of

problems: the growing claims citizens made on the state, and therefore the demand for increased power and resources in its hands in
order to enable the state to bring about complete social democratization alongside the political. However, it was not until the 1930s that
the composition of government was such as was needed to give those
reforms substance. The 1920s became, after the break caused by the
war, a period of hesitation and halting advance, marked by an over-
heated economy and a state of political checkmate which was doomed
to culminate in the crisis and transformation which followed.

5

WELFARE WITH A SKEW

THE industrial society differed from its predecessors in the swiftness of its changes. It follows from this characteristic, which we
illustrated in the previous chapter, that the 'fully matured'
industrial society of the 1960s presents an essentially different picture
from that of around 1908. All that the two have in common is the
rapid, remorseless process of change.

If this fundamental characteristic remains, it also follows that the
society of another decade or two will differ in essential respects from
the one in which we now live. The result of several centuries' developments which we now can see, is only a short, ephemeral 'final' result.
It is already in the process of changing into something new, part of
which we perhaps can guess at, or even predict, although the core of
the change is beyond our grasp.

We do not have to go all the way back to the period following
World War I to marshal support for the above arguments. The
swiftness of change is also apparent within a much shorter time perspective. If for instance, around 1945, just after the guns had again
been silenced in Europe, some Swede had predicted that his country
would look today as it actually looks, his compatriots would have
thought him out of his mind. His theories would have been too
fantastic, too daring.

This is not to suggest that the change has been so sweeping as to
result in an 'unhistorical' state, one that lacks ties with the past. On
the contrary, the past is still very much with us, conditioning us for
good and ill. Even if it is not the principal factor at work, it cannot
be ignored. Therein lies the explanation for many of the distinctive
features which, although part of the Western traditional development,
yet are uniquely Swedish, just as the same shaping force has been at
work in all other Western countries to give them *their* distinctiveness.

In certain respects these historical links explain why some changes in Sweden were so rapid and far-reaching.

It is important to bear these factors clearly in mind. Both the historical, the process that has been operating for centuries, and the new, or that which was new only a short time ago, are inextricably intertwined in the society we meet today—and will still be so two or three decades hence. When for want of better words we speak of an event as epoch-making or revolutionary, we are not saying that it explains everything or even the greater part, or that it would have become as important as it did if a great deal else that was new and old had not been operative at the same time. In the economy, in the social reality, in the political strivings and in the distribution of governing power, this mixture of the old and new is always at work. It helps to explain the pronounced conservative trends in the midst of rapid change.

How, then, does Sweden of the 1960s differ from Sweden at the beginning of the twentieth century? What can we identify as the main features of the change that has occurred?

Sweden now has more than 7·8 million inhabitants as compared with 5 million around 1900. Where 55 per cent of the population used to live off agriculture and its subsidiary occupations, less than 10 per cent do so today, that is, less than a million people as against three million sixty years ago. Today's agriculture returns more than twice the yield of fifty or sixty years ago because it has so largely become industrialized, and because there has been a continuing trend away from smallholdings towards large farms run as businesslike enterprises. Industry's share of the population has risen from 30 to about 45 per cent, and employment in public services and the professions from 6–7 per cent to about 20 per cent. The cities and towns have experienced vigorous growth. Some 80 per cent of the people occupy less than 20 per cent of the country's land area, with three metropolitan regions showing the densest concentrations: Stockholm, Göteborg and Malmö. A relatively densely populated belt, 250 miles in extent, is in process of cutting across central Sweden from Stockholm in the east to Göteborg in the west. The region around Malmö is also becoming densely populated.

Where 1,000 students once completed their secondary education and 500 graduated from the universities every year, the figures today are around 25,000 and 8,000 respectively. These figures do not include the various equivalents to a professional education which earlier did not exist or were held to be inferior. Nine years of basic schooling are now compulsory, and a growing number elect to pursue their education beyond the ninth year.

A continuing increase in incomes and material standards has enabled large sections of the Swedish community to rise above poverty and insecurity to a life of full employment, decent wages and security. This does not mean that poverty is entirely abolished. Even in our prosperous society there exists a residue of people who have failed to keep up with the rest or—to put the matter differently—who have not been given adequate help. Although the majority live at a far higher level than fifty or sixty years ago, there are large groups who suffer material hardships in relation to the average standard that has been achieved.

The male industrial worker has raised his real annual wage by 120 per cent since 1910. Since hours of work have been considerably reduced in the meantime, his real hourly rate has risen by all of 250 per cent. That still does not give the whole picture. Wages can now be calculated for a nation in full employment. The spectre of constant unemployment, or what Karl Marx called the 'industrial reserve army', vanished several decades ago.

Other groups have improved their material standards by the same percentage or even higher. A large white-collar stratum, often better off financially than the workers, but not always, has emerged, and many of its members have come from working-class homes. On a rough calculation, there were ten workers for every white-collar man sixty years ago. By the mid-1960s the ratio had dwindled to one-and-a-half to one.

A system of social insurance has evolved which, if nothing more, has at least resolved the most perplexing problems of security for the great majority. Sweden now has schemes to guard against the financial consequences of old age, ill health, and unemployment. Families with children receive allowances from the state. A vacation from work is guaranteed under law and paid for by the employer. The Swedish labour market has become thoroughly organized, with unions representing not only manual workers, but also salaried employees and professional workers. Collective bargaining is conducted with reference to all categories of employees, including those on the payrolls of central and local government. Sweden has become the prototype of the welfare state organized from top to bottom.

Today's Sweden is often interpreted abroad as a country of near-exotic qualities. Observers point to her high standard of living, her advanced welfare policy, the ordered tranquillity and harmony of her labour market, her policy of peace, agreements and compromises. The ratings have fluctuated, ranging from epigrams like 'land of the middle way', 'the land of balanced forces', 'the politics of com-

H   225

promise', and 'land of idyll' to disquieting descriptions of a country where social security is supposed to destroy diligence and thrift, and engender crime, neuroses and an alarming number of suicides.

The one extreme of judgment is as absurd and biased as the other. To say that the truth lies somewhere in between is not to take refuge in another platitude, but rather to suggest that the actual reality is much more complicated and far more difficult to assess. It is much less suited to headline slogans or to 'general theories' about the welfare-state experiment than any thumbnail descriptions are capable of indicating, whether they be flattering or the contrary.

Before we proceed to describe this complicated reality, let us see how 'it all came about' in the light of what has already been portrayed in this book.

To begin with, the course of events since World War I has followed all lines but a straight one. Of certain areas it can be said that the trend is fairly consistent, although hardly even or continuous. A theoretical curve describing economic activity would be full of notches and the upward acceleration of the past twenty years has in fact been exceptional. When it was observed above that the real annual wage of industrial workers has risen by 120 per cent since 1910, we should add that this wage actually dropped slightly in the first ten years up to 1920 and that it rose by only 3 per cent during the 1930s. It rose during the 1940s and 1950s by more than 30 per cent, which is at a more accelerated rate than ever before. But World War I and the Great Depression cut deep notches in the real-wage curve.

These notches were not only related to wartime isolation and slumping business conditions. They also signified a different turn in the direction taken by economic activity, especially difficult for a country as dependent on exports as Sweden. The restrictions on economic internationalism imposed by protective tariffs, beginning in the later 1880s, were like a ripple on the water compared with the far-reaching change-over to national self-sufficiency forced by World War I, especially after unrestricted submarine warfare was proclaimed in 1917, and by the crisis of the 1930s.

To some extent, no doubt, the situation during World War I was caused by Sweden's own actions. As the policy of neutrality was interpreted by the Hammarskjöld government, it was also rigidly applied in the commercial sphere, so that Sweden cut off most of her trade both with the Entente and the Central Powers. The policy of protecting agriculture had fallen far short of attaining complete self-sufficiency. Nearly 30 per cent of the bread grains consumed in

Sweden just before the war had to be imported. On top of that, the wartime blockade indirectly hurt livestock production, which normally had sufficed to meet the domestic needs, by impeding the imports of concentrated feed and maize. Industry was directly affected by sharply reduced imports of fuel, lubricants, spare parts and machinery. Even though it was possible to maintain the level of national income in spite of these difficulties (indeed, it rose by about 1 per cent per year), it declined in relation to the gainfully employed population, which was increasing by more than 1 per cent per year. The losses in foreign trade and production largely occurred during the latter part of the war. During its first two years Sweden could even profit from her privileged position as a neutral country and boost her exports. Since imports fell off rather promptly after the outbreak of the war, the result was that Sweden became an exporter of a considerable amount of capital.

Sweden's transition from net importer to net exporter of capital was accentuated during the 1920s, once the crises of readjustment after the war had been overcome. The change, considered in relation both to the war years and to earlier conditions, may be illustrated by the following series of indices on the volume of industrial production developments, exports and imports from 1923 to 1929.

Year	Volume of Industrial production	Volume of exports	Volume of imports
1923	100	100	100
1924	114	119	109
1929	160	185	144

The gross national product rose during the same period by more than 4 per cent per year, or slightly more than 3 per cent for every gainfully employed member of the population.

The return to 'normal' after the fairly violent inflation of the post-war years was marked by a return to the gold standard, in practice in 1923, although not legally ratified until the following year. This move presupposed that a deliberate policy of deflation would first be carried out. The resumed gold standard was not an instrument for achieving improved balance in other respects, but rather a target whose realization meant the acceptance of greatly scaled-down prices, considerable unemployment, and extensive elimination of less competitive enterprises in the economy. As Professor Erik Lundberg has pointed out in his book, *Konjunkturer och ekonomisk politik*

227

(Business Cycles and Economic Policy), it was characteristic of a monetary system under the gold standard that economic policy was not really pursued with any cognitive goals in mind. He writes:

'The goal was simply—without having to be made explicit—to conduct the kind of economic policy that could maintain the gold standard. The excellent thing about the gold standard was that it presented the central authorities and the *Riksbank* with the smallest possible problems. Automatic mechanisms predominated and a minimum of active intervention was the ideal.'

Like all centrally decreed policies, of course, this one worked both for good and ill. A total assessment depends on how one evaluates the operation of its different parts. However, certain observations can be made concerning the general characteristics of the economic conditions of the 1920s.

Government policy or, if one chooses, the absence of such a policy over and above adherence to the automatic mechanism of the gold standard, succeeded to the extent that industrial production rose relatively fast, the balance of foreign trade was restored, large amounts of capital could be exported, and extensive re-allocation gains were achieved by means of rapid rationalization of the private sector. The rationalization of those days manifested itself in the widespread closing down of factories and the formation of new, more efficient enterprises with a more modern production apparatus and structure, as well as the measures taken by old companies to modernize and reorganize their production. Accordingly, the really big changes took place in the large enterprises that were already established. The assets created abroad by exports of capital materialized in the formation of foreign subsidiaries by Swedish industrial firms. The first steps in this direction had actually been taken before World War I. A number of Swedish groups (affiliated companies) became 'world names' not only by selling in other countries, but also by establishing manufactures abroad. Among the more eminent are such names as SKF, the makers of ball and roller bearings, Separator in dairy apparatus, and the Swedish Match Company, which under Ivar Kreuger enjoyed a virtual world monopoly of match sales by methods that a later decade found debatable.

All these developments, however, should be set off against the high level of unemployment that persisted throughout the 1920s. About 10 per cent of the trade unionists were without jobs, in part because of the seasonal fluctuations peculiar to the construction industry.

Furthermore, the pressure of low food prices on the world market created a state of continual crisis in agriculture. Thousands of people fled the farms for other occupations, a trend accelerated by the great gulf between wages and incomes. But for the unemployment that plagued the non-farm sectors, the rural exodus might have been even greater. Besides, the relatively favourable development and rapid expansion of the economy in general, did not necessarily apply to all its constituent parts. Thus the iron industry operated under worrisome conditions, with widespread stagnation as the result. In the forest-based industries, the situation was also difficult, although the rising production of pulp, paper and furniture meant that there was no economic loss in the industry as a whole.

The 1920s were also politically troubled, with ministries following one another in fairly rapid succession, and most of them holding minority mandates. The Liberal Ekman government of 1926–28 and 1930–32 has entered the annals as a classical example of 'tussock-hopping', that is to say of conducting politics of balance, which permitted it to stay so long in power—in so far as one can speak of 'power'—at a time when the very institution of government was enfeebled. The state of checkmate which generally prevailed in the Riksdag after universal suffrage was enacted in 1921 was ultimately to be traced to the fact that large groups simply did not bother to vote. The shift towards the Social Democratic party, which ought to have followed naturally, considering the social composition of the Swedish population, was less extensive than expected, since many of its presumptive supporters did not vote. Throughout the 1920s voter turnout never exceeded 70 per cent; a proportion of 75 per cent was not reached until 1936.

Various circumstances interacted to create this situation. A certain indifference to politics, which at bottom may have stemmed from ignorance and indolence, was probably nourished by instability at the ministerial and parliamentary level. That made politics less exciting, drearier and less important: after all so little was happening politically. In economic policy, the gold standard had set up rules for passive policy, and that was that. In social policy, almost nothing took place. At the behest of a royal commission headed by Richard Sandler, the issue of nationalization had been put on ice and was eventually dropped from the agenda altogether. There hovered a dismal air of marking-time over the 1920s, at the same time as industry and commerce were undergoing an extensive transformation.

The war and its aftermath had been a heyday for profiteers and speculators, people who became rich from shortages, usury and the

229

quick conclusion of shady deals. This spirit of exploitation persisted into later years and celebrated some of its triumphs even in the most distinguished business circles.

Perhaps the most triumphant of them all was Ivar Kreuger, who also suffered the most spectacular fall, ending with the dramatic suicide in Paris on March 12, 1932. His story is fascinating chiefly because of the dramatic course of its events: the construction engineer and match manufacturer from little Sweden who became one of the world's mightiest financiers, hailed as a benevactor by governments, and then so suddenly exposed as a ruthless swindler.

Against the background of the 1920s, the life of Ivar Kreuger would have been equally remarkable even without the dramatic finale. In the closing years of the decade he started to act as a vehicle for international transfers of capital, in particular from the United States to Europe, and gradually did so on a scale that bears comparison with the Marshall aid which came in the wake of World War II. On the basis of money borrowed in America, a single privately owned Swedish company lent 75 million dollars to France, 125 millions to Germany, and numerous sizable amounts to other countries.

Ivar Kreuger was a child of the 1920s, and a quick sketch will suffice to explain how he was enabled to perform as he did. The 1920s were a fragmented decade in the field of foreign trade and international capital movements. Despite the efforts of many, the barriers erected in wartime had never been completely demolished. A decisive obstacle was the American tariff policy. Further complications ensued from the indemnity to be paid by Germany under the Versailles Treaty, and the peculiar British currency policy. The result was a clear distortion in the trade relationship between Western Europe and the United States.

Commerce could be stopped easily enough, but little could be done to prevent the escape of capital or tax evasion. It was this fact that set the stage for the passive side of the Kreuger concern, that is, for his borrowings abroad, especially in the United States. Kreuger securities were ideally suited to speculation in a decade supplied with a surfeit of speculators. At the same time that stock market quotations were held at very high levels, and thereby favoured a speculation which was further inflamed by fantastic dividends, these securities were primarily bought so as to be placed in a no man's land and thereby evade taxes. For Kreuger, the development of an effective match industry with such unique speed, apparently aimed at achieving a world monopoly, enabled him to combine the speculative zeal of borrowers with their confidence. Among successful stock market speculators—a class of people often given to simple-minded faith— Kreuger was regarded as a financial wizard, a man for whom nothing was impossible. After the 1927 loan to France, approved and carried out by Kreuger after large American interests had refused, the enormous confidence he had built up was reinforced. In a statement made the day after his death, Eli F. Heckscher spoke of 'the imperial dignity which international stock-market jargon sought to bestow on him'.

Obviously, it took more than borrowing and the speculative zeal of others to keep Kreuger going. Solid assets were also required, and here he had his industrial 'empire' to show. In due course he acquired control over several other Swedish companies, among them Boliden, Cellulosabolaget and L. M. Ericsson. However, these acquisitions cannot be explained with reference to the need for investing profits. On the contrary, the foreign loans confronted him with great financing difficulties, which generated a sequence of plunging quotations and purchases in support of the market, culminating in the liquidity crisis that spelled his definite fall. But the solid assets were necessary to maintain confidence. Where else would the securities and high dividends have come from, and how else could Kreuger lend money at relatively low rates of interest?

However, Sweden and those parts of Swedish industry singled out to serve Kreuger's interests, proved far too small a base for these operations; much of the 'underlying values' consisted of castles in the air, and the deficiency was concealed by a long, intricate and never entirely unravelled series of manipulations with different dummy companies placed round and about Europe.

On the other hand, it would be unjust not to take into account the great benefits wrought by Kreuger's transfers of capital, especially on the French and German economies. Heavy infusions of capital were needed to put the European economy back on its feet, and restore balance and function to the system of international payments. Had the infusions been even greater, and had a more extensive inflationism been adopted forcing the abandon of the gold standard and making higher employment levels possible, a great deal would undoubtedly have looked different. The crisis of 1929 could have been avoided, and Nazism would presumably never have been given the chance to usurp power. It is quite clear that Kreuger himself had such cause and effect relationships in mind when he pleaded for a more expansive and inflationist policy, quite apart from what he may have hoped to gain thereby for purposes of saving both himself and his financial policy. For certainly there were also idealistic motivations behind some of 'the wizard's' manipulations.

In any case, the doings of Ivar Kreuger were calculated to impart a special nimbus to the Sweden of this decade. They were held to foreshadow the advent of a new era of greatness, but this time in the economic sphere. The comparisons were sometimes rather extravagant. A good example comes from the poet Sten Selander, who in an interview on March 13, 1932, was quoted as saying:

'It was a bullet that ended Sweden's former age of greatness: the bullet fired on the evening of November 30, 1718. Today the echoes of another shot reverberate round the world. Will that too mark the end of a great Swedish age?'

Had Kreuger lived, in other words, he would supposedly have made Sweden the financial centre of the world.

Many people reaped quick fortunes from Kreuger shares and debentures, and many were willing to stake their all in the expectation of big new profits. The corks of champagne bottles popped, caviar abounded in profusion, and cabarets and revues enjoyed a golden age. At the Vasa Theatre, Margit Rosengren and Lars Egge sang 'The Last Waltz'; Gösta Ekman and Tollie Zellman acted out *A Comedy at the Castle,* from the stage of the Oscars Theatre; and a film with Lars Hansson, *Sin,* was playing to packed houses at the Röda Kvarn cinema. The first 'talkie' was shown at Children's Day celebrations in October 1928. Riches so quickly earned had to be ostentatiously exhibited. In a setting of widespread poverty, large-scale unemployment, political deadlock and general gloom, the diamond rings shone so much more brightly, the black muskrat fur looked so much warmer and more genuine on the older ladies, and the minivers and silver foxes so much more becoming on the younger women. The swallow-tailed coat and high hat were in fashion, and their wearers would drive between parties in a Daimler-Benz, Oldsmobile or Buick. In October 1928, Merz, the racing-car driver, received permission from the country authorities to drive the first Mercedes Sport on a Swedish highway. Men began to abandon the austere black and grey for bluish colours in their suits and coats.

The 1920s were a wonderful time to live in for the very few, an oligarchy that looked forward to a future where stocks kept eternally rising in value and never ceased to pay handsome dividends. As to the future that fate actually had in store, of this there was little or no premonition. The newspaper *Dagens Nyheter* showed a picture of two broadly smiling boys and noted how sympathetic they looked; they were the sons of Benito Mussolini, attending a meeting of the Young Fascists.

The crisis was unleashed by the Wall Street crash. At 12.30 p.m. on October 24, 1929, the New York Stock Exchange shut its public gallery, feeling that visitors must be spared the scenes of wild panic and plummeting shares enacted within. That, of course, could not cushion a much larger, world-wide public against the crash—or against feeling that it had ushered in, if not actually caused, the Great Depression. The roots of the Depression went deeper than a precipitate drop in stock quotations. Economists who took the market crash as their starting point and predicted a quick recovery, with 'prosperity just around the corner', were right in so far as events taking place in a stock exchange did not have to mean so very much. It was merely that at the bottom of the crash lay profound economic changes: in particular, each year the increase was smaller in the demand for cyclically sensitive goods, such as cars and houses, and a general congestion of international trade with over-valued rates of exchange for the pound and distorted capital movements. Once the crisis became an accomplished fact at the beginning of 1930, its spread was also rapid and extensive.

Sweden was drawn into it by way of her exports. As late as the summer of 1930 and indeed a good part of 1931, the home-market industry maintained its high production level from 1929, and thriving business at home also served to sustain imports. Exports were falling ominously, however, and that in addition to the trend in imports opened the dikes through which falling external prices inundated the Swedish economy. When the international wheat market collapsed in 1930, it aggravated the crisis that had plagued agriculture throughout the 1920s. Unemployment began to increase during the summer of 1930, and by the end of the year the crisis was a fact. Unemployment among the trade unionists, averaging at 11 per cent from 1926 to 1930, rose to 19 per cent between 1931 and 1935, exceeding 23 per cent in 1933. For every 100 vacancies there were 228 applicants in the late 1920s, but 441 applicants between 1931 and 1935, a figure which has never been surpassed. As exports declined and imports remained unchanged, reserves of foreign exchange were being drained. To add to the difficulties, the Kreuger companies increasingly resorted to domestic supplies of credit as the international capital market began to fail them. The resulting pressure ultimately had an impact on the *Riksbank*. Since the Kreuger borrowings went towards meeting international obligations, a further strain was

H*   233

imposed on an already taxed exchange reserve. Out of a reserve that held 300 million kronor in the spring of 1931, these borrowings laid claim to nearly half. On September 27, 1931, after nothing had come of efforts to float government loans in the United States and France, and by which time the exchange reserve had dwindled to 30 millions and holdings of gold to 198 millions, the Bank authorities decided that the time had come to leave the gold standard. At the same time they raised the Bank Rate to 8 per cent after having previously lowered it in successive stages. They feared the imminence of inflation —and the measures provoked by this fear no doubt deepened the crisis and prevented recovery. For some time to come, that shot fired in Paris on March 12, 1932, was to worsen the situation both in real and psychological terms.

In the general election of the following autumn, the Social Democrats won 104 of the 230 seats in the Lower Chamber. Although improving on their performance in the 1928 election they were still in a minority position. However, by virtue of the so-called crisis-deal with the Agrarian party in 1933, the Social Democrats managed to gain the parliamentary base for a ministry which was to open up a new era in Swedish politics, and introduce during the 1930s something new in the national life. The modern 'framework planning', and the initial breakthrough of welfare policy took place during the 'thirties, even though the beginnings look both modest and uncertain from the perspective of our day. The basis of power was permanently altered, both in a parliamentary and in a deeper political sense. The mixed society slowly began to take shape.

However, the actual break with the past was strongly influenced if not entirely dominated by that same past. A clear interrelationship thus existed: the new was dictated by the old. It was the failure of the 'twenties, finally exposed by the Great Depression, which compelled a reappraisal and made the new politically possible and necessary. New economic theories, in large part formulated by the so-called Stockholm School, and given a more radical bent by J. M. Keynes in 1936, also gave the politicians knowledge and an ideological foundation for their endeavours. A different look at the budget and its effects on the national economy provided scope for a new kind of financial policy, where deficits in the state treasury could actually be used to stimulate business and trade. The attitude towards social policy changed in response to these new economic patterns of thought. Expenditure on social welfare could be seen, not as a mill-stone round the neck of economic progress, but as a stimulus to demand and investment in a recession, and hence as a means to reduce unemployment, boost production, and raise the national income. However, the old balanced-budget theory died hard, and to get around that obstacle the Government had to devise the expedient of working with two budgets: one, a regular operating budget marked by strict economies; and the other, an extraordinary capital budget that could be made deliberately expansive.

So manifest was the need for government action that even though specific measures could generate fierce political controversy, a nearly unanimous endorsement could be fashioned for some of the fundamentals involved. The important thing here was not to make too explicit in words what one actually thought. A useful propaganda aid was given by the reformist strivings abroad, in particular the New Deal expounded by President Franklin D. Roosevelt of the United States when he took office in March 1933. Fear of Nazism and Fascism no doubt entered in, too. The pro-reform 'social liberalism' which emerged contained an element of 'lecture-room socialism', one of whose propelling forces was the realization that social improvements would help to build up a front line of defence against contagion from the south.

Another problem that called for urgent attention was the stagnation in population growth. Here, too, even the ultra-conservatives could be made to feel that reforms were justified. If opposed in principle to anything that smacked of political radicalism, they were still amenable to arguments that Sweden needed a growing population, the better to preserve Swedish culture and uniqueness.

However, as the husband-and-wife team of Gunnar and Alva Myrdal pointed out in their book of 1934, *Crisis in the Population Question*, the validity of old theories was being re-examined in all spheres precisely because the birth rates of the 'twenties and 'thirties had fallen so steeply. In any event, they said, the time had come for such re-examination. The working classes had to be dissuaded from their recently embraced neo-Malthusianism, the doctrine that levels of living could be raised by practising birth control. Given the adoption of a radical policy of redistribution, a new technology provided adequate resources for larger families and improved material standards at the same time. The conservatives would also have to appreciate that poverty did not spring from moral turpitude, indolence and wastefulness, but from institutional and economic and political conditions which could and should be changed. If the population question were considered in this entirely different light, it could provide the dynamite charge to remove the obstacles to a new social and economic policy. *Crisis in the Population Question* outlines

235

most of the new redistributive and welfare schemes which were carried out during the next three decades.

The population rise during the nineteenth century and the opening years of the twentieth stemmed wholly from a declining mortality. Birth rates stood still at a lower level than in previous periods and even dropped from 34 per thousand in the latter part of the eighteenth century to 31 by around 1850, and thence to 26 at the beginning of the twentieth century. Then a much sharper decline set in: between 1911 and 1920 the birth rate was 22 per thousand, from 1921 to 1930 between 17 and 18 per thousand, and from 1931 to 1940 between 14 and 15 per thousand. The turn taken by these rates depended in part on declining mortality in the higher age groups. While the number of births in relation to child-bearing ages did not drop as much, the downward trend was alarming enough. Thus 137,000 children were born in each of the century's first ten years, but only 85,000 in 1933.

Sweden was by no means alone in this experience, though as the 'thirties opened she ranked high in the dubious low-nativity stakes. France had long been characterized by a declining birth rate, and the same phenomenon had appeared during the interwar years in one country after the other—the United States, Britain, Germany, the whole of Scandinavia. One can speculate about the causes, as so many others have done already: depressed business conditions producing unemployment, and a sense of insecurity among those who had jobs. But there is certainly no clear evidence of any connection between the birth rate and these factors. The continuing urbanization may have been relevant: whereas children in the old agrarian society were regarded as future assets to help work the farm, every new child in the industrial society was more readily seen as an extra burden for family maintenance. However, that thesis does not quite hold water. As we observed earlier, a great surplus of labour also existed in agriculture, which means that the burden of maintenance should have weighed heavily there, too. The propaganda on behalf of birth control methods may have played a role even for people who never used contraceptives, by further diffusion of information on the classical method for limiting the number of children. Then, too, nativity is evidently subject to the dictates of fashion.

In any event, it was thought that propaganda and different efforts to improve the material standards of families with children would induce the birth rate to rise. A particular stimulus towards this end was the increase in the number of marriages—even though the decline in relative birth rates derived from falling nativity within marriage and not from a lessened incidence of marriage; on the contrary, the 'twenties and 'thirties witnessed a rise in the proportion of women marrying, especially in the group aged twenty-five years and younger.

It was not only, however, a matter of increasing the nativity rate. There was also the question of improving conditions for the children who already existed, and of using financial incentives for families with children as a device to regulate the business cycle.

That was because a population with a shrinking base generally tended to depress the economy. It reduced the demand for housing accommodation, the need for teachers and schools. A number of goods and services in the 'economic-indicator' class suffered a declining demand by comparison with a vigorously expanding population in the younger ages. Given these considerations, it was important at a time of falling nativity to encourage the consumption among existing families with children. The socially deserving cause could be linked with the economically sensible course.

A similar line of reasoning could be applied to the opposite end of the population pyramid. Older manpower found it more difficult to obtain well-paid jobs than younger people, if indeed jobs could be obtained at all. In times of slumping business, the first to feel the pressure of imminent layoffs were the old and 'has beens'. Pensioners and other old persons represented a steeply declining purchasing power. From this point of view, there was an important difference between the population of 1910, where of every 1,000 persons 84 were past sixty-five and an additional 123 past fifty, and the population of 1935, where 92 out of 1,000 were past sixty-five and 124 more past fifty. An official policy on unemployment ought to bring more older persons into the labour force, with unemployment benefits and higher old-age pensions given to non-workers so as to boost their purchasing power to reasonable levels. Here too, social merit and economic sense were combined in the new outlook.

These two considerations were also united in a third sector: agriculture. If farmers received higher incomes they could step up their demand for both consumer goods and capital investments in their holdings. The industrial enterprises which stood still or operated at half capacity would receive orders, could employ more people, and in turn inject new life in other factories by ordering more capital goods from them. Above all, a powerful stimulus would be given to construction, a key indicator in the business cycle.

An ideological dilemma arose on the last point for the Social Democrats who were to implement the new policy. All the attractions of political tactics lay there for them to exploit. By helping agriculture they could bind the Agrarians as a supporting party and thereby gain a parliamentary base for the other reforms. The economic inter-relationships, as they now were beginning to be perceived, also seemed to justify such a policy. Militating against it was the old free-trade ardour of a party which first and foremost represented the large and not especially well-off groups of consumers. This counter-current ran all the more strongly since the Social Democrats had fought a last-ditch campaign against protectionism, having run on a platform of free trade which protested against the safeguards set up earlier for agriculture. In the words of the newspaper, *Arbetarbladet*, written in May 1933, it was difficult for the Social Democrats to back a policy calling for:

'a considerable rise in the price of those foods which play an impor-tant role in the household budgets of our humblest families. . . . Let us nevertheless make sure that the arrangements do not follow the pattern of that southern European nation, where all the people live by taking in one another's dirty wash.'

It required a rather difficult process of readjustment, vividly described by Ernst Wigforss in his *Memoirs*. What was once anathema now had to be accepted: in 1930 the flour mills were required to mix a specified percentage of Swedish grain in the milling of imported wheat and rye; minimum prices for wheat and rye were fixed by ordinance; and in 1932, the manufacture of sugar was put under monopoly and export subsidies attached to livestock production. It was not only the tactical considerations of parliamentary alliance with the Agrarians which helped to facilitate the readjustment. The Social Democrats were also motivated by an ideological predilection for state intervention in economic matters and by their knowledge of interacting factors in the economic picture.

The Agrarian party offered resistance too. A general 'bourgeois' attitude pervaded its ranks. The Agrarians vaguely favoured economic liberalism in all sectors except their own. They did not take kindly to the Social Democratic insistence on an expansion of state intervention in business in the form of public works, which would employ people at ordinary market rates of pay; in particular they objected to establishing these rates at the wages of common labour. As these Agrarians saw it, public works were emergency projects, and as such should be paid for at emergency (i.e., lower) rates; otherwise workers would have no incentive to move over to regular jobs at the first opportunity.

Be that as it may, an agreement was finally reached after long negotiations. It was quickly christened 'cow-lition'—a pun on Coalition, the official name of the agreement between the Social Democrats and the Agrarians. This agreement, augmented by special concessions for agriculture, fulfilled what the Social Democrats had proposed earlier. By and large, it signified a vigorous expansion of state activity, financed by an extraordinary capital budget; the regulation of milk production and an excise on butter, chiefly designed to boost animal husbandry; a 20 per cent increase on the income tax; and higher taxes on beer, spirits and tobacco. But the minister of finance, Ernst Wigforss, could not push through his proposal for higher taxation on inheritances in the form of death-duties; the Agrarians objected to a levy on the sum total of inherited wealth as opposed to the separate taxation of each bequest. On the other hand, the ordinary taxes on inheritances and property were raised by different stages.

Taking the policy as a whole, it would have been quite impossible if the gold standard had been retained. However, its result was also a higher degree of self-sufficiency and a less internationally dependent economy. The change becomes readily apparent when the figures cited earlier for industrial production, exports and imports for 1923–29 are compared with their counterparts for 1929–39. An index value of 100 has been assigned to both 1923 and 1929:

Year	Production		Exports		Imports	
1923	100		100		100	
1924	114		119		109	
1929	160	100	185	100	144	100
1930		102		91		103
1937		151		119		130
1938		153		105		135
1939		166		116		158

An important role for greater self-sufficiency was played by public activity and public services. These could neither be exported nor imported. An automatic corollary of increased public activity was to place a larger share of resources beyond the realm of international contingencies, as it were.

The expanded production for the home market which resulted, took place both in the old exporting industries, making them turn more 'inward', and in the consumer goods industries. An important factor here was the increase in housebuilding: from 1923 to 1929 its volume increased by 37 per cent, from 1929 to 1939 by 153 per cent.

It is clear that this partial reorientation of focus imparted a more diversified pattern to production than would have resulted from increased international specialization. Briefly, Swedish industry began to do a little of everything rather than much of very little.

Industry had approximately doubled its output from 1890 to 1913. After the stagnation of war and its aftermath, output rose by 60 per cent from 1923 to 1929, and from 1929 to 1939 by a further 70 per cent. The real national income, however, lagged behind, rising by no more than 26 per cent in 1923–29 and 43 per cent in 1929–38. The differences are accounted for by the far less favourable development in other branches of the economy, agriculture in particular. During the 1920s farms did not increase their production at all, whereas industry could all along benefit from the falling prices of raw materials which hurt agriculture so much.

Moreover, most of the rising national income during the 1920s benefited mainly the wage earners in industry. The gap was narrowed again in the 1930s when farmers and labourers in agriculture had their incomes raised at a faster rate than industrial employees. The closing gap did not reflect any accelerated productivity in agriculture, but rather the crisis policy which protected farmers against foreign competition. It can therefore be said that the 'horse-trade' between farmers and workers greatly favoured the farmers.

This situation inevitably affected the whole atmosphere of society. Perhaps we should first note that a farmer-worker alliance in politics would never have been forged if this atmosphere had not essentially changed beforehand. Politically speaking, the farmers and workers had traditionally stood on opposite sides of the barricades. The fight for suffrage and social reforms had largely been waged against the farmers as the most deeply entrenched members of the Establishment. The social differences were also great. After all, the new industrial working class sprang from the lowest classes in the agrarian community, where they had been treated as social outcasts, oppressed, and held in contempt by the farmers. The trade union movement had fought its most bitter battles against the farmers in trying to organize field labourers. And as we noted above, the barb of Social Democracy's free-trade arrow was chiefly pointed at farmer interests.

Certainly the crisis agreement could be interpreted to mean that the Social Democrats and Agrarians were 'scourged' into each other's arms. However, matters were not as simple as that. The Agrarian party had begun to acquire a different social content from that of the old Ruralist party. Landowners and the really big farmers rallied round the Conservative banner, almost to a man. The Agrarian party had a more 'working-class look', a trend spurred by the chronic crisis in agriculture. Of great importance, too, was the formation of farmer producer cooperatives, built up during the'twenties and given greater organizational strength in the 'thirties. For all the differences of structure and objectives, these cooperatives imparted a quality of trade unionism and unionist mentality to Swedish agrarian society, and as such could instil feelings of kinship towards Social Democracy and the regular trade union movement. As the Social Democrats had done in relation to *Landsorganisationen* and its member unions, so the Agrarians began to view their unionism as a strong organizational and personal springboard for the political arena. The two parties spoke in part a common language, alien to Liberals and Conservatives.

This sense of community was reinforced by the government coalition which the Social Democrats and Agrarians formed after the general election in September 1936. The election was a success for the Social Democrats who had been defeated in the Riksdag in June 1936 on the issue of national defence and then on a proposed reform of old-age pensions, a defeat which had compelled their resignation. They won 112 seats in the Lower Chamber, while the Agrarians won 36 seats, the same number they already had.

Naturally, the increased cooperation and understanding between the Social Democrats and Agrarians should not be taken to mean that they lived in perfect harmony or agreed on all matters of principle. When the issue of pensions came to a showdown in the late spring of 1936, the Agrarians allied themselves with the other non-socialist parties. Indeed, whenever more far-reaching measures of social policy were involved, the Agrarians still retained their traditional conservatism. The fear of higher taxes and hence of more extensive intervention in income distribution, was one they continued to share with the Conservatives and Liberals. In this way the coalition acted as a break on reform policy. It was the price Social Democracy had to pay for carrying out policies in the desired direction and still be able to stay in government. None the less, the opportunity was provided to embark on this 'socialist' course, to try out experiments which turned out to be far less devastating for nation and economy than their opponents had first feared. It is interesting to note that, during the election campaign of 1932, the leading newspaper of liberal persuasion, *Dagens Nyheter*, saw fit to pin the label of 'straitjacket socialism' on the measures to protect agriculture taken by the incumbent Liberal Government.

Just how much of the credit for recovery belonged to emergency policies of government and how much to the concurrent upward course of the international business cycle is debatable. We shall not attempt an evaluation here. Given the (then) existing interaction between home affairs and external events, we cannot strike a balance among the different factors. The essential thing was that a steady improvement set in from 1933 onwards, in spite of a certain jerkiness in cyclical movements. As the decade neared its end, the unemployment rate dropped to around 10 per cent, bringing it down to the same levels as of the late 'twenties. Some members of the opposition thought the figures low enough to warrant a repeal of the public works programme. A series of tax increases, some of them designated as extraordinary or temporary, were adopted without incurring the dire consequences for business predicted in opposition circles. Here, however, firms were partly compensated in 1938 when they were permitted to make a free evaluation of their inventories. Considering the government policies as a whole, they can be described as successful, whatever role the feverish rearmament policy of Nazi Germany may have played in improved international business. The municipal elections of 1938 also signified a major victory for the Social Democratic party. For the first time in its history it attained a majority of the electorate.

Ernst Wigforss, writing subjectively from his long Social Democratic experience, describes the period from the crisis agreement up to the outbreak of the war as the 'years of success'. Notwithstanding the inevitable setbacks and obstacles, the party felt it was on the right road and, on the whole, successful. Even if protests were voiced when the bills had to be paid, the majority of reforms received overwhelming parliamentary endorsement. Debates over taxes might wax fierce, but then the other side could be told that it shared the responsibility for increased expenditure. Although the Social Democrats were formally right in this, the argument was somewhat dubious, since the government was engineering all the reform initiatives. Even so, the argument indicated an essential change in the political atmosphere: the 'thirties had succeeded in establishing social reforms and state intervention in the economic sphere as a 'natural' policy. In this respect a measure of 'coat-tail-riding' had proved to be politically necessary within the space of a few brief years. Speaking for the liberal school, Professor Bertil Ohlin, destined before long to head the Liberal Party, accepted the new interventionist ideas, in terms of 'framework planning', in his book from 1936, *Fri eller dirigerad ekonomi* (A Free or Planned Economy); at the same time however, he repudiated nationalization of industry and a socialist ideology of equality and income-levelling.

This ideological influence, this indoctrination, had a most important impact on Swedish politics in the thirties—although its evaluation depends on one's political persuasion. More significant than the actual measures taken, although they too were very important, was the ideology which made the thirties a watershed in politics, in social affairs, and (though to a lesser degree) in the economic sphere.

There was nothing uniquely Swedish about this. Similar changes took place in virtually all the highly industrialized countries, and not least in the United States under Roosevelt and the New Deal. However, it is no exaggeration to say that such politics were pursued more resolutely in Sweden, and were subject to fewer controversies than elsewhere.

Perhaps the differences were smaller in Sweden, because the party destined to do the innovating had already shared the responsibilities of government on a number of different occasions. At all events, it felt increasingly integrated in the community after the enactment of universal suffrage at the beginning of the 'twenties. The trade union movement, which was an inseparable part of this party, had also achieved a high degree of integration. It no longer felt beyond the pale, if indeed it ever had been—apart from brief periods of conflict. Additional proof of the integration came in 1938, when the central organizations of labour and management, LO and SAF, agreed at Saltsjöbaden on procedures to regulate collective bargaining and direct action. Indeed, the interpretation put on all this cooperation has often swung to the other extreme, implying that all is peace and harmony on the Swedish labour market. The integration process was further facilitated by the tendency of other groups, representing the 'higher' social categories, to organize along union lines. Mention has already been made of the producer cooperatives in agriculture. In 1931 the salaried employees in private employment joined forces in a central organization, Daco, and in 1937 their counterparts in national and local government formed TCO, *Tjänstemännens central-organisation* (the Central Organisation of Salaried Employees); the two were merged into a larger TCO in 1944. Organizational changes were following hard on the heels of the political.

However, the processes of economic and social change did not keep in step; nor did they always move in the same direction.

The state's influence over the economy increased through the general economic policy and the expansion of the public sector: but

243

there was never any question of trespassing on the economic power constellations. Private enterprise had to adapt itself to a new market situation provided by the state, but it was free to do so in its own manner, as in the past. Private entrepreneurs stood the same chance of profiting from the decisions they made, or ran the same risks of losing. The preserves of private enterprise were not encroached on by any public acts of coercion.

Although they had not been intended to do so, the new policies operated in part to reinforce the ascendancy of entrepreneurs and the owners of capital. The strong tendencies towards greater self-sufficiency and the growing volume of state orders protected many companies against external competition. The formation of mergers and cartels was encouraged by this protection. Stabilization and consolidation tended to replace the brisk turnover of the 'twenties, characterized by very high rates in the birth and death of businesses. In the 'thirties, private enterprise found a better climate, and the power groupings were accordingly made more secure. If by socialism is meant the nationalization of industry, or any other comparable transfer of economic power from private enterprise to the state, then the course of events during the 'thirties was anything but socialistic, however Cassandrian the images that were conjured up in political debate.

Neither can it be said that the measures to regulate economic activity and to legislate welfare were particularly profound in their social effects. Naturally, the decline of unemployment levels normal for the previous decade was a big improvement in relation to the crisis which actually existed. But as the 'thirties ran their course, unemployment was not to drop any further. The new social policy did not have time to work extensively, either. There had been talk about and initial action towards the building up of social reforms, which by contrast with the earlier lecture-room socialism, sought to redistribute incomes and material standards. Nothing was done, however, beyond adding a little to the basic security in existence. A law on voluntary unemployment insurance was passed in 1934. A new scheme of old-age pensions was adopted in 1935, and its benefits increased in 1937. Provision was made in the same year for pre- and post-natal benefits to mothers, and loans were introduced to help newly-married couples set up house. Grants to the children of widows and invalids, and to orphans were increased, also in 1937, together with advance allowances to children born out of wedlock. Further, the 1937 Riksdag voted subsidies for school lunches, with amounts to be allotted on the basis of need. In the housing field, a system of

244

state loans for construction in urban areas was devised in 1933, and special subsidies were added in 1935 for the accommodation of large families. Twelve days of paid vacation for one year of work were stipulated in 1938.

To a very great degree these reforms were of the kind we usually call selective. Benefits were paid out according to need, or otherwise only to special groups who were thought to be in special need of assistance. The transfer payments, as far as they went, had a clear redistributive effect. However, since the amounts involved were so small, their effect on the aggregate income picture was negligible. The total transfer payments via national government, municipalities and county councils, which in 1929 came to around 275 million kronor or scarcely more than 3 per cent of the national income, amounted in 1935 to 403 millions or 4·9 per cent, and in 1940 to 658 millions or 5·1 per cent of the national income. Although the increase was great, the result was still very modest.

However, that must not be construed as evidence of feeble socio-political ambitions. On the contrary, the reforms in hand were part of an extensive programme for the future. This planning was to yield significant dividends from the late 'forties onwards, after the interruption caused by World War II. In 1933 a Royal Commission on housing amenities was appointed, followed in 1935 by the Population Commission. They worked partly within the same terms of reference, namely the population issue, which had come to predominate in social affairs after the Myrdals had sounded their alarm. By 1938, when the Population Commission disbanded, it had presented no less than fifteen printed reports and a long series of unpublished studies, dealing with such matters as sex and abortion, public support of family formation and confinement, the location of industry with reference to rural depopulation, and savings. In 1938 came the Social Services Commission, which pursued its investigation until 1951 and recommended, *inter alia*, reforms in old-age pensioning, health insurance, accident and industrial injuries coverage, and unemployment insurance. However, it was to be vouchsafed a postwar government to put the recommendations of this vast inquiry into practice.

Just how much this activity was delayed by the war years is impossible to say. We can merely certify that they halted the work of reform in both the socio-political and economic spheres. The war necessitated price control, rent control, food rationing and other emergency measures. Naturally, it also impeded imports and exports. All this had distinct yet immeasurable repercussions on the Swedish economy for a fairly long time to come. As to food rationing, it could work hardships at times, but there was nothing like the intermittently severe shortages during World War I. The years from 1939 to 1945 were far less difficult, both because a high degree of domestic self-sufficiency had been attained, and because the administrative machinery for rationing worked well enough to discourage hoarding and price speculation. Yet these years imposed their strains and stresses too, and full recovery was not made until the beginning of the 'fifties. At the same time, Sweden enjoyed a privileged position: she was spared actual war. The end of the war left her population and economy intact, with none of the displacements and dislocations experienced by other countries involved.

In describing Swedish development during the period of armed neutrality, we shall briefly touch on only those few features which had significance for the post-war scene—for a Sweden that was to look quite different in many ways.

First of all, there were the costs incurred for the defence of neutrality. They necessitated a tax burden and a growth of the public sector (albeit a special and extraordinary part of it), which would certainly have dismayed large groups if the interests of national security had not been of paramount importance. The nation became accustomed to high state expenditures and taxes, a fact that had crucial bearing on the programmes of welfare 'rearmament' initiated after the war. All sections of the community had learned to do their sums with quite different figures from those of the past. The size of these figures, which would have horrified people in the later 'thirties, looked perfectly safe and reasonable towards the end of the 'forties, They had, as it were, merely been transferred to new sections within the frame of public expenditure.

No doubt a sense of affinity and solidarity created among different groups during the war years, was especially important in this connection. The emergency military service had achieved a levelling-out, not in terms of income or distribution of power, but socially in terms of mixing. People from different walks of life, who in ordinary circumstances would have had little to do with one another except in a superior-subordinate relationship, became confreres in the same unit, sharing the same duties; often, the hierarchy for giving orders reversed the positions of civilian life. The seeds were planted for contacts, equality of status, and even fellowship cutting straight across the lines of social and economic classes. At the same time, many of the wealthy were given an insight into the living conditions and problems of the 'people' which created lasting social impressions.

246

It came to be appreciated that life could be hard on people through no fault of their own. Many may have felt a distaste for class distinctions which they had earlier found to be so natural as to give them little thought. The professor and company executive were on Christian-name terms with the worker and the office clerk; and even if the fellowship were limited to the military and seldom extended into civilian life, the experience was a new one and decisive in a society still permeated with civil-service traditions, the arrogance of class privilege, and the secluded freemasonry of working men. Indeed, is it possible to make too much of the new experiences and lessons in living together which this phase of history provided?

That changes in attitudes had been wrought was unmistakable, even though they could not be measured; and they were bound to affect events in the world of party politics. The wartime coalition government, comprising all parties in the Riksdag except the Communists (naturally regarded as unreliable), had established a political truce. More important, the coalition seemed to be functioning smoothly, with a high degree of collaboration across party lines. The ideological differences did not have to disappear, or be entirely concealed for that reason. However, practice was acquired in the arts of cooperation and compromise, and the merits of political opponents could be appreciated at a political level. The result was the creation of an atmosphere which undoubtedly enveloped the body politic and increased understanding for the requirements of solidarity.

In any case, it would be difficult to conceive of the parties rallying so unanimously to the cause of social welfare, in the midst of tough political battles during the 'forties and 'fifties, had the years of wartime emergency not conferred these experiences. Taxes did not horrify as before. The requirement of solidarity and at least some measure of equality was felt by the majority to be natural in a new way.

Also significant were the erroneous assumptions about what the return of peace would bring in its train. A repetition of the 'twenties was expected after World War II: first a period of high purchasing power and boom, followed by stagnation or falling demand and then, unless vigorous measures were taken to stimulate the economy, extensive unemployment. A government committee appointed to study postwar planning worked for a time with this perspective in mind, and its views lay behind the audacity which marked economic policy in the immediate postwar years. The wheels were to be kept in motion at all costs, the better to prevent recession and unemployment. Major social reforms were legislated in fairly short order: an

247

increase in old-age pensions, family allowances, free lunches in every elementary school, and free textbooks in all the schools which provided compulsory education. A few selected statistics perhaps best illustrate the development. In 1940 welfare expenditure totalled 5·1 per cent of the net national income and in 1950, 9·9 per cent. As here used, 'expenditure' pertains solely to the payments made by national government, municipalities and county councils; excluded are the insurance benefits to which the beneficiaries themselves have contributed, and which therefore in principle do not alter the distribution of incomes. In 1965 the welfare expenditure had risen to 13 per cent of the net national income, if calculated according to the same method. If the insurance benefits which are not financed by taxation are included, the expenditure accounts for nearly 17 per cent of the net national income, or 13 per cent of the gross national income.

These reforms signified, at least initially, a considerable improvement in income for large groups of people. Regular sources of income rose rather quickly at the same time, partly by virtue of higher wages, and partly because of full employment which offered remuneration to all those able and willing to work. Given the tolerably decent standard of living which already existed, the result was not only a rise in purchasing power: new needs also manifested themselves, so that the economic demands of large groups of people took an entirely new turn. In the field of private consumption, people wanted such things as motorcars and houses. In public consumption they were interested in better medical care, more education, and similar 'heavy' items. Further, in consequence of large-scale population shifts, many local authorities faced the necessity of investing huge sums in community facilities.

Of absolutely decisive importance was the policy of full employment, both for the general rise in the standard of living and for the greatly changed pattern of consumption it entailed, and for the inflation issue which was to become the chronic problem of economic policy in the postwar period. Unemployment among trade unionists, which had fallen to around 10 per cent in the late 'thirties, rose by a couple of units during the first war years, but then dropped to around 8 per cent in 1945. After that, the curve declined steeply, reaching 3 per cent in 1950 and falling below 2 per cent after 1955. While these figures do not measure unemployment with minute precision, they are quite serviceable as indicators of the general trend; the more sophisticated methodology of labour-force surveys was not applied in Sweden until 1955. Actually, the changes by comparison with the 'thirties are greater than the cited figures indicate, since they say nothing of qualitative developments. Unemployment as from the late 'forties has been of the short-term 'rolling' type, reflecting the displacement of manpower in the wake of continuing structural changes. It has lacked almost completely the character of protracted under-employment and recurring seasonal unemployment, both of which used to be the scourges of the labour market. To a large extent this qualitative change has been made feasible by an entirely new kind of active labour-market policy, involving re-schooling and transfer of released manpower to expanding sectors of the economy.

This full employment, which of course essentially was possible through buoyant international business activity, has drastically altered the actual social environment. A job—or the certainty of finding a new job if the old one comes to an end or no longer suits the individual—has not only conferred an economic security that used to be the privilege of relatively few. Full employment has also conferred previously unattainable independence on large parts of the population: they have the option of deferring their entry into the labour market so as to improve their education, or they can more safely take the risk of investing in the education of their children. Employees feel themselves to be on equal terms with their employers (where the latter used to say, 'You're fired!', the former can now say, 'I quit!'); they enjoy the security of planning their personal investments and personal consumption; theirs is the feeling of being wanted on the labour market, rather than having to accept the first job offered to them.

Full employment in Sweden has been accompanied by greater social security in the wake of continuing reforms. A compulsory system of national health insurance was introduced in 1956, and a national supplementary pensions scheme took effect in 1960. A paid vacation of three weeks was enacted in 1951, extended to four weeks in 1963. In 1950, basic education was prolonged from seven to nine years, and is now increasingly given in a single institution, the comprehensive school. Programmes of state assistance to pupils and students have been successively improved, though the earlier plans for paying a direct 'study wage' have been abandoned; instead, students qualify for an allowance plus a loan which runs without interest and the repayment of which is extended over a long period of time, tied to the cost-of-living index but related to income earned in later years.

As a result of this reform work, a high degree of social security has been achieved. Swedes are insured for most of the income lost (up to a specified ceiling) from illness, unemployment, and old-age disablement. They are partly compensated for the direct costs incurred by the bringing up of children. Places in schools up to and including the gymnasium and its equivalents are free, and programmes of higher education are heavily subsidized. Labour-market policy operates to provide certain guarantees for retraining and assignment to new jobs in the event of unemployment. Hospitalization is free, and the cost of medicine and doctor's care in out-patient treatment is covered by subsidies. Benefits from social insurance are augmented by a programme of public assistance, which provides a degree of minimum security when particular types of insurance do not apply.

This 'Social Sweden' is new, having evolved as depicted above, over four decades. Yet the structure is not complete. It does not cover all kinds of risks, and in certain spheres the benefits or allowances are very low. Poverty is not completely abolished. However, the system underwrites the major risks that in times past were left for each and everyone to solve to the best of his ability and pocketbook, and against which large groups of people could not guard themselves at all.

A contention that has been frequently made during the creation of this 'Social Sweden' is that security of such broad scope would have devastating effects on incentives to work and to save, that a large army of work-shy would sprout forth. Such forecasts have proved quite erroneous, at least up to the present time. Whatever tendencies may have manifested themselves in this direction, they have statistically been drowned in full employment, a virtually unbroken upward curve of private savings, and tremendously heightened aspirations for the schooling and training that qualifies for more interesting and better paid jobs. The losses that arise intermittently in the form of voluntary unemployment, that is, from the frequent changes of jobs and workplaces, have been small as compared with what a drop of one or two per cent in the general employment level would entail. Since the different types of insurance compensate for only between 60 and 85 per cent of lost income, and since the insurance sums are geared to previous income and, as regards supplementary pensions, the income earned over many years, the incentive to work is ample. Many married women, coldly calculating in the expectation of better health insurance and a supplementary pension, have elected to return to the labour market. Social security has not lessened the inducement to work and advance, as is so often alleged in foreign debate on the risks of the welfare state. On the contrary, it has further spurred the diligence of a diligent people.

This does not mean that full employment and welfare programmes have eliminated all the problems of economic policy. Actually, they have instead indirectly caused major difficulties in the striking of sectoral balances in the Swedish economy. These difficulties were summarized by the Prime Minister, Tage Erlander, in 1956 in the words, 'the discontent of impatient expectations'. At the same time he was identifying an important factor in the inflation which has characterized so much of the postwar period. Here we meet the Galbraithian dilemma, albeit in a different guise, for Sweden is committed to giving the public sector its due share of expenditure, but at the same time has been less eager to finance it. The problems involved are crucial: how shall national and local government acquire the resources to meet the new demands of a welfare economy? And since a large slice of the cake for the public sector inevitably infringes on private consumption, how can a fair share of resources be allocated to the community for industrial investment?

These are questions that have challenged virtually all the modern industrial nations since World War II. Inflationary tendencies and economic over-heating have had to be struggled with everywhere, at least intermittently. A number of circumstances have been peculiar to the Swedish development, however. One is that the social insurance schemes in use before the adoption of national supplementary pensions in 1960, which are entirely paid for by employer contributions, were financed less from contributions and more from taxes, in comparison to schemes in other countries. Conceivably, this preference for tax financing has made it politically easier to introduce and expand the social reforms; the costs do not show up as quickly. A second circumstance peculiar to Sweden is that the public sector, apart from the transfer payments, has grown faster and answers for a larger portion of the national product in Sweden than in any other Western European country or in the United States, in spite of that country's much higher share for defence expenditures. Thirdly, up to the mid-'fifties Sweden rigidly maintained a low interest level, which meant that much of the national debt found its way back to the *Riksbank* and thus had to be financed by the note printing press, instead of private savings. In order to keep interest rates down, the *Riksbank* had to make supporting purchases so as to keep exchange rates up. Fourthly, a very large part of housing construction has been financed by state loans, at the same time that rents have been kept down both by direct price controls and by subsidies. A perpetual inflationary gap has thereby been created, a gap expressed in housing queues longer than would have existed otherwise, as well as in a surplus of purchasing power aimed at other goods and services.

Fifthly, Sweden, by virtue of non-involvement in World War II, started on her postwar course with a material standard that already was so relatively high that she ran into the special problem of prosperity at an earlier stage. The continued increases in this standard brought about a new pattern of consumer demand: as from the early 'fifties, a fast-rising rate of motorcar ownership (now the highest in Europe), a rapid development of a large number of consumer durables, increased demand for more spacious accommodation and improved amenities in housing, and a violent expansion of educational facilities. The last-mentioned is worth singling out to illustrate the speed with which the 'new standard' has come to focus on previously minor sectors. As late as the 'forties educational debate centred on the problems of how parents in the 'lower classes' could be persuaded to let their children study. It was assumed that social lags would be more difficult to overcome than economic. So the educators, university authorities, and in the final instance the state, were caught napping. An endless procession of mothers and fathers, with their children in hand, literally pounded on the doors of the secondary schools. By the mid-'sixties, four children in ten completed the equivalent of a gymnasium education as against one in ten twenty years earlier.

Owing to rapidly increasing demand, several of the important public services are not always readily available to those who want them. A special type of welfare queue has come into being, as manifested in a shortage of teachers, instructional materials and school premises; a shortage of housing in the large urban areas; congested traffic on streets and highways; a shortage of hospital beds, doctors and nurses; and the presence of many would-be borrowers in the capital market. The public and private sectors have become keen competitors for the country's available resources. It has proved difficult to end this competition, because the public claims on these resources have actually been caused by growing private appetites: large-scale public investments are required to meet the demands posed by intensive urbanization, the expansion of education and motorcar ownership, and the increased public services people want in the form of better medical care, better old-age care, better social counselling, and so on. It is safe to say that the public-private competition has been intensified by the aforementioned special Swedish method for financing social welfare and a great number of public services. It has stepped up the demand for these services, since they are offered free or at low cost. At the same time, for general political reasons and in deference to certain economic realities (for example, corporation cost levels, effects on savings, wage and salary administration, etc.), it has proved difficult to maintain a tax level that not only defrays state expenditure but also permits an increase in the sum total of national savings. Both state and local authorities have shown a marked tendency to mortgage money left over from years of heavy budget surpluses in new expenditure.

Since 1949 the consumer price index has risen by around 100 per cent. In other words, the value of money has fallen by half in a little less than twenty years. There is no question but that depreciated money constitutes one of the dark sides in Sweden's postwar picture. That she has been able to keep her exports up and her foreign payments in reasonable balance is due to the existence of severe inflation in all the modern industrial states—and elsewhere, too.

However one assesses this development, the general consensus is that it can be regarded as a virtually built-in cog in the mechanism of Sweden's welfare state as it has functioned to date. By means of different compensations in the form of index-tied benefit scales, many of the political obstacles that might otherwise have cropped up have been removed. Competition between the different central organizations of employees, and between their affiliated unions, has generated strong upward pressures on the wage side. Here a continuous inflationary gap has resulted from the emergence of a large public and private service sector, which devours manpower and in which productivity increases are difficult or impossible to attain. Employees in the service trades have demanded the same pay rises as those working in trades where real provision can be made for them because of measurably great productivity increases.

In an economy of full employment, where vital sectors are chronically short of labour, the big organizations have lost their capacity to act as a counterweight in wage policy—a capacity which they still retain in many other respects. Instead, though it has by no means been their deliberate intention, they have come to form what might be termed a conspiracy against the value of money. It will have become clear from our historical account that inflation is anything but a new experience for Sweden. But the special variety of it that has dominated the past twenty years—the inflation of welfare, full employment and strong unionism—has at least the virtue of novelty, if no other. To no little extent the wage system has functioned in such a way that by means of a sliding wage scale and piece-work results, the pay rates in many industries are much higher than those agreed on by negotiation. The market trend in wages and salaries has more or less put the unions out of work as arbiters of the pay envelope.

At the same time the unions representing employees in the service trades, certain low-wage enterprises, and national and local government have been able to push up rates above increases in productivity; the resulting inflationary pressure has thus retained a high degree of determining power for these unions. Parallel with this development, the white-collar unions, impelled by a more or less explicit desire to offset the effects of graduated taxation, have managed to achieve an influence, quite outside the parliamentary arena, which runs counter to the income-equalizing aspirations of government authorities. The responsibility therefore lies with the state insofar as it has not applied sufficiently strong weapons of economic policy to guide the acts of these unions in the desired channels. Political difficulties, however, have militated against the adoption of such a course. Even though most people dislike inflation and often enough criticize it in general terms, they do not dislike it strongly enough to compel resolute action to stop it. There are good grounds for believing that the Swedish people would object much more strongly to the austerities which an anti-inflation policy would impose.

Marketing, political organizational, and political sociological factors are here in conflict with the theories which sustain full employment and welfare policy, insofar as the gaps in income between different groups of earners have tended to widen, at least since the beginning of the mid-'fifties. In the meantime the benefits of social security have exerted no more than a small equalizing effect where the vertical income differences are concerned. To the extent these benefits are financed from direct taxes, they equalize incomes only at the basic insurance level. The principle applying to the income-related additional insurances—that is the different classes of health insurance, unemployment insurance and supplementary pensioning—is to let the benefit stand in proportion to the contribution. The effect here has been a horizontal rather than vertical equalization; the income earned by one person during his working lifetime is levelled out, but not the income as between different categories of earners. On top of that, many of the benefits offered by the public sector, such as grants to education and the like, have been utilized in relatively greater measure by the already affluent, who thereby receive a substantial 'discount' to offset the progressive rate of taxation. In real terms therefore, the vertical equalization wrought by taxes has fallen short of the distributions shown by the official tax tables. In other words, the image of the modern welfare state as 'levelled-out' and 'classless' (evaluations that have often appeared in descriptions of Sweden in the 'fifties and 'sixties) is exaggerated, to say the least.

Indeed the history of this welfare state up to date does not confirm such judgments, but refutes them emphatically.

The statistics on income are impaired by many weaknesses. They are based on income tax returns which have afforded opportunities for evasion, both legal and illegal. Comparisons based on a specific year can hit wide of the mark, since the incomes of certain groups tend to vary. At the bottom of the income scale we may find many earners who do not normally belong there: the ill or unemployed, whose social benefits are not recorded as income; the military conscripts who suddenly drop out of civilian life to take basic training or refresher courses; and the students in the universities, who before long will be earning much more.

A look at the net tax assessments for 1962 shows that about 5,000 of the 4·3 million persons earning more than 2,400 kronor a year had an income in excess of 100,000 kronor. They comprised 0·1 per cent of all earners and accounted for 1·6 per cent of the aggregate reported income. Between 50,000 and 100,000 kronor was earned by 31,000 persons or 0·7 per cent of the total, with 4 per cent of the income. Less than 15,000 kronor was earned by 70·5 per cent of the total. They represented 43 per cent of the aggregate income of 51,000 millions assessed for income tax purposes. Only half of the net tax assessments accrued to 80 per cent of the earners.

In the taxation of net wealth or property, which begins above a stipulated minimum of 80,000 kronor per person, somewhat more than 2,000 of the 186,000 taxpayers in this class owned assets worth one million kronor or more. Assets worth between one-quarter and one million were owned by about 24,000 persons. It is illuminating that of the 2,000 fortunes in the one-million class, 1,000 belonged to persons who earned at least 100,000 kronor in income, and a further 684 fortunes to persons who earned between 50,000 and 100,000 kronor a year. The fortunes yield returns, not least in the form of well-paid positions in the firms where they are situated.

Exact comparisons with corresponding data for 1908 (cited earlier) cannot be made owing to unsatisfactory statistics and the different statistical techniques employed in the two years. Generally speaking, however, the rungs of pre-tax income do not appear to have moved significantly towards equalization in the more than fifty years which have passed since 1908. The levelling-out is more pronounced after deduction of tax.

However, if account is taken of the higher concealed benefits in 1962 (there was no reason to hide benefits in 1908), the 'discounts' on taxes mentioned earlier, and the particularly heavy burden of local taxes on the lower income groups, the levelling-out again becomes less pronounced. Whatever yardstick one applies in this respect to gauge the changes from the semi-industrial society existing shortly after 1900 up to the present welfare state, and whatever one feels about the desirability of carrying income equalization to great lengths, the basic fact stands out clearly enough. In an economy where 80 per cent of the earners vouch for half of the income only, the other half of it earned by the remaining 20 per cent, of whom fewer than 4 per cent lay claim to 15 per cent of it, it would be absurd to suggest that income equalization had progressed very far in Sweden. In 1962, a direct tax of 50 per cent did not operate until assessed income had reached the figure of 120,000 kronor. At the level of 18,000 kronor, the direct tax came to 21 per cent for married persons and 30 per cent for the single. At the same time indirect taxes and fees which had little progressive effect and no doubt worked regressively in many cases, provided the national exchequer with 50 per cent of its tax revenue. Out of all the taxes payable to national government and local authorities, progressivity accounted for a very small percentage only in 1962.

When we turn to the practical economic development during the post-war period, that is, development which has underlain the change in material standards and the rising national income, we find two persistent trends: the one, structural change in industry on a large scale; the other, innovations in technology of far-reaching effect. The most expansive corporations have increasingly applied new technical advances towards a greater degree of capital utilization. Naturally, it is difficult here to identify just what is cause and what is effect. In many cases, growing demand has led to increased investments and high capital intensity. On the other hand, it is not uncommon for technical innovations to pave the way for a strengthened market position and improved sales results. Or it sometimes happens that a company, caught in a competitive squeeze with a diminishing demand, will ruthlessly cut costs through rationalization and find itself in the capital-intensive group as a result.

Agriculture is among the sectors marked by stagnation and even decline. Since the beginning of the 'fifties, levels of employment and production in such a labour-intensive branch as dairying have fallen sharply, while output of meat has increased. According to the most reliable recent statistics, agriculture in the mid-'sixties engaged about 7 per cent of the gainfully employed population, used between 5 and 10 per cent of the total capital stock in the form of buildings and machinery, and occupied about 15 per cent of the aggregate land area. These production factors were supposed to have made a contribution of about 3·5 per cent to the gross national product or, if the agricultural contribution is estimated according to world market prices, somewhat under 2 per cent. Again according to world market prices, labour productivity could be estimated at about one-fourth of that attained in other sectors of the economy. In terms of Swedish prices, which were higher owing to special protection against imports, labour productivity was about half of that in other sectors.

Agriculture continued to be dominated by small holdings and the distribution of acreage was still unfavourable. Large areas that were ill suited to cultivation were included in the arable.

It is beyond the scope of this book to discuss how much of this situation has derived from an unfavourable economic structure with its roots in protective tariffs dating from the 1880s and 1930s, and how much might have been different in the absence of this protection. We shall have to content ourselves with such facts as are available.

A first observation we can make is that the protection of agriculture has not seriously deterred the flow of manpower from farms to other branches of economic activity. From the viewpoint of the agrarian community, perhaps, the age composition of those remaining on the farms was unfavourably affected by this protectionary policy. A farm operated along more businesslike lines and more efficiently organized in general might have acted as a stronger inducement for young men to stay on. Be that as it may, the rural exodus has proceeded at an accelerated rate; during the 'forties the farm labour force diminished by between 1 and 3 per cent per year, during the 'fifties by 3 to 5 per cent, and during the first half of the 'sixties by 5 to 8 per cent per year.

Since at the same time neither production volume nor agricultural processing values have appreciably changed since the beginning of the 'fifties, the productivity of farm labour has increased at a rapid rate that has outstripped even that of industrial labour, although it was still low at the mid-'sixties. One reason for the improved productivity, despite the increasingly unfavourable age composition of farm labour, is the disappearance of many small holdings on marginal land. All told, the number of farms had dwindled from 300,000 to 200,000, that is, by one-third from the mid-'forties to the mid-'sixties. The many closures, which became particularly noticeable as from 1960, related chiefly to holdings of less than 10 hectares of arable (one hectare equals 2·471 acres). Improved productivity can also be explained with reference to greatly increased capital investments in the form of machinery and different growth-promoting chemicals.

The forests account for nearly one-third of Swedish export revenues; about half the output of the forest-based industries is shipped abroad. Since the war, however, the Swedish role as supplier of the world market of forest products has declined relatively; this trend has accelerated in the 1960s and indeed applies to Scandinavia generally. In consequence Sweden no longer takes the lead in setting prices as she once did. On the whole, the basic operation of logging or timber-cutting has also stagnated. Even though there was a relatively sharp upswing from a nadir in the mid-'fifties, the volume of logging around 1965 did not exceed the average for 1900 to 1950 by more than a few percentage points. Here again, however, labour productivity has risen owing to mechanization and greatly improved transport conditions. Large sums have been invested in road-building. The forest tractor, the car and the asphalted roads have more and more replaced the horse and the waterway as transporters of timber from the felling areas to the sawmills and pulp factories. By and large, however, these cost-reduction measures have been applied only in the past few years. From all indications, the pace of rationalization in forestry proceeded more slowly than in agriculture up to the end of the 'fifties. It appears that the fragmentation of land ownership has proved to be a severe barrier to higher productivity on a more extensive scale. In the mid-'sixties, 50 per cent of the forested acreage was held by private owners—the 'woodland farmers'; corporations held 25 per cent, the crown 20 per cent, and other public owners 5 per cent. A considerable portion of the state-owned forest was characterized by low yields; the state's 20 per cent of total forested acreage was matched by only 12 per cent of the forest value. The present pattern of ownership has largely remained unaltered since the turn of the century. In the past few years, however, the fragmentation has been counteracted: the woodland farmers in certain areas have formed associations for the purpose of managing their forests and marketing the timber in common. From a technical and administrative point of view, this step amounts to a 'kolkhozing' of farm woodlands which signifies important rationalization gains. At the same time, however, the corporate ownership of forests is divided among some thirty firms—a large number, which also militates against improved efficiency.

On the other hand, the industrial side of the forestry business has committed itself so much more earnestly to scientific management. Heavy spending on new plant and equipment has been characteristic of the pulp and paper mills together with the shutdown of small and outdated production units, and a high capital intensity. By the mid-

'sixties it was estimated that between three and four times as much productive plant per employee was invested in these industries as in manufacturing generally. Expansion and rationalization have been particularly intensive in the paper industry. Indeed, the whole post-war period has witnessed a continuing trend towards a greater component of domestic processing, with a growing share of production assignable to board and paper and a lesser to pulp. In the making of pulp itself, there is increasing emphasis on the more highly bleached pulp, while an offshoot line of production, fibreboard, has already been classified as an industry in its own right.

The rate of return from pulp and paper production has gradually declined under the pressure of greater competition. This of course accounts for the increased rationalization, but the dwindling rate of return has entailed difficulties in financing the investments which rationalization requires. In such a situation, the solution offered by the extensive consolidation of forest holdings both by private and corporate owners may well be impelled by its own law of necessity.

A similar spur towards concentration has certainly not been lacking elsewhere on the Swedish industrial scene during the past twenty years. The mining companies, steel mills, metal works, engineering plants and shipyards—big exporters all—have run into tougher foreign competition, and their plight is anything but helped by the cost of inflation that has prevailed ever since the beginning of the 'fifties. This does not mean that times have been hard or that future prospects look dim; but the pressure to improve and rationalize has never let up.

In the mining industry, improved methods of separation and dressing have greatly increased the feasibility of exploiting iron-poor ores. An important example of what this means is provided by the Stråssa mine in the Bergslagen region of central Sweden. The mine was shut down in the early 'twenties when only about 35 per cent iron could be extracted from the ore. Operations were resumed in 1959 and large investments have permitted an extraction rate of between 60 and 70 per cent, which is roughly the same yield as the iron-rich ores of Norrbotten province in the far North.

A revolution has taken place in boring and drilling techniques. The old hand-held steel drills have given way to compressed-air machines, capable of drilling hundreds of metres of boreholes per day. This has made for improved yields: by the mid-'sixties, iron ore was being mined at the rate of 30 million tons per year, as compared with an average 18 million tons in the 'fifties and 10 millions in the 'forties. Whereas increased production in the 'fifties required a larger labour force, the fast-rising output levels of the 'sixties have been attainable with fewer hands. As a result of the new methods and of large-scale investments, labour productivity has risen at a swift rate.

Production in the basic metal industries has described an accelerated upward curve. At the mid-'sixties more than 3 million tons of forged and rolled finished steel were produced as against 1·6 million tons in the 'fifties, 920,000 tons in the 'forties, and 650,000 in the 'thirties. Amalgamations and mergers have proceeded briskly in the iron and steel industry ever since the 'thirties, when mill closures made frequent front-page headlines. Even in the mid-'sixties, however, operations were still spread out over a fairly large number of plants, with the three largest accounting for about half of the total output. The rate of capital intensity soars higher and higher. In 1966 the value of plant investment per employee was more than twice that in industry as a whole.

In the engineering or metalworking sector, a quite different course of development has been taken by the shipyards. Up to the outset of the 'sixties, Swedish shipbuilders managed to hold their own fairly well in international competition—mostly from Japan—thanks chiefly to heavy demand from Norwegian shipping companies. But the rate of return on investment has fallen steeply. Further, the increasing compulsion to grant long-term credits (in marked contrast to an earlier day when heavy prepayments could be demanded), has put the yards in an increasingly precarious financial position. Up to the mid-'sixties, Sweden was still able to hold her own against most other countries in the shipbuilding business. However, it is by a very narrow margin as compared with the late 'forties and early 'fifties, when the wealth rolled in with seemingly no effort. The change has since then already been dramatic and extensive, and in the long run perhaps very serious.

A far more auspicious situation exists in other branches of the engineering industry. Sizable increases in production have been recorded, averaging at 8 per cent during the 'sixties. If the shipbuilders and motor vehicle manufacturers are excluded, the engineering industry exports about 40 per cent of its output. Demand for its products has kept pace with the general rise of affluence in the large industrial countries. West Germany, Great Britain, the United States and other Nordic countries are the leading buyers. The engineering industry has grown faster than industry as a whole, and has been particularly adept at boosting its exports. A universal tendency towards international trade in metal-worked products is very much in evidence. At the same time, however, the rate of return has at times been less favourable. Since engineering plants are by their nature labour-intensive, they cannot readily offset mounting payrolls with the same facility as, for instance, the pulp and paper mills or the corporations in the basic metal industries. None the less, developments have moved steadily in the direction of greater mechanization and capital utilization. In the main, the pace-setters are still the large firms based on engineering 'genius': ASEA (heavy electrical equipment), SKF (ball bearings), AGA (electronics), Electrolux (home appliances) and Volvo (motor vehicles).

Turning to the home market industry, the postwar development in several of its areas of classical endeavour has been poor. To a great extent that is the result of the earlier 'hothouse' climate under which it had thrived. The winds of competition from abroad and of keener bidding for manpower at home from more expansive sectors have led to lost markets, low yields and shutdowns or mergers. Hardest hit were the shoe and textile manufacturers. The 'fifties inflicted a direct depression on the textile industry, with extensive structural change as a result. Some one hundred companies were forced out of business, and about fifty branch establishments disappeared. The number of people employed fell by about one-third. A measure of stabilization was attained at the beginning of the 'sixties in the wake of severe cost-reduction programmes, growing domestic consumption and increased exports. Not a little of the credit for this achievement goes to the traditionally high quality standards of Swedish ready-to-wear clothing.

Towards the mid-'sixties the food processing industry contributed about 10 per cent to the total value of processed production. A relatively large part of its output, about 20 per cent, went to foreign markets. Nearly three-quarters of the exports consisted of dairy and meat products. The industry as a whole has increasingly concentrated on the sale of products with a higher processing component, a consequence not only of the tendency to consume more food outside the home, but also of the demand by women for lighter household chores. As a result the processing value of that industry has risen much more quickly than its market value.

A relative newcomer on the Swedish industrial scene is the manufacture of chemicals and chemical products (except for such established branches as matches and explosives). During the 'fifties and 'sixties this industry has expanded at buoyant rates, averaging at 5 per cent in the early years and soaring up to about 8 per cent more recently. The increase in output has been most striking for pharmaceutical products.

The development of the different industrial branches described above has required the expansion of two basic spheres: energy supply and transportation. Hydroelectric power has been harnessed at a forced pace. The total quantity of electricity generated, at 5,000 million kilowatt hours in 1930, rose to 10,000 million kWh in 1940, 20,000 million kWh in 1950, 40,000 million kWh in 1960, and 50,000 million kWh in 1965. In 1965, however, this domestic production still satisfied only about 35 per cent of the energy requirement. A few percentage points were added by wood and peat. About 60 per cent had to be imported, with oil meeting half the total energy requirement and coal and coke about 10 per cent. A modest beginning in the construction of nuclear power plants can also be noted.

In transportation the expansion of motorcar traffic has been the predominant development. This concerns passenger cars in particular, but has by no means lacked importance for the transport of goods. In the fifteen years from 1950 to 1965, the private passenger car is estimated to have increased its share of the total mileage travelled by individuals from 33 to 85 per cent. Out of the total traffic in goods, measured in ton-kilometres, the railways accounted for about half in 1965, as against 40 per cent for trucks and 10 per cent for merchant vessels. One-third of the freight carried by the railways consisted of Lapland ores; the transportation of other commodities was shared about equally between road and rail.

The conveyance of goods has described a sharply rising curve. In 1950 it reached nearly 14,000 million ton-kilometres, rising in 1960 to 20,000 millions and in 1965 to 27,000 millions. The actual increase in production was naturally a very important factor. Demands on transport have, however, increased at a faster rate than required by increased industrial production alone. Various other circumstances have prompted the increase, among them the concentration of industry, greater demands for the bringing together of the intermediate products coming from subcontracted firms, the sale of more highly processed and heavier products, and increased demands for service.

As a matter of course the expansion and concentration of industry, the large-scale shifts of population, and the increased transports have given an added incentive to the construction industry in all its ramifications: houses and flats; factories, stores and other establishments of industry and commerce; schools, hospitals and other communal buildings; and the power stations, water and sewage mains, roads, bridges, underground railways, harbours and other civil engineering projects. As thus defined, the construction industry employed some 340,000 persons by the mid-'sixties, considerably more than the number engaged in agriculture. Somewhat less than half of this work force was engaged in building construction, and not quite half of this half in house-building. The latter, which produced an average of 50,000 flats a year from 1946 to 1955, achieved an annual output of 64,000 flats in 1956–60 and 80,000 in 1960–65. About one-third of the total investment in new building and civil engineering projects has gone to the housing sector. The construction of schools, hospitals, nursing homes and local government offices has accounted for about 15 per cent of the total. Roughly the same share has gone to streets, highways, water supplies, and sewerage, while 18 per cent has gone into the construction of facilities for industry and commerce.

The statistics are imperfect and less precise when we look at the private services sector, defined to include the distributive trades, banking and insurance, property management, consultant services, the hotel and restaurant business, domestic help in the home, and the pursuit of literary and artistic activities. By and large the distributive trades (wholesaling and retailing) appear to have engaged 12 per cent of all the gainfully employed in 1950 and 13·5 per cent in 1960; the proportion has presumably remained the same since then. When we include all the services mentioned above, the gainfully-employed share in 1950 came to nearly 15 per cent in 1950, slightly more than 19 per cent in 1960, and just short of 20 per cent in 1965. Thus a certain stagnation in the number employed has set in during the 1960s, during which the number has only just kept pace with total production increase. It is chiefly explained by the sweeping programmes of cost reduction that have been carried out since the later 'fifties in retailing, banking and insurance—enterprises which normally required much manpower. As in the manufacturing industry, the structural picture has come to be characterized by shutdowns, amalgamations and the emergence of large corporations. Even so, the staffs engaged by banks, insurance companies, property management companies and consultant firms swelled from about 62,000 in 1950 to 108,000 in 1965. On the other hand, domestic service in the home engaged 64,000 persons in 1965 as compared with 90,000 in 1950.

A handful of giants now dominate in wholesaling, though it is worth noting that two of the biggest are owned by associations of retailers. The expansion of department stores, multiple concerns, supermarkets, and self-service stores has been extensive. The number of retail establishments declined from roughly 85,000 in 1950 to

70,000 in 1965. The consumer cooperative societies, comprising the largest single form of business organization in retailing, must be noted particularly in the trend towards concentration. At the beginning of the 'fifties they had more than 8,000 stores, which were reduced to 6,500 in 1960 and 4,000 in 1965; a figure of 1,500 stores is predicted for 1970. In the mid-'sixties the consumer cooperatives transacted upwards of 20 per cent of the country's retail business and more than 25 per cent in food alone.

The public services—education, health and medicine, national defence, public administration and so on—have greatly expanded in both absolute and relative terms. In 1965 they contributed more than 10 per cent to the gross national product, equivalent to an increase of nearly 50 per cent in the value added since 1955. In that year the public services engaged 340,000 of the gainfully employed; in 1965, 470,000. An analysis of public expenditure in 1965 in the operating and investment sectors shows the following:

	Operating expenditures, in per cent	Investment expenditures, in per cent
Education	27	24
Health and medicine	21	15
Social services	8	4
National defence	14	44
Other	30	13
	100	100
	14,500 mill. kr.	5,750 mill. kr.

As we had occasion to observe earlier, the public services by their very nature do not lend themselves to rationalization schemes. Better education requires more teachers per thousand students; improved medical services more doctors and nurses; an expanded social counselling service more people qualified to help clients; and so on down the line. Accordingly, increased productivity is a term of little relevance for this sector. Its meaning could of course be stretched to include a higher quality of instruction in the schools, or better treatment and amenities for patients in the hospitals—but that does not show up in the statistics. At the same time, however, there is no denying that there has taken place a considerable increase in productivity as thus defined, and it must certainly be taken into account as one of the significant contributors to the rise in national living standards.

Given such methods and instruments of measurement as are available to us, the national gross product of 90,000 million kronor achieved in 1965 breaks down as follows by employment and the value added to goods and services:

Industrial Group	Number employed	Per cent of value added
Mining and manufacturing	1,150,000	36
Power and gas	50,000	2
Building and construction	340,000	10
Farming and fisheries	275,000	3
Forestry and logging	70,000	4
Distributive trades	460,000	14
Transport and communication	270,000	10
All private services	325,000	10
All public services	470,000	10
Totals	3,410,000	100

Any generalizations about the Swedish postwar development as outlined above are bound to be vague and somewhat arbitrary. It all depends on one's own set of value judgments. Many participants in the public debate have assailed what they regard as an inflation of the public services, perhaps not so much because they believe these services are unnecessary, as because of the heavy taxation they incur; it is also argued that many of these services should be 'de-socialized' and adapted to consumer demand at freely set market prices. However, the disputants seem fairly well agreed on one characteristic of the development, excluding Sweden's strong commitment to the public sector, namely that it is highly 'Americanized'. The underlying ideas, the methods, and the general impulses for structural change have emanated in great measure from the United States—often, it would seem, for reasons of fashion rather than rational motivation. This represents a vast difference by comparison with the period at the juncture of the nineteenth and twentieth centuries, when Germany played the role of pivot marker for the Swedish economy; it will be recalled that Britain had performed a similar role in earlier periods. Not so long ago, one of our leading newspaper columnists had occasion to remark 'Next to Sweden, the United States is the most Americanized country in the world', an observation that contains much more than a germ of truth. It often happens that Swedish businessmen are quicker to put American ideas into practice than their counterparts on the other side of the Atlantic. However, where American industry gives priority to mass production for enormous markets, Swedish industry has preferred to base its planning on special inventions and designs. Greater reliance is put on engineering 'know-how' and on the 'genius' enterprises' markets whenever ordinary products run into excessive difficulties.

II

The evolution of a welfare society has been accompanied by a growing accretion of power to the state and its primary institution, the executive of government. At the same time, important private concentrations of power have accrued to large interest organizations, especially those of labour and management, and to a lesser degree in consumer cooperation and agriculture. A similar aggregation of monolithic interests has taken place in the business community, often ahead of the rest; pre-eminent here are such trade associations as *Industriförbundet* (mining and manufacturing concerns), *Grossistförbundet* (wholesalers) and *Köpmannaförbundet* (retailers). Large companies and combinations of companies have merged into larger units, whose financial affairs not infrequently are dominated by a few large commercial banks and their holding companies.

When we proceed to analyse the aggregation and distribution of power in present day Sweden, a couple of points should be borne in mind so as to keep matters in proper perspective. Comparisons with a 'liberal' society of an earlier day have all too easily taken an exaggerated and over-generalized form. Today, there is a similar tendency to overestimate the increase of power that has accrued to the Government, interest organizations and corporate managements.

Before the emergence of the welfare state, power and influence were highly concentrated, as we have seen, in the hands of a few civil servants, entrepreneurs, owners of capital and politicians, who mostly shared a similar social background. Apart from the more affluent farmers, who enjoyed a special political status because of their long-standing enfranchisement, the great mass of people had no say in the running of their country's affairs. On the eve of the franchise reform embodied in the Act of 1866, Baron Erik Leijonhufvud predicted that the industrial working class would long be worse off than any other group ever had been, and subsequent events proved him right. The working man was the object of legislation but had nothing to say about its formulation, unlike the farmers, who had had their say ever since the first Riksdags were convened in the fifteenth century. The democratic rule that no one shall be governed by persons beyond his control did not apply to the new working class. A tiny group at the top of the social and economic pyramid exercised a virtual monopoly of everything: the shape of the economy, political influence, culture and learning.

Economically, too, the Swedish community was far less 'atomistic' than is often claimed. A distinct animus towards monopoly pervaded those enterprises which spearheaded the trend towards increasing industrialization. Owing to the relative immobility imparted by technical factors and high fixed costs, almost every captain of industry held an initial monopoly which lasted much longer than was warranted by his being the first man to make a certain product, or perhaps the first to exploit an invention or new design. The impact of foreign competition was held at bay by poor communications, which often engendered regional monopolies within the country. Beginning around 1900 the element of monopoly or quasi-monopoly assumed its most striking aspect in the 'genius' or invention-based companies. As was noted in the previous chapter, the high profits and re-investments of profits which this power concentration made possible were important factors in the rapid industrial expansion and in the uneven distribution of income and property.

This concentration of power in the hands of a few had no counter-weight of importance to offset it. The state power and the interest organizations were weak. It could also be said, speaking schematic-ally, that the central authority was wielded by the managing directors of industry and commerce.

A completely different kind of balance characterizes the welfare state. The present scene, one might say, consists of enormous blocs of concentrated power which have largely achieved a state of equili-brium. On the one hand, augmented power is vested in the state and the Government, but on the other, the large organizations are better equipped not only to influence the central authority, but even to thwart it. It can be contended that the new equilibrium was born out of equilibrium by the alliance which has existed all along between the Social Democratic party and the workers' trade unions. This alliance obviously has had great significance in the formulation of long-range policy. In a number of cases it has enabled the national labour federation, *Landsorganisationen* (LO), to obtain by legislation what could not be obtained at the conference table. Sometimes, LO has had its way in collective bargaining merely by threatening to resort to government legislation. However, it would be a mistake to infer from the alliance that LO and the Social Democrats work in harmonious unity like a pair of horses in harness.

267

The different functions the two have to fulfil, have of necessity created certain tensions and conflicts. LO has been able to work with a membership cadre that is economically, socially and politically more homogeneous than that of the Social Democratic party, which relies much more on marginal groups to help maintain its dominant authority. The Social Democrats, moreover, have shown a propensity —common to almost all democratic parties in office throughout the world—to govern 'above party' in the name of national unity. Naturally enough, this aspiration, manifested with varying degrees of awareness and zeal in different issues, has offered virtually all the major interest groups special opportunities to 'take part in' government as balancing factors.

This system has acquired its own name, 'Harpsund Democracy', in reference to the prime minister's residence in the Södermanland province. The inference is that the week-end conferences which Mr Erlander is in the habit of holding at Harpsund with representatives of different organizations have greater bearing on the government's political actions than the attitudes, debates and negotiations of the Riksdag. Whether that is true or not, and it should be noted that the government cannot act without the support of its party caucus in the Riksdag, the essential significance of Harpsund Democracy is that it illustrates the working of 'countervailing power': before proceeding to act on an important matter, the government takes pains to assure itself of support from all the large interest groups, or failing that, to forearm itself against any serious opposition that such a group is likely to offer.

However, the balancing scales can also be knocked askew, and this has definitely been true of official policy on wages and income during the postwar period. Further, a corollary of every balancing system is the imposition of considerable restrictions on the central authority. We shall consider the more important restrictions below.

One of these has been strictly political in nature. Although the Social Democrats have held executive office uninterruptedly since 1932 (apart from a few summer months in 1936), they have commanded a parliamentary majority for twelve years only, from 1940–52. The party has at no stage commanded a majority in both chambers simultaneously; the closest they came was in 1940–44, with half the seats in the Upper Chamber and a great majority in the Lower (130 seats of 230); and in 1944–48, with half the seats in the Lower Chamber and a big majority in the Upper. Long stretches of incumbency have been shared with other parties: the Agrarians from 1936 to 1940 and again from 1951 to 1957, and all the non-socialist parties from 1940 to 1945. In only four elections, 1938, 1940, 1942 and 1962, have the Social Democrats won more than half the votes cast. It is impossible to determine to what extent this position on the margin has compelled the party to compromise with its ideology. The existence of real obstacles would also have compelled the more cautious exercise of power even with greater strength in the Riksdag. At all events, it is quite wrong to suggest that this position can be reconciled with absolutism, especially with the theories of 'one-party rule' expounded by the Norwegian historian, Jens Arup Seip. As a matter of course, the very possession of ruling power has provided an inside track for influencing the course of events. To a great extent however, the Social Democratic party has seen itself confronted with two alternatives: either to proceed cautiously, and hence to accept great limits to its power; or to throw caution to the winds and risk getting thrown out. For this reason the opposition has had means to exercise a countervailing power. The Swedish system of checks and balances has its own built-in institutional arrangements: negotiations between party leaders, compromises worked out in standing committees and, not least, the participation of parties in the official inquiries which usually precede legislation.

In turn, of course, this distribution of power at the top has imposed a considerable restraint on the full exercise of formal sovereignty. The counteraction of concentrated power *within* the state has also checked the further arrogation of power *to* the state.

Nor has the party-political balance operated as the only restraining factor. The Riksdag's traditional claim to supreme authority has ruled out the accretion of powers to the government that might normally be expected to follow from the higher level of public expenditures. Swedish Riksdag members have opted for reduced political efficiency rather than the surrender of any of their prerogatives to the government, such as the exclusive power of the Riksdag to levy taxes and its right to inspect the accounts of state-owned companies.

When the Riksdag is spoken of as an obedient 'forwarding agent' for a government having a parliamentary majority, a point often made in Swedish debate, the reference is to the fact that government bills are seldom defeated in the Riksdag. However, it can be argued with equal validity that the Riksdag does not baulk because the government has plumbed its sentiments beforehand. As a rule, bills are not tabled until the party's own parliamentary faction has been won over, and, in important cases, not until after negotiations have been held with other factions and their views and objections have been taken into account. Since the opinions of the large interest organizations are also very often tested in advance, the so-called 'forwarding agency' delivers unto law not the will of an all-powerful government but rather the compromise that emerges in a system of countervailing power.

This system is frequently made out in foreign debate to represent a sort of golden mean, a miracle of harmony, and an idyll of the Middle Way. These views are typically embodied in the *Politics of Compromise*, a celebrated book on Swedish politics written by Dankwart A. Rustow. However, it can be contended with equal justice that the compromise itself and the power it stands for, may have been a political ideal realized at the expense of more resolute political action, and hence an indirect cause of the economic and social imbalance—inflation, unevenness of income distribution, and a meritocracy of the educated—which has come to characterize the Swedish welfare state at the same time.

Another restriction on the further accretion of power to the state has been the traditional independence of the Swedish civil service and the social and political ties of its leading administrators. Two questions may be raised here. Might it not be assumed that the civil service, in trying to get its proposals through and to act obligingly in general, has become more subordinate to the government in fact than on paper? And after so many years in office, might not the Social Democrats be expected to exercise their right of appointment so as to staff the top administrative posts with 'the right people'? There is no evidence of any pronounced trend in that direction over the past thirty years. The traditions of the different civil service departments have proved too tenacious. Even though many members of the ruling party have reached high administrative positions, their number is very small if the party's long period in office is considered. On the whole the politics of balance have been applied as far as political appointments to high posts are concerned. If a Social Democrat has been made the director general of a department or the governor of a county, then the next vacancy in either post will be reserved for a non-socialist politician or a civil servant. Of the twenty-four governors in office on January 1, 1967, ten were former Social Democratic politicians. What is perhaps even more important than this alternation of precedence is that the majority of senior public officers have not taken the path of politics at all. They have risen through the ranks of the civil service and their political allegiance has been unknown and usually vaguely anti-socialist. And once installed as county governors and directors-general, the Social

Democrats (and that also goes for the members of other parties) completely adopt the traditions of their office, and look upon themselves as civil servants. For them, it becomes axiomatic to uphold the same non-political independence of judgment as the 'true' civil servants—and no one has expected them to do anything else.

On the other hand, a certain accretion of power to the public administration has taken place in a couple of other respects. During the postwar period the government has deviated to some extent from the principle on which the Swedish civil service has long been erected, that is, the distinction between governing and administering. Decisions long regarded as the province of civil service departments have been centralized in the government ministries, giving rise to a considerable degree of ministerial rule. This process has gone to different lengths in different administrative spheres, and has been anything but consistent. Nevertheless, it has unquestionably served to converge more power upon the government, a power perhaps exercised in reality more by ministerial secretaries and under-secretaries than by the ministers themselves.

A phenomenon of greater importance than the foregoing, however, has been the power of the state to engage local authorities as arms of administration. It is estimated that the organs of local government spend about 80 per cent of their expenditure on objects prescribed by the central government. This system has had a double effect. Within the limits imposed by state-assigned duties, the municipalities are in a better position than the civil service departments to act on their own initiative. They usually contribute from their own funds to the different objects of public expenditure. At the same time, since the municipalities have generally been led by elected Social Democratic officials, the government has had access to an administrative machinery with the same political philosophy and intentions. It is no coincidence that the deliberate building-up of this system was begun during the thirties, when the new policies were introduced and began to concentrate on the big new issues of social welfare, housing and education.

This does not mean that the local authorities have always submitted easily to state dictates. On the contrary they have exerted important influence at the centre by virtue of huge representation in the Riksdag and in party executives. Any move that looks like infringing on local honour or interests is sharply opposed. When accord exists, however, the role of municipalities as state executors has made it easier in practice to implement government policies than might be the case if the executors had been hostile or indifferent.

271

The maintenance by private enterprise of its own capitalistic organization has imposed another important restraint on state power. Apart from the nationalization of some railway lines, the establishment of *Norrbottens Järnverk* (a pig-iron producer) and *Statens skogsindustrier* (a forestry enterprise), and the exercise of a stock option in Luossavaara-Kiirunavaara AB (LKAB), (owner of the great iron ore mine in Kiruna)—a government interest dating back to 1907 and then initiated by the Conservative prime minister, Arvid Lindman (1862–1937)—virtually nothing in the way of socialization has been undertaken by the Social Democratic government. The import of the stock option in LKAB was to equip a single private company, Grängesberg, with a vast sum which it could spend on erecting a new steel plant at Oxelösund, on the Baltic coast south of Stockholm, and on the joint-venture Lanco project in Liberia.

It stands to reason that the expanded public sector has conferred more power on the state. In effect, of course, it has socialized a growing part of the income earned by individuals. But its significance for the distribution of power is not as great. Most of this money is returned to the citizens in the form of transfer payments or as public services. These commitments are fixed; the state cannot manipulate them for other ends. In one sphere, namely the funds built up by contributions to the supplementary pensions scheme, there was theoretical scope for abuse of power, but the government waived this possibility when it stipulated special regulations for the trusteeship of these funds.

If large power blocs can thus be said to counter-balance one another, a distinct tendency towards far-reaching concentration of power *within* these blocs would appear to be in the making. We therefore have reason to look more closely at each of the blocs in turn.

By far the largest are the labour-market organizations. However, the countervailing power they exert against one another is not solely restricted to the classical pattern of labour versus management. The different organizations of employees, LO (wage-earners), TCO (salary-earners) and SACO (professional workers)—to name just the big three—are also mutually opposed. They fight not only over the total pay available, and the aggregate amount of fringe benefits, but also with equal intensity over how much the one group can carve out for itself at the expense of the others. Were we to resort to Marxist terminology, we would say that Sweden's class struggle over the past two or three decades has been waged to a far greater extent between different classes or groups of employees than between employees and

272

the capitalists or employers. The persistent inflation has added further fuel to the flames. Together, the employee organizations have been able to wrest gains in excess of the actual scope permitted under conditions of a stable currency. Continuing inflation has acted as a further spur: to be on the safe side a group will demand more than it expects to get, lest it be fooled by other, more pushing groups. The result of the in-fighting is to make all groups march in the same direction. When the management lacks the strength to resist, disequilibrium sets in. The 'conspiracy' against stable currency becomes a *fait accompli*.

Considered from another angle, this state of affairs may be taken to mean that the leaders of employee organizations wield too little rather than too much power. Beyond a point they cannot resist the pressure exerted by fervent affiliated groups, who themselves may not represent more than a minority of the total membership. In a field as crucial as wage policy, the internal power basis of the organizations has proved to be rather weak. Democracy, in the sense that strong opinions among the members make themselves known to the organizational executives and largely determine their actions, has evidently functioned very well—perhaps far too well if the considerations of public interest are taken into account. The leaders of LO and TCO do not decide the wage and salary demands; their affiliated groups and members do that for them. The efforts that have been made by the large organizations to coordinate their collective bargaining have been motivated not so much by the expectation of being able to squeeze more out of management, as by the hope of avoiding the rivalry described above. It is felt the inter-group planning will make it easier to keep the aggregate of contractual pay rises within a limit which better corresponds to economic balance in the community. On the whole, it is difficult to generalize about the concentration of power that has taken place in the large labour-market organizations. They are built up like Chinese boxes, with local chapters fitted into national associations, which in turn are fitted into congresses or confederations as the largest box. The confederated organization, however, functions both directly—through the executives of the affiliated associations—and indirectly through its own representative assemblies to which the affiliates elect delegates in proportion to their size. Members of the central committees or executive bodies are thus elected officials, and not appointees of any affiliated association. However, it is not uncommon for these central executives to be dominated by 'heavyweights' among the affiliates, which also deliver all the dues to the confederations.

At one and the same time, therefore, the confederation is 'owned' by the affiliates and above them in rank. An identical relationship applies to the affiliate (a national union, for instance) and its constituent locals or chapters. This dichotomy makes possible a strong accretion of power when the central executive is unanimous. If any one or more of its members is opposed, however, the resulting fissure can crack right down the whole structure. LO has drawn its own conclusions from this perilous portent: if agreement cannot be reached on a question, it is left to 'ripen', according to trade union terminology. Before important matters are decided, all the association chairmen are sounded out for their opinions; they meet in a special body for this purpose, and while their recommendations in theory are advisory only, they would in practice seem to be decisive in the majority of cases. In other words, we have here a rather pronounced system of checks and balances, where the degree of power actually vested in the executive leadership depends to a great extent on the importance of the men who compose it.

In the exercise of internal democracy, individual members can bring their influence to bear in more ways than by the formal casting of votes. They often express their opinions at chapter meetings or at local inter-union assemblies, which convey them to the national associations and confederations. Generally speaking, however, this concerns especially active groups. Provision is also made for the more direct communication of opinion. Factory workmen may express their opinion to the union representative who will pass it on if there is any substance to it. Union officials are thereby apprised of what is 'stirring' in the ranks, and they are usually sensitive to such opinions. After all, they are elected to represent their members as 'ombudsmen', not to rule them. At the same time, of course, the leadership tries in different ways to guide this opinion, to prevail on members to accept the policy it seeks to conduct, and perhaps even make this policy look like what the members want.

The end result of all this is that the power structure is somewhat divided. In matters which more directly touch member interests, the procedure calls for caution, a sensitive ear, and patiently exercised influence. Democracy is a living force. However, if members ignore an issue out of indifference or ignorance, then the executive leadership can speak with the authority of the whole organization behind it and no advice is asked from anybody. As far as the outside world is concerned, the statements made on these occasions are also interpreted to reflect the views of not only the LO-leadership or TCO-leadership, but of the 'workers' and 'salary-earners', too. It would then appear that the internal power structure of the labour-market organizations shows up best at the top whenever the issue involved least affects the direct interests of members. There is nothing strange about that; but it must certainly be taken into consideration in any appraisal of the real importance of internal power and its exercise.

An answer to the question of how far the concentration of power has proceeded in private enterprise will greatly depend on the kind of yardstick chosen to measure it.

If we take as our starting point the number of corporations and their size, the tendencies towards concentration are strong enough, but this concentration has as yet not occurred very extensively.

However, if our approach is that of the financial power wielded over corporations and the instruments available for directing their affairs, both the postwar tendencies and the actual achievement by the mid-'sixties, then the degree of concentration is striking. According to a 1966 study of listed companies made for this book, one person served on no less than 60 of their boards of directors. Seven directors served on between 30 and 40 boards, nine on between 25 and 30, and thirteen on between 20 and 25 boards. Various reasons can be given to explain the demand for so many of the same men: their financial interests in these corporations; their skill and capability, which made their services highly desirable; the unstated yet implied offer of reciprocal rewards ('you let me sit on your board and I'll let you sit on mine'); and a penchant for emblazoning the names of distinguished businessmen on the directorial roster. Perhaps the import of a board chair was not especially great in a number of cases. All the same, the total picture is clear enough, in spite of various explanations and the operation of different effects in individual cases: a small number of persons hold disproportionately large power in the business community. The picture emerges with particular force for Stockholm's Enskilda Bank and its corporate family. Its chief executive, Marcus Wallenberg, was the man who held the 60 directorates. Ragner Söderberg, a close relative of the Wallenbergs, held 39, Jacob Wallenberg 23, and Marc Wallenberg 22 directorates. Among the enterprises they were connected with were such important companies as ASEA, Atlas Copco, Alfa Laval, Astra, Stora Kopparberg, Swedish Match, Bolinders, Svenska Järnvägsverkstäderna, Scania-Vabis, Svenska Fläktfabriken, L. M. Ericsson, Saab, Svenska Diamantborrningsaktiebolaget, and the largest insurance concern, Skandia. The head of Handelsbanken contented himself with nine directorates, among them the boards of Eriksbergs, IBM, Mo och Domsjö, Svenska Cellulosa (the largest forestry enterprise), Swedish

Esso and Svenska Metallverken. Fifteen directorates were held by the head of Skandinaviska Banken, including such companies as Billeruds, Kockums, Skånska Cement, Swedish Match, Grängesberg, Swedish Unilever, and the Skandia group.

It will be noted that the leading men of the largest banks sometimes meet on the same boards. If we extend our purview to include the other top-ranking executives of these banks, it turns out that their fraternization is by no means unusual. The different groups compete with one another, as do some of the corporations within their fold; but many financial and personal threads converge—a fact that has facilitated the mergers and working agreements which, not least during the 'sixties, have become almost staple fare for the business pages of Swedish newspapers.

Here too, however, checks and balances have asserted themselves —and are still doing so. When reference is made to the ten or fifteen families that are supposed to have Swedish industry and commerce under their thumbs, one must qualify this statement by adding that the control of these families is not all-embracing. Collaboration and common financial interests on certain front sectors do not prevent internecine conflict and competition on others. A broad spectrum of the business community stands outside the large power groups or in non-dependent relation to them. In the mid-'sixties there were about 500,000 enterprises, including the country's 200,000 farms, which employed less than 26 persons. About 10,000 had between 26 and 500 employees, while not quite 400 enterprises had more than 500 employees. About 300,000 of the enterprises were single pro-prietorships or family-run businesses. Frequently, too, the small firms depended on the large, working as their suppliers or dealers and receiving credits from them. Yet these small enterprises constituted a fairly significant 'free' sector in the business world. Together, they wielded a not inconsiderable power through their own interest organizations: the producer cooperatives in agriculture, the Central Federation of Master Craftsmen and Small Industries, the Swedish Retail Trade Federation, the Federation of Swedish Wholesale Merchants and Importers, and the purchasing chains owned and operated in common by independent tradesmen.

The inner accumulation of power within the business community is unmistakable, but its full concentration is far from being achieved. However, the tendency certainly appears to have proceeded further there than within the interest organizations, both in regard to the business community as a whole and as regards its component power blocs on their own.

A high degree of autocratic rule governs in the individual corporation. Supreme authority is vested in the board and managing director. If the corporation is dependent on a holding company, investment trust or commercial bank, the authority is vested in these, and exercised in the same dictatorial manner. The fact of ownership and ability to grant credit provides all the power which existing market conditions permits. No provision is made for democratic control. The board and managing director are answerable to the shareholders at annual meetings, but the elections at these gatherings are often dominated, if not entirely run, by a few holders owning large blocks of shares. True, the shares of many corporations have been widely diffused among large numbers of people, each holding shares in small amounts. But that does not lessen the concentration of power. Quite the contrary: the more widely dispersed the shares are, the less of them it takes—perhaps no more than 5 to 10 per cent of the total share capital—to gain full control over a corporation. Indeed, it is quite likely that the past ten to fifteen years of growing public investment in equities has reinforced the autocratic quality of corporate ownership. Most of this investment is not direct, but is in the form of stock purchased in a mutual fund, the idea being to spread the risk more effectively than would be possible for an individual investor. The right to vote in these funds is pro-rated by the amount of stock held. But the fund executives or their proxies vote at the general meetings of the corporations whose shares they administer for their investors.

The cooperative enterprises are more democratically structured. They are owned by their member-customers and governed by a representative system. Here again, however, the authoritarian element is strong. The need to run the cooperatives as businesses has necessitated, or at least has been made to justify, the delegation of large discretionary power to managements. *Kooperativa Förbundet* (KF), the Swedish Cooperative Union and Wholesale Society, has a board of directors consisting entirely of staff men, the heads of its different departments. The chairman, who in effect is also managing director, is thus controlled by a group who actually work under him. KF's administrative council, constituting a kind of super-board, has a membership of which half are salaried employees of the consumer societies. Even so, the ordinary members hold a latent potential for taking over as a last resort. The executive head of KF or Folksam (the cooperative insurance company) never attains the same sovereignty enjoyed by the big 'families' of the business community.

Some essential differences emerge when we compare the power

system of private enterprise with that of the interest organizations. In the latter, the officials are chosen by the people they 'govern' and are subject to their control. No one holds the highest posts through inheritance and money as in the typical corporation. If an official loses member confidence he may not be elected at the next of the regular elections. The organizations also have rules for defining the procedures for decision-making, the persons to be heard, and the business to be transacted by those in higher authority, for example in the general assemblies and congresses. While all these safeguards do not totally incapacitate an official, they do circumscribe his power. Under such circumstances, the executive head of an interest organization often feels himself confronted with the same problem as the politician: either he conducts a very cautious policy to ensure his stay in office; or he exercises his power fully for a short time and stands a real risk of losing the next election. To be sure, the differences between the interest organizations on one hand and privately owned and cooperative business on the other may be hard to grasp, and public discussion on these different power positions has often equated them as being fully comparable. Yet the differences are there, though more by virtue of the democratic order prevailing within the interest organizations and the greater pressure on their leaders to live 'politically' to hold the confidence of members.

One sphere where the concentration of power is—and has always been—particularly high is the press. Sweden admittedly has a great many daily newspapers. Between 75 and 80 per cent of the circulation is accounted for by non-socialist daily newspapers, whereas the Social Democratic party with its near-50 per cent of the electorate controls only about 20 per cent. The trade-union papers no doubt counter-balance this situation to some extent. However, they in turn are offset by the weekly magazines, which though formally 'neutral' are almost wholly permeated with bourgeois sentiments. In terms of circulation almost half of the weeklies come from one family-owned publishing house. The same family also owns the country's two largest daily newspapers.

Given the disproportionate percentages cited above, the true significance of the press for today's power politics is, of course, debatable. If roughly 50 per cent of the people vote Social Democratic but only 20 per cent of the newspapers are Social Democratic, and only 20 per cent vote for the Liberal party although it is backed by 50 per cent of the papers, what influence does the press then have?

As a first answer to that question, we can say that the voting figures would look different if, say, the Social Democrats had no

278

newspapers at all. The party's strong organization and the support it gets from labour would then avail little. A more specific answer, however would look first of all to more indirect effects. The existence of a Social Democratic press compels other papers to quote, paraphrase and debate its contents, and induces them in different cases to take a stand they might not take otherwise: but because of their preponderance, the non-socialist papers have also compelled the Social Democrats to modify many of their policies or put them in different words, so as to get the best possible press. Otherwise, the Liberal and Conservative papers would make it difficult or impossible for the Social Democrats to get their messages across in the same way as they might have if, say, they accounted for half the daily circulation. While all the research in this field indicates that political editorials influence no more than 10 to 15 per cent of the readers, that relatively limited proportion consists of a large number of people who create opinions at different levels. The arguments they assimilate from reading newspapers are passed on. It becomes easier to advocate opinions, often already held in the first place, which are put into articulate form by editorials. However, even the news pages, which directly reach more readers, are often politically tinged by the selection of subject matter, the typography of headlines, and turns of phrase in the articles. In any analysis of the power structure of Sweden's welfare state, it is impossible to overlook the enormous preponderance of the Liberal and Conservative press—whatever the drawbacks or merits ascribable to it according to one's own views. Just how important this situation has been cannot be assessed. Yet there is no doubt that it has eroded Social Democratic ascendancy, perhaps not so much at the polls as in manifestations of public opinion. The party has been forced towards greater caution in its exercise of power. In the big controversy over supplementary pensions during 1959, the Social Democrats were able to win no small measure of support for their plan when the largest opposition newspaper, *Dagens Nyheter*, bolted the non-socialist camp; that, in any event, was how the matter was interpreted by both the Social Democratic and opposition party strategists. This interpretation evidently had bearing on the conduct of politics irrespective of whether or not it was correct.

Given the complex power structure of the Swedish welfare state, it is only natural for the power relationships to shift as different issues become topical and different combinations of 'weights' and 'counter-weights' arise. Even though a certain 'regular' distribution exists, it is far from constant, as has been demonstrated in the party politics by the government coalition of Social Democrats and Agrarians in the 'fifties, and by the opposition coalition in the 'sixties of the Liberals and Agrarians (who since 1957 have called themselves the Centre party). However, the large labour-market organizations also lend themselves to varying groupings. The Social Democratic plan for supplementary pensions was backed by LO (wage-earners) and SACO (professional workers). TCO (salary-earners) adopted a formally neutral though substantially affirmative stand, while its largest member unions were opposed. In regard to the hotly debated issue of surtax, both TCO and SACO have long held different views from the Social Democratic government, whereas LO appears to have been more Social Democratic than the Social Democrats themselves, that is, opposed to any easing of graduated rates of surtax.

Of more importance than these groupings, however, has been the great balance of power: between the political power represented by the Social Democrats and the economic power represented by the business community, with due allowance for the curtailments on both sides as described above. Frequent reference has been made to this balance as an example of the 'mixed economy'. The term is correct as long as its reference is restricted to mean a combination of free enterprise with an extensive public sector embracing considerable components of state and municipal enterprise. There is no question but that the state operates in such a system to influence the conditions of industry and commerce by virtue of its general economic policy, its competition with private enterprise, and the orders it places with manufacturers. Nevertheless, this influence is very limited. Businessmen are completely free to invest as much as they like in what they like, and to locate plants where they like, subject only to the market forces under which they work. Besides, the capital at their disposal exerts both a direct and indirect political effect. It can be spent to mould public opinion, and in that case may be fed into either obvious or more subtle channels. Economic power arms the business community with a vast potential for acquiring the expertise it considers necessary, with less concern than the state for formal qualifications and pay standards.

The popular image of near-perfect harmony between political and economic power in present day Sweden no doubt stems from the special but protracted situation of a party that has been in power for as long as most people can remember. Foreign balance-of-power theoreticians derive particular nourishment from a mental image of workers in government who stand up as equals of the owners and managers of banks and corporations. Naturally, the picture does

280

contain a germ of truth, but it is a truth chiefly valid on the psychological level. It has been possible for a man to enjoy a sense of equality
and equilibrium when he has had political power in his hands. That
feeling has mattered a great deal for the continued integration of
Sweden's labour movement with the community.

Nevertheless, at the same time it is also true that this balance has
tottered precariously. One of the chief objectives of official policy, for
which other objectives have had to be sacrificed or subordinated, has
been to promote rapid economic growth. This focus of effort has led
state authorities to proceed with extreme caution where intervention
in business is concerned. Apart from the social security commitments
and some channelling of credits to finance residential construction,
they have left the business community very much alone. Its freedom
of action and power positions have not been encroached upon.

Considering the demand for economic growth, the cautious policy
is presumably justified. It is likely that disruptive effects would
follow, as a short-term result at any rate, if corporate freedom of
action were sharply circumscribed or if drastic surgery were practiced
on the pattern of the economic distribution built up by the market.
But whatever the criteria of evaluation applied to this aspect of the
matter, it is with reference to such considerations that official policy
has been conducted. Further, it is clear that the result as regards
power and income distribution, has been a greater measure of status
quo than would have followed if, say, certain egalitarian demands
had acted as primary determinants instead.

An important corollary of the present power structure, considered
in the form of large counter-balancing blocs, has been an inherent
tendency for these blocs to merge in a governing cadre of 'upper set'
persons in national and local government, the corporations, and
interest organizations. They comprise a new 'class' of politicians and
high-level functionaries: an Establishment, in other words. Although
more differentiated in its social origins than the old rank-ordered
society or the emergent industrial society, it is still an Establishment
standing over and above the citizens and employees, with heavy
components of a scientific and academic meritocracy. Let us take a
typical list of the guests invited to attend an official dinner given in
honour of a foreign prime minister or president. There we find the
cabinet ministers, party chairmen, parliamentary speakers, and other
Riksdagsmen, a few under-secretaries of state, ambassadors,
directors-general in the civil service, the president of SAF (Swedish
Employers' Confederation), the chairmen of LO, TCO and SACO, two
or three generals in the armed forces, several professors, the managing

281

directors of the large banks and of a number of the industrial giants, the editors-in-chief of leading newspapers (with all parties represented), and other guests of comparable status. Almost all of them have met one another before at similar gatherings; they more or less share the same idiom, and often take advantage of the occasion to conclude an amicable deal or perhaps to start new quarrels. While there is nothing shady or corrupt about that, it does convey the same flavour of accord and power grouping across boundary lines which once marked the Establishment over which Axel Oxenstierna, Magnus Gabriel De la Gardie and their fellow nobles presided. Just as the different members of this nobility used to represent separate interests and ideologies, and quarrelled over them, so do the members of today's élite, whether driven to do so by nature or by occupational interests. For all their divergencies, however, they form a special group, having high position, high income and personal distinction in common with one another. Theirs is a social freemasonry that extends from the prime minister to the professor, from the bank director to the LO chairman, from the ambassador to the man in charge of the Federation of Swedish Rural Districts, from the editor-in-chief of the leading Conservative paper to the Communist leader. It is a power structure that cuts right across the more formalized structure described above, a kind of special social group outside and above the ordinary social classification.

It is impossible to assess the significance of the emergence of this new élite in today's welfare state. Basically it is far less of a composition of individuals than the upper class of earlier times: except for the men of capital in the business world, its members derive their authority and social position from the different power blocs they represent. Obviously, a measure of social status is forever conferred by a period of high office. But on the whole a former chairman of LO, an ex-cabinet minister, or a retired managing director becomes a nobody, unless he occupies a new office where he can represent a power group. Even persons of the greatest influence, such as those who have sat in the inner sanctum of government for long years, are no longer power factors once they are pensioned off. At best they become the fitting objects of tribute at political party or union congresses. The members of this new élite are seldom men of independent means; it is in their functioning as a kind of upper-class meritocracy that they have their power, and the power they exercise depends on the power of the interests and sections of the community they represent.

When we say that the modern welfare state is characterized by an incomplete yet far-reaching balance of power between different interests and groups, we are also saying that this society has perforce begun to be characterized by a high degree of conservatism. Traditions and patterns of thought from a more or less proud past engender sluggishness and immobility. That is true not least of the political parties, the large interest organizations, and within the idealistic popular movements. It becomes possible to wrench free of old policies and notions only slowly, and inch by inch. The hold of the past is perhaps least strong in the business community, where constant readaptations are forced by technological innovations and economic pressures. A cult of flexibility also appears to have seized business leaders, at any event in the large corporations; some of its manifestations would certainly appear to be imbued with the zeal normally associated with couturiers. 'Modernization' and 'reorganization' have become the new catchwords.

As a matter of course, these technical and economic changes in the business world have urged on new ideas in politics. New theories and arrangements have indeed made headway everywhere, also in the interest organizations and social movements. The Swedish trade unions, for example, have shown a remarkable tolerance towards cost-reduction programmes and technical innovations.

Yet the overall impression remains of a society that has been rendered highly conservative by the countervailing force which different power groups exert against one another, each in its own 'sluggish' way. It often takes long periods of instruction, persuasion and indoctrination before any more ambitious organizational, administrative and political changes can be carried out. It would not be stretching the logic of language too far to suggest that the prevailing balance has contained the seeds of its own imbalance, since new needs cannot be promptly fitted into the system without making themselves felt as foreign intruders. It is tempting here to draw a comparison with the old rank-ordered, craft-guild society, which as we have seen could not incorporate new factors without serious disturbances. Today's conservative element in the midst of fast-moving changes is reflected not only in attitudes and opinions. It has also had its impact on social grouping and status. The welfare state of the 'sixties is still very much a society of class differences.

III

According to a method of classification common in Swedish social statistics until well into the 'fifties, about 10 per cent of the population

283

in the early 'sixties belonged to a category called social group I. Its members consisted of professional workers, higher civil servants, and executives of companies having at least 200 employees. They earned high incomes or were men of property. Social group II, usually described as the middle class, embraced 35 per cent of the population. The remaining 55 per cent made up social group III and included the 'workers'. This is a highly debatable classification, to say the least.

Many members of social group III earned higher incomes than a great many in social group II; perhaps their social status was correspondingly higher too, at least as they themselves and those around them perceived it. But if group III is augmented by the lower half of II, both income distribution and social evaluation remain substantially the same for the composite. The members of social group I are generally identical with the highest 10 per cent of income-earners. Together with the lower half of II, the members of III occupy the bottom half of the income pyramid. The upper portion of II belongs to the intermediate layers, even though some of its members have slid down to the low-income groups and some in social group III have hoisted themselves up to intermediate ranking.

By reason of political or union commitments, many manual workers have gained a kind of status elevation to social group II, though they still carry on as workers. They mix at the conference table with company managers or with department executives at least, and with people of both I and II in municipal and county councils. Others have climbed higher, having become Riksdagsmen, cabinet ministers, senior civil servants and the like, or gained leading office in the labour movement and thereby given evidence of social mobility. There are not so many of these people as one might think. In 1961 only 2 per cent of the Upper Chamber members were real labourers, while a corresponding proportion within the Lower Chamber remained fixed at between 4 and 5 per cent. Of the parliamentary secretaries on party and trade-union staffs, numbering 31 in the Upper Chamber and 55 in the Lower, about 60 had started their careers as manual workers. For the majority of them, however, the shop lathe was a distant memory, and there was little likelihood that more than a handful would ever return to an industrial trade. It is considered more natural to arrange some white-collar job for a Riksdagsman or union official who faces imminent resignation rather than have him go back to a trade he last pursued perhaps twenty or thirty years ago.

In 1961 only 30 per cent of the legislators came from working class homes, while 20 per cent came from the upper class. The cabinet, as composed on January 1, 1967, contained only five ministers who were workers originally. Ten of the remaining twelve had a university education; the other two included a former low-ranking civil servant and a man who had started out in business for himself. Of the ten university graduates, two came from lower civil service environment, the others from upper middle-class groups or social group I; none came from working-class homes.

The overwhelming evidence suggests that social mobility has been anything but extensive in the political sphere. Indeed, the overall impression is that of stagnation as compared with the 'thirties and 'forties, when the Riksdag contained a higher proportion of workers and the Social Democratic government was much less academically tinged. In 1937, 13 per cent of the Lower Chamber seats were held by workers.

A clearer picture of non-mobility emerges from a 1957 study of 245 big-business leaders. Only $3 \cdot 5$ per cent of them came from working-class homes, while $44 \cdot 5$ per cent came from social group I. The fathers of 30 per cent had owned or managed the affairs of corporations employing at least 200 persons; the fathers of an additional 10 per cent had owned or managed enterprises with between 10 and 200 employees. Nearly 80 per cent of the 245 held degrees, usually in engineering or business administration.

To judge from the Swedish business scene as it appeared in the late 'fifties, the surest way of reaching the top was to let oneself be born in a family whose father owned or managed a large-scale manufacturing enterprise; better still, as shown by 10 per cent of the cases, the father's father should likewise have tried his hand at owning or managing, preferably both. The third generation could always help his own cause along by taking an academic degree, preferably in civil engineering.

Background was almost equally important for a distinguished career in the state bureaucracy. Of the roughly 200 'top people'—cabinet ministers, under-secretaries of state, heads of administrative departments, directors-general, county governors, army or air-force generals, admirals and persons of equal standing in active service in 1965—more than half were the sons of big businessmen, professional men and higher civil servants; a mere twenty stemmed from working-class homes. The latter group have their political achievements to thank in great measure for their advancement. Ironically, the 'politization' of certain high posts has more greatly favoured the upper class than the higher levels of the middle class. People who aspired to reach the top by climbing the civil-service ladder could enter at a higher rung by making sure that their parents belonged to social group I and by completing a university education themselves. Those who sought to advance extra quickly and surely were well advised to combine these requisites with a period of activity in politics. Perhaps the most elegant combination during the 'sixties was displayed by the youngest member of the cabinet: born of a well-known and extremely wealthy upper-class family, academically educated in Sweden and the United States, married to a woman of nobility with her own university degree, already a veteran at the Social Democratic hustings, and exceptionally gifted.

Considering that the Social Democrats have held office for so long, why has greater social mobility failed to follow as a first step towards a more general levelling of classes in Swedish society? Questions of this import have been asked in more than one research study, in more or less astonished tones. As regards social mobility, that should cause no surprise. The very fact of long incumbency has persuaded many people, caught up in careers and of family backgrounds suited to studies and high-ranking office, to join the Social Democrats (whether from conviction or for speculative reasons), who have had use for highly qualified persons in their service. At the same time, the observance of a 'fair' allocation of political appointments between the parties has further impeded social mobility: the Liberal and Conservative aspirations for high office have almost exclusively come from the upper class or the better-situated middle class. Besides, with the possible exception of the ministries, political allegiance is immaterial for civil service appointments. The demands of formal qualifications operate so high up on the ladder of promotion that eligibility has become restricted to university graduates. Lest the latter observation be misinterpreted, it should be pointed out that, as late as 1965, about 40 per cent of the undergraduates came from social group I and only about 20 per cent from working-class homes. Thus the low degree of social mobility no longer appears so remarkable.

Yet by international standards the Swedish universities and professional schools draw on an unusually broad social spectrum. The crucial question then is: how will the different types of courses, the new programmes of state aid to students, and the evidently great thirst for education in all sections of the community affect recruitment and social mobility? Although the discussion of future developments does not properly come within the scope of a historical account of this type, it would be interesting to touch on them in so far as certain trends have already manifested themselves.

First of all, it would be absurd to assume that the broadening of education will not have an impact on social mobility and stratification. Since no reserves to speak of are left in social group I, whose young people enter higher education almost to a man, the range of recruitment automatically widens as more students matriculate. However, insofar as it is at present possible to make tolerably well grounded observations, it seems likely that the effects will not be as undirectional and homogeneous as the ideological premises of the new educational policy have assumed.

Opportunities will be more equally aportioned than before, and the long three to four generations that once had to be traversed from working class to middle class, and thence to upper class, will certainly be shortened for a very large number of cases. The working man will no longer have to await his grandson or granddaughter before he gets a professor, a director-general, or a captain of industry in the family. Indeed, his own children may very well attain such positions without causing anything like the sensation they would today. Nevertheless, for a long time to come the working man's son or daughter will have to command energies and talents above the average. Compared with the children of a professor or corporate manager, nothing will be handed over on a silver plate. Even though the proportion of under-graduates coming from working-class or middle-class homes will increase sharply, the fact remains that only a slight number of the children in these groups study, whereas nearly 100 per cent of the children from social group I will do so. Moreover, the broadening of education shows tendencies which create new problems of social stratification. The students who do not graduate for one reason or another will have to take the jobs with less pay and prestige attached to them. More than that, they will have to take these jobs because they were tried and found wanting. At the same time those who are most successful and attain the finest positions, with the highest repute, the fattest salaries and the greatest power, will have less cause to thank their lucky stars for having been born in the right family. To a greater extent they can experience success as self-merited, as a fair reward for capability and diligence. One cannot disregard the risk that this stratification, precisely because of its greater 'fairness', will become more ruthless, more socially cruel than that hitherto existing, where everyone knew that success and failure to a great extent depended on circumstances beyond the individual's own control. From a special but important point of view, this problem has already begun to trouble many in the trade unions. How are they going to get capable leaders who can preserve labour's political influence, and keep the organization together, when broadened educational opportunities absorb the most talented working-class children and propel them towards careers as engineers, physicians and company executives—careers that look more promising than trade unionism?

It is, of course, conceivable that greater educational opportunities will pave the way for a greater degree of economic equality. The supply of highly trained manpower would increase so greatly, thanks to the opportunity for advanced studies for all talented, that the salaries and perhaps social prestige attached to today's 'higher' occupations would no longer be so exclusive. But that assumption may be rooted more in egalitarian wishful thinking than in sound reasoning. The experience gained to date is that the need for higher-calibre personnel is rising at a faster rate than student enrolment. More important, however, is that the demand for top talent in different fields may well continue to outrun supply. In that case, a broadened 'higher' stratum would include an 'upper' group possessing special prestige, economic position and power. Given the tendencies observable to date, there is no lack of scope for such possibilities.

Concerning the extent of the development by the mid-'sixties, it must at all events be noted that social mobility in Swedish society was still extremely limited. Presumably, although any comparison is difficult to make, it was more limited than in the 'twenties and 'thirties when the final breakthrough of the labour movement temporarily increased this mobility. On the other hand, a different kind of stratification has taken place, though it would be misleading to include it in the concept of social mobility: the increase in white-collar workers or salaried employees, recruited from the ranks of wage-earners or manual workers, who in consequence have become much reduced in proportion to the total population. It is estimated that about half of the salary-earners in 1965 came from working-class homes.

The extent of the social change resulting from this shift has been the subject of much discussion. It is supposed to have had great significance, according to the findings of a study published by Fritz Croner at the beginning of the 'fifties. In accordance with the definitions employed to identify a separate working class, it would be justifiable to speak of a white-collar class having its own characteristics. Croner differentiated the two classes with reference to financial circumstances, levels of education, career opportunities and way of life. Further, he used these criteria not only to distinguish salary-earners as a separate social class, but also to give sharp outlines and a clearly positive content to white-collar class feelings.

If the developments in the late 'forties were headed towards the formation of a uniform white-collar class separated socially from the working class, which in itself is extremely doubtful—they have not subsequently seen fit to abide by Croner's conceptual scheme. The sharp increase of white-collar groups has made them increasingly fragmented as regards economic position, career opportunities and education. Further, the salary earners who bear the closest affinities to the wage-earners have greatly increased their relative proportion of the total group. This means that, as the salary-earners have grown in an organizational and technical sense, more and more of their number have come to lack both the career opportunities and the special responsibility—the position of trust—which would bring about a socially significant difference vis-a-vis the manual workers. The office clerk, shop assistant or television cameraman differ far less from the 'average worker' than from such salary-earners as graduate engineers, university lecturers, civil-service departmental heads, or secretaries in the Swedish Central Organization of Salaried Employees. Besides, the greater extension of fringe benefits, in particular supplementary pensions and the provision of paid vacations under law, have made the differences between manual workers and the growing army of clerks smaller than they may have looked at the beginning of the 'fifties. That has further neutralized the value of switching over from a blue to a white collar.

Especially striking are the differences within the white-collar population itself: between the holders of executive positions and those who are engaged in routine, clerical occupations; and between salary earners of varying educational backgrounds. These differences are far more important than those between wage-earners and low salary-earners if reference is made to alienation, that is, the distance from control over the production process in which one takes part. G. K. Chesterton once ironically observed that millions of women suddenly demanded the right to make their voices heard, whereupon they took jobs as stenographers. The same can also be said of most of the people who in the past thirty to forty years have become salary-earners instead of wage-earners. Perhaps their control over the production process has not diminished, but it certainly is no greater. How much more can the typist, shop assistant or TV cameraman decide than the skilled labourer? How much closer do these salary-earners feel to their productive tasks?

The formal statistical distribution between wage-earners and salary-earners thus demonstrates little if any change in the actual class structure of society. This conclusion would seem to be the most correct when viewed from the production aspect, as it were.

The same conclusion is reinforced when we look at the consumption aspect. Large numbers of salary-earners do enjoy a level of income and material standards which does not differ from that of a large number of wage-earners. Both groups have been able to raise their consumption substantially during the past twenty years. But many wage-earners and lower-ranking salary earners have done so in fairly equal degree, allowing for some important variations within each group. Therefore, it is not likely that any new feelings of class between them can have been engendered, and any class differences on objective grounds become even harder to find.

Nothing new has occurred in the political sphere, judging by the proportion of votes cast for different parties, to suggest that a new alignment of classes has resulted from the swelling numbers of salary earners. To be sure, behaviour at the ballot box does not exactly coincide with social classification. However it does not stray too far, and if a large white-collar class with sharply outlined class feeling has emerged, it would surely be reflected in the election returns. Yet in spite of the great expectations held by the Liberal and Conservative parties since the 'forties, the elections of subsequent years offer no supporting evidence. When, as in the local elections of 1966, the Social Democrats had poor returns, all the categories of earlier voters contributed to the reduced margin: young people, irrespective of their social-group affiliation; salary earners; better-off-wage-earners and perhaps above all, their wives, who demonstrated a political weariness; worse-off wage-earners who failed to vote at all to a larger extent than usual, and so on. A certain trend, related to increased party mobility generally, has been observable in connection with migration to the large and middle-sized towns, since that has changed the living conditions of voters and loosened the former hold of the party and union apparatus. However, declining party loyalty has evidently applied to all parties and social groups; and does not at all indicate the existence of a strong subjective feeling of class on the part of a new and growing population of higher-level salary-earners.

The actual groupings have not been materially affected by today's process of structural change in the economy, with altered work functions in manufacturing industry and a rapidly expanding services sector, which by the mid-'sixties had reduced the ratio between wage-earners and salary-earners to $1 \cdot 5:1$ from 10:1 sixty years ago. After the three decades during which the welfare state had evolved, the working class and the lower middle class were still distinguishable from the upper middle class and upper class. They could be distinguished from these 'higher' groups in respect of all the four criteria employed by Croner: financial position, level of education, career opportunities and way of life.

A frequently made contention is that class equalization has gone especially far on the consumption side. In their role of consumers, the professor and company executive are supposed to be indistinguishable from the manual worker and the lower-grade white-collar worker. The latter, too, can afford a smart suit, a car, a weekend cottage, and the luxury of dining-out. It is indeed evident that some of the earlier outward class manifestations have disappeared and that the financially weaker groups are now enjoying a higher standard of living, while the more affluent are less status-conscious and less conspicuous in their consumption. However, one does not have to scratch too far beneath the surface to see that the differences are significant.

The more affluent differ from the wage-earners and lower-grade salary-earners in essential aspects of their consumption patterns. Mixed patterns are admittedly common: for example, the presence of many children in a high-income family will sometimes be reflected in a lower-than-average consumption, or the earnings of several breadwinners in the same family may have an opposite effect. Other things being equal, however, there is still a world of difference between annual incomes of 75,000, 30,000 and 20,000 kronor, which after tax deduction amount to about 40,000, 20,000 and 15,000 kronor respectively. The sectional head of a civil service department, with a family of the same size as a metalworker's, has two or three times as high a purchasing power. He lives in a better dwelling and eats better, yet will usually spend a lesser share of his net income on housing and food than the wage-earner; the differences thus increase once the necessities are satisfied and 'extra' purchasing power is left over to be spent on leisure, culture, amusements, travel, status and so on.

As already indicated, the pattern of income and consumption does not necessarily follow these nominal examples. The incomes earned by working wives contribute correspondingly to the level of living. In some cases the 'higher' groups will include a lower-grade white-collar component by virtue of the gainful employment of a wife or child. The man who heads a section in a civil service department may have a clerk-wife and typist daughter: occupationally that puts the

291

wife and daughter in the lower middle class, but socially and according to patterns of consumption the family belongs to the upper class.
Such mixtures are not particularly common, however. Instead, it is
becoming much more usual for university-educated men to marry
university-educated women. The greater likelihood, therefore, is that
the gainfully employed wives in social group I will be working in
group I occupations, such as teaching, medicine, higher positions in
the civil service, and the like.

That brings us to another pattern of 'consumption' which to a
very great degree is divided along status and social lines. The old
nobility deliberately strove, with legislative aids as well, to keep their
blue blood unsullied, by debarring marriage outside their own order.
The Swedish social groups of the 'sixties do not lag far behind in this
respect. Girls from wage-earner and lower white-collar homes usually
become the wives of wage-earners and lower white-collar workers,
while the daughters in social group I marry the sons in the same
group. In a study dating from 1953, Michael Wächter found, not at
all unexpectedly, that girls with fathers on the same social level
made 'better' matches the higher their educational attainment, while
girls of the same educational attainment made 'better' marriages the
higher the social status of their fathers. In other words, a girl could
bring off the 'best' match if she were university educated and had a
father who occupied the uppermost layer in social group I—and she
often did bring it off, if by the 'best' is meant that the husband combined high education, high income and a position of authority with
superior background. The picture does not quite tally, though, since
the men in the highest positions usually do not possess all the
variables which condition this status at one and the same time: that
is, the highest education, the greatest power, plus the finest official
title, plus the highest income. A justice of the Supreme Court earns
a high salary, but much lower than that of the big-company managing
director, who often holds no more than a degree in civil engineering.
The professor ranks below the Supreme Court justice and earns less
than the managing director, but surpasses them both in educational
achievement and on the vocational rating scale of the man in the
street. In many cases the professor and other university teachers will
have wives who hold degrees. The average company manager tends
to prefer a girl with 'excellent family background' to the girl with an
academic degree. It appears that the old proverb, 'like will to like',
is valid, and the result certainly makes for lesser social mobility and
more rigid stratification than if 'mixed marriages' were more common.
The children grow up in a more homogeneous environment when

the father and mother 'belong to the same kind of people', and that in turn determines the kind of people they will associate with in the overwhelming majority of cases.

The social-group classification we have employed above coincides fairly well with the occupational classification employed in the Swedish population censuses. As will have emerged from our account, both suffer from the same shortcomings. Wage-earners and salary-earners are recorded as separate and distinct social groups, despite the fact that, with reference to important criteria—place in production, degree of alienation, education, career opportunities, income and way of life—it would be more correct to draw the line somewhere in the middle of the white-collar corps. Such a boundary is also open to debate of course. The different groups intermingle and merge in a way which makes all boundaries defective in one or more respects. Nevertheless, the transformation, if you pass from one boundary to the next and compare two groups separated by an intermediate group, is pronounced and fairly uniform. Continuous changes occur along the way from the least-educated and lowest-paid with the most monotonous, arduous or dirtiest jobs at the bottom end of the scale; thence to the fairly well-paid skilled worker; and from there by way of accountants and production engineers up to the top layer of company managers, directors-general and professors, high politicians and organizational leaders. It is by no means a matter of indifference in the welfare state what social group one belongs to—as the perhaps impossible dream of equality and the classless society prescribes. On the contrary, it is a matter of great significance.

Paradoxically enough, this stratification has in one way been accentuated rather than diminished by the public mechanisms for welfare. Swedish social policy is based to a great extent on the principle of safeguarding material standards. If a beneficiary is deprived of income because of unemployment, illness, old age and the like, he shall be compensated in relation to the income lost. There have been sound reasons for adopting this system; but its effects very much recall the code of the former rank-ordered society that every man had the right to get a standard of living according to his family's social status.

However, as it may be said of many other characteristic features of the welfare state, so may it be said of the social structure that big new changes are possibly waiting round the corner. The welfare state is young. It has a long way to go before taking on final shape—if a final shape is attainable at all. Rapid changes on the business scene, in politics, in the balance-of-power system, and in the mixed economy that has prevailed during the postwar period, can fast alter the picture we have before us today. The lines of divergence that may lead to new constellations and groupings are not only being generated from within. Influences from abroad are also at work, and more powerfully than ever before: the economic unification of Western Europe; Eastern Europe's rapid transformation into highly industrialized welfare states; the insistent clamour of the under-developed countries for development; partnership and equality; and perhaps the most important of all, the advance of technology, with inventions and discoveries of a hitherto unknown impact.

6

O BLESSED LAND

I F this portrayal of Swedish society as it developed from the great-power era to today's welfare state has been chiefly a tale of perpetual change, it has at the same time told of certain constant factors that have determined Swedish life and work over the course of these three centuries.

There is nothing contradictory about this statement. It merely signifies that the changes, however tremendous they were, also had coherence and continuity. By way of summing up there is reason to draw attention to these connecting threads which run through all the changes.

One way of explaining the factors of continuity is to say that Sweden has been a singularly fortunate country.

She has had the fortune to own two immense natural resources, forests and iron ore, which for more than three centuries have enabled her to maintain an eminence on the world market out of all reasonable proportion to her population. That eminence first laid the foundation for political greatness and later for a relatively high prosperity.

She has been fortunate in having good communications with the outside world, coasting two seas that have played and still play decisive roles in European civilization.

These natural resources and trade position have created outward ties and interests which have induced foreign capital and talent to offer their services in the promotion of Swedish economic advance. At the same time the facts of geography have helped to protect her against conquests and aggression. On the whole, her wars have been fought in the satellite provinces or beyond, and for more than 150 of the 300 years covered in this review, Sweden has not been involved in any wars at all.

Perhaps fortune can also in part be held responsible for those circumstances of the late Middle Ages and under the Vasa kings, whereby Sweden's peasants were never feudalized or deprived of their political rights, but could assert themselves as a franchised order—a position of authority which was able to resist encroachments during the great-power era. The existence of a free peasantry set a distinctive stamp on Swedish social and political history until well into the industrial era, not only as a priceless value in its own right, but also as insurance against overly inflamed social clashes and conflicts. Since the time of Charles IX, Sweden has experienced only two 'illegal' upheavals of state; both were bloodless, and neither was a revolution triggered off by social antagonisms.

If by fortune we also mean historical stability and the absence of lacerating inner strife, then Sweden has been fortunate to enjoy religious unity ever since the Reformation. The unity, obviously, has been obtained at a price, in the form of intermittently rigorous dogmatism and the loss of enriching debate between different schools of religious thought. Yet it has unquestionably helped to make the Swedish 'monolith' that much easier to erect.

Another achievement, though here it is perhaps truer to speak of skill rather than fortune, is the system of public administration built up under Gustavus Adolphus and Axel Oxenstierna, the essential features of which remain with us today. By international standards, this system has presumably succeeded unusually well in combining independence with loyalty towards the holders of political power. A large part of the explanation may derive from the strong legal structure which was built into Swedish public administration from the beginning. The civil service departments were called upon to secure for the subject the rights guaranteed him by the law of the land. Yet surely of great importance also, is that both the public administration and the central authority have largely abided by the reciprocal rules of the game. When Charles XI and Charles XII sought to 'politicize' the administration, they were forced to take the roundabout path of creating extraordinary agencies. They could never completely overcome the opposition put up by the old independent departments.

The labour movement which accompanied the upsurge of industry tended to feel 'outside the community' in hard-pressed situations: but it soon chose to conquer this community from within, not by upheavals but by democratic and parliamentary action. At no time does the movement seem to have felt totally segregated and alien. Its leaders took especial pains to maintain calm and order, rejecting all revolutionary tendencies, during the general strike of 1909. Their skills were perhaps best demonstrated during the embitterment which followed the Ådal riots of 1931, when military troops killed five demonstrators who had attacked a group of strikebreakers. More inflamed souls could justifiably criticize union officials for philistinism and bureaucratic obedience to the law. The result, in any event, was further integration and a successive reform work, in which change and continuity could be combined. That may have been possible because industrialization in Sweden was spared the worst social misfortunes that plagued its advance elsewhere, in particular the mass agglomeration of people in urban wens, condemned to breathe the belchings of coal chimneys and endure the dirt and perils of coal mines.

Given this background, it is perhaps understandable that many foreign observers—and Swedish too—should call attention to the 'idyllic balance' of Swedish development as compared with the more disturbed conditions in other countries. For when all is said and done, the Swedish development has been unusually balanced by international standards, though the balance is far from complete, and at times obscures the significant conflicts beneath the surface.

It is sometimes contended that the affluent nations have valuable lessons to offer the under-developed countries in their aspirations towards economic growth and well-being. That may well be true, but a study of the Swedish experience is not likely to prove particularly rewarding for this purpose. The few parallels that may exist become insignificant against all the dissimilar factors, which consistently reveal the poorer nations to be at a disadvantage.

At about the middle of the nineteenth century, when increased population, fragmented land ownership in agriculture, and widespread proletarianization combined to produce the most serious situation, Sweden may have had birth and death rates which closely resembled those of today's under-developed countries. Indeed, Malthus had several decades earlier referred to Sweden as one of the most telling proofs of his theory. But the Sweden of that day was not 'under-developed' in our sense of the term. Her people were not illiterates. Her public administration had developed for two hundred years to a high degree of effectiveness and was almost completely free of corruption. Her exporting industries had proud traditions to point to, and resources of enterprising spirit and craftsmanship on which to draw for meeting the big changes that lay ahead. They could compete in familiar, well-established markets. At their disposal were merchant and banking houses with seasoned experience and relationships that had been cultivated over a period of at least two hundred years.

Further, domestic markets stood open for the industries which were to join the exporting industries in starting the new development: a fairly broad middle and upper class on the consumer side, and basic industries needing machinery, repairs and servicing in the sphere of enterprise.

Agriculture, burdened by overpopulation and widespread pauperization presented a situation that could be called 'under-developed' in the middle of the nineteenth century. However, the differences as against today's under-developed countries in similar circumstances are still very great. By virtue of large foreign loans and falling prices in the grain market, Sweden had the means to import considerable quantities of foodstuffs to feed the rural manpower that migrated to industry. Even though the situation occasionally became critical for agriculture, the problem could be solved by the voluntary exodus of large numbers from the farms, a concurrent increase in the food supply, and the fairly rapid adoption of more efficient methods of agricultural production. Sweden thereby avoided the vicious circle which afflicts some of the under-developed countries: the need for industrialization and eased pressure on an overpopulated agriculture to get people to move over to industry, parallelled by the overwhelming difficulty during a long period of transition of producing more food to feed the growing industrial population. An extensive emigration to the United States also helped Sweden to solve the problem.

Political conditions in Sweden were stable. Foreign industrialists, businessmen and investors had no revolutions and nationalizations to fear. Knowledge of the new technology and new management techniques could be freely obtained from the industrially more advanced countries, Britain in particular.

The old guild system which formerly applied to the practice of trades had been dissolved, a fact which probably made opposition to the new factory system less formidable than it might have been otherwise. Moreover, the same time the habits and traditions of cohesion, discipline and bargaining technique evolved by the guilds later came to benefit the emergent trade unions. The temperance and dissenter movements had initiated a training for democratic citizenship which within a few decades proved very useful to the new labour movement.

It would be wrong to underestimate the difficulties and conflicts, the growing pains that were visited upon Swedish society during the process of industrialization. The exodus of millions from an overpopulated agriculture to the new enterprises and industrial towns entailed a difficult and, for many, hopeless process of adjustment. In its wake came a new class grouping, at first characterized by social rootlessness, a sense of alienation, and fear of the new and the rapidly changing. Yet the new environment conferred such palpably great benefits by comparison with the environment in which today's under-developed countries are struggling, that almost all attempts to draw parallels look meaningless.

The privileges of West European civilization—and here we also include the 'new Europe' on the other side of the Atlantic—had perhaps accrued in richer measure to Sweden than to any other country. Sweden came to enjoy a disproportionate share of its advantages. However, after the dreams of first-class power status had evaporated, she was relieved of having to assume a full share of the responsibility.

This privileged position has no doubt influenced Sweden's view of herself and of the world around her, producing a feeling of isolation and self-sufficiency. One of its manifestations is the secure hold which the policy of neutrality has upon voters at all the elections of recent times. In the final analysis, it may well have been the uneasy conscience flowing from this privileged provincialism which made Sweden support the League of Nations so ardently during the inter-war period, and the United Nations afterwards. Perhaps it is for the same reason that her people generally tend to become deeply involved in events taking place in remote lands, while observing neutral silence towards events taking place at close quarters.

Appendix I

Vasa Dynasty
Gustavus I, regent 1521–23, king 1523–60
Eric XIV, 1560–68
John III, 1568–92
Sigismund, 1592–99
Charles IX, regent till 1604, king 1604–11
Gustavus II Adolphus, 1611–32
Christina, 1632–54 (regency government, 1632–44)
Palatinate Dynasty
Charles X Gustavus, 1654–60
Charles XI, 1660–98 (regency government, 1660–72)
Charles XII, 1697–1718 (regency government, 1697)
Ulrica Eleonora, 1719–20
Frederick of Hesse, 1720–51
Holstein-Gottorp Dynasty
Adolphus Frederick, 1751–71
Gustavus III, 1771–92
Gustavus IV Adolphus, 1791–1809 (regency government, 1792–96)
Charles XIII, 1809–18
Bernadotte Dynasty
Charles XIV John, 1818–44
Oscar I, 1844–59
Charles XV, 1859–72
Oscar II, 1872–1907
Gustav V, 1907–50
Gustav VI Adolph, 1950

Appendix II

L. De Geer, 1876–80
A. Posse, 1880–83
K. J. Thyselius, 1883–84
O. R. Themptander, 1884–88
G. Bildt, 1888–89
G. Åkerhielm, 1889–91
E. G. Boström, 1891–1900
Fr. V. v. Otter, 1900–02
E. G. Boström, 1902–05
O. Ramstedt, 1905
Ch. Lundeberg, 1905
K. Staaff, 1911–14
Hj. Hammarskjöld, 1914–17
C. Swartz, 1917
N. Edén, 1917–20

Hj. Branting, 1920
L. De Geer (the Younger), 1920–21
O. von Sydow, 1921
Hj. Branting, 1921–23
E. Trygger, 1923–24
Hj. Branting, 1924–25
R. Sandler, 1925–26
C. G. Ekman, 1926–28
A. Lindman, 1928–30
C. G. Ekman, 1930–32
F. Hamrin, 1932
P. A. Hansson, 1932–36
A. Pehrsson-Bramstorp, 1936
P. A. Hansson, 1936–46
T. Erlander, 1946–

Appendix III

National Coalition, no Social Democrats	July–October 1905
Liberal	Until May 1906
Conservative	Until October 1911
Liberal	Until February 1914
Conservative	Until March 1917
Conservative (Caretaker Government)	Until October 1917
Liberal–Social Democratic	Until March 1920
Social Democratic	Until Autumn 1920
Non-party Government	Until Autumn 1921
Social Democratic	Until April 1923
Conservative (+1 Lib. & 1 Agrarian)	Until Autumn 1924
Social Democratic	Until June 1926
Liberal (offshoot party + 1 regular Liberal)	Until Autumn 1928
Conservative	Until May 1930
Liberal (offshoot party)	Until September 1932
Social Democratic	Until June 1936
Agrarian	Until September 1936
Social Democratic + Agrarian	Until December 1939
Coalition, no Communists	Until August 1945
Social Democratic	Until September 1951
Social Democratic + Agrarian	Until October 1957
Social Democratic	Since October 1957

INDEX

303